Cutting Through Ego and Revealing Fearlessness:
Chod Practice According to Jigme Lingpa's
Bellowing Laugh of the Dakini

by
Ven. Khenchen Palden Sherab Rinpoche
and
Ven. Khenpo Tsewang Dongyal Rinpoche

Cutting Through Ego and Revealing Fearlessness:
Chod Practice According to Jigme Lingpa's
Bellowing Laugh of the Dakini

by
Ven. Khenchen Palden Sherab Rinpoche
and
Ven. Khenpo Tsewang Dongyal Rinpoche

Edited by Members of the Samye Translation Group
Ann Helm, Steve Harris, Ani Trime Lhamo,
Arriane Emory, Cynthia Friend, Nancy Roberts,
Amanda Lewis, and Lama Pema Dragpa

Cutting Through Ego and Revealing Fearlessness:
Chod Practice According to Jigme Lingpa's
Bellowing Laugh of the Dakini

Copyright © 2019   Khenpo Tsewang Dongyal Rinpoche

All rights reserved. No part of this material may be reproduced in any form or by any means, electronic or mechanical, including photocopying, recording, or by any information storage and retrieval system, without prior written permission from the authors.

Published by Dharma Samudra.

Padma Samye Ling
618 Buddha Highway
Sidney Center, NY 13839
(607) 865-8068
padmasambhava.org

ISBN-13: 978-1-7335411-2-1

The Venerable Khenpo Rinpoches request that you please not practice these Chod instructions unless you have received empowerment, transmission, and teaching on Jigme Lingpa's *Bellowing Laugh of the Dakini* by a qualified lama who holds this lineage. Thank you.

DEDICATION

Dedicated in the honor and memory of His Holiness Dudjom Rinpoche, Venerable Khenchen Palden Sherab Rinpoche, Lama Chimed Namgyal, and all the lineage holders of these secret teachings, as well as all the devoted practitioners of the past, present, and future.

Contents

Dedication vi
Acknowledgments xiii
Preface xiv

Part 1:
Introduction to the Practice of Chod

**Chapter 1: Understanding the Place
of Chod in Buddhist Practice** 3

    Developing the Correct Motivation for Practice 4
    The Wisdom Dakini 5
    Chod Empowerment, Transmission,
       and Instructions 9
    All Dharma Practices are Chod 10

Chapter 2: History and Lineages of Chod 15

    Guru Padmasambhava and the Early Lineages 15
    Padampa Sangye and Machig Labdron:
       The Later Lineages 16
    Male and Female Chod Lineages 22

    The Life of Machig Labdron 22
       Birth and Early Life 24
       Training 29
       Adult Life 33
       Teaching Activities 35

Great Masters of Chod 39
    The Early Lineage of Chod 39
    The Later Lineages of Chod...................................40
    Longchenpa 41
    Jigme Lingpa 43
    The Longchen Nyingthig...44

Chapter 3: Essential Elements of Chod Practice..............47

The Proper Practitioner..47

The Philosophical View of the Four Demons 49
    The Demon of the Aggregates................................49
    The Demon of Death..50
    The Demon of Negative Emotions 51
    The Demon of Distraction......................................52

The Chod Practitioner's View
    of the Four Demons 53
    Tangible Demons 54
    Intangible Demons..54
    Demon of Exhilaration..54
    Demon of Pride 55

How To Cut Ego-clinging...56
Ritual Objects of Chod Practice 58
The Eight Worldly Concerns..60

Preparing to Practice Chod 61
    The Challenges of Chod Practice............................62
    Signs and Obstacles...63
    Choosing Practice Places...66
    A Warning About Power Spots...............................69

Summary of Preparations 69

PART 2:
DETAILED COMMENTARY ON THE SADHANA *BELLOWING LAUGH OF THE DAKINI*

Chapter 4: Preparing and Overpowering Practices 75

Sangwa Yeshe Khandroma 76

The Four Styles of Walking 84
    Walking with Great Confidence in the View 85
    Dakini Walk 85
    Black Snake Walk 85
    Crazy Elephant Walk 86

Dancing on the Demons of the Five Continents 86
    The Three HUNG Syllables 89
    First Dance on the Eastern Continent 90
    Second Dance on the Southern Continent 92
    Third Dance on the Western Continent 93
    Fourth Dance on the Northern Continent 94
    Fifth Dance on the Central Continent 96

Staking the Tent 99
Dissolution Stage Practice 102

Chapter 5: Preliminary Ngondro Practices 105

Visualizing the Objects of Refuge 105
    Taking Refuge and Developing Bodhichitta 107
    Mandala Offering 108
    Guru Yoga and the Dissolution Stage 109

Contents

Chapter 6: The Main Practice 113

Three Stages of Bodhichitta 113

Creation Stage: Troma Prepares the Offering 118
    Troma Offering Mantra 120
    Preparing the Four Feasts 122
        White Feast 122
        Red Feast 123
        Striped Feast 126
        Black Feast 127
    Four Groups of Guests 130
        Honored Guests 130
        Qualified Guests 130
        Guests of Compassion of the Six Realms 131
        Obstructing Guests 131
    Inviting the Guests 133
    Offering and Distributing the Feasts 136

Dissolution Stage: Dzogchen Meditation 140
Provocations and Challenges 140

**Chapter 7: Concluding Dedication
and Aspiration Prayers** 151

Special Instructions for Concluding Retreat 157

Part 3:
Practical Advice for
Beginning Chod Practitioners

Chapter 8: Brief Overview of Chod Practice 163

Chapter 9: Frequently Asked Questions
    about Chod Practice 165

Dedication of Merit 187

Appendices

Entire Sadhana of *Bellowing Laugh of the Dakini*
    revealed by Rigdzin Jigme Lingpa 191

*Song of Supplication of the Creation and Completion
Stages of Machig Labdron* by Raga Asye 239

Endnotes 257
Bibliography 272
List of Figures 274
About the Authors 279
Padma Samye Ling Shedra Series 285
Other Publications by the Authors 287
Opening the Door of the Dharma Treasury 289
Padmasambhava Buddhist Center 290

Acknowledgments

These teachings are primarily drawn from a retreat that took place in Grants, New Mexico in July 1991. Additional materials came from teachings in New York in April 1991, in Denver in October 1993, in West Palm Beach, Florida in 1999, in Tennessee in 2014, and at Padma Samye Ling in New York in 2005, 2014, and 2015. Further material has been generously provided in discussions with Ven. Khenpo Tsewang Dongyal Rinpoche.

The Venerable Khenpo Rinpoches would like to thank the many students who have helped to produce this publication. The original 1991 New Mexico, 1991 New York, and 1993 Denver teachings that form the backbone of this book were transcribed and edited by Ann Helm, Pema Dorje (Steve Harris), Ani Trime Lhamo, Arrianne Emory, and Lama Pema Dragpa. The 1999 Palm Beach Dharma Center teaching was transcribed by Marjorie Soule. The 2005 Padma Samye Ling teaching was transcribed by Beba Pema Drolma. The 2014 PSL Chod Ritual Retreat was transcribed by Shane Kennedy. The 2014 Nashville teachings were transcribed by Kirk Lawson and Charles Hudson. The 2014 Padma Gochen Ling teachings were transcribed by Louise Kohler. The 2015 PSL Summer Dzogchen Retreat teaching was transcribed by a team of transcribers that included Ani Joanie Andras, Cindy Feldman, Cynthia Friend, Bonnie Holsinger, Paul Jones, Melina Sierra, Carol Stromek, Jacob Wise, and Dan Zellan. The text for this volume was synthesized and edited by Cynthia Friend and Nancy Roberts. The final edit and preparation for publication was completed by Lama Pema Dragpa. The final peer review was done by Amanda Lewis. Pema Dondrub re-typed the *Bellowing Laugh of the Dakini* Chod sadhana included in the appendices. Ann Yegorova laid out the book for publication.

Preface

Why do we practice the Dharma? The "Dharma" means love, kindness, compassion, joy, and appreciation. We want to activate, deepen, and engage these basic qualities so that we can radiate them more powerfully to other beings. For us, this is more than a casual notion. We practice positive qualities to become stronger practitioners, so that we can really make a difference for ourselves, our families, friends, neighbors, and for everyone. This is what makes our lives meaningful. But as we progress, we don't change the way we are: we always remain very humble and simple.

This motivation is at the very heart of Chod practice, and directs all our growth. First, we learn the meaning of Chod practice. Later, we learn and practice how to do the ritual ceremony. Even though it's good to perform the ritual and play the drum and all that, the meaning is more important than the ritual details. Using ritual implements can accelerate or activate our development. But ritual will be just a superficial, relative activity until we develop an understanding of the meaning. Understanding the meaning is what brings realization of the absolute level. It is very important to combine the relative and absolute levels as much as we can.

Where did Chod practice originate? Although a few skeptical scholars have questioned whether Chod was originally a Buddhist teaching at all, this teaching came from Buddha Shakyamuni. Over the course of his lifetime, he gave every type and level of teaching. Chod practice is part of the teachings that are now called the Vajrayana, which has been upheld and practiced continually over the centuries by generations of masters. The practice of

Chod was brought to Tibet in the 8th century at the time of Guru Padmasambhava, King Trisong Deutsen, and the Abbot Shantarakshita.

Over time, four different lineages or traditions of Chod came to Tibet from India. (1) The early translations are Guru Padmasambhava's Chod practices known as *chos chod*. He left *terma* that have been discovered over time by a sequence of tertons. (2) Brahmin Aryadeva gave the teaching known as *tsig chad chenmo*. (3) Padampa Sangye's Chod practice is known as *Shije* [zhi byed]. (4) And Naropa's Chod practices are called *sang chopa* and *rong nyon chenmo*.

Who then made Chod practice famous? It was the great master and wisdom dakini Machig Labdron. She was born around 1103, lived around 99 years, and entered mahaparinirvana in 1201. She is one of the most renowned female masters in Buddhist history.

She once gave a teaching in which she described her past lives, identifying herself as an emanation of the Buddha Tara. She also said, "In one of my previous lives, I was Mayadevi"— meaning that she had been the mother of Buddha Shakyamuni— "and I was Gangadevi when I spread the Buddha's teaching, and I was Sukhasiddhi, one of the most famous wisdom dakinis. When Buddhism came to Tibet, I was Yeshe Tsogyal, and now I am Machig Labdron." Another teaching said that on the outer level of external appearances, she was Machig Labdron, on the inner level she was Tara, and on the secret level she was Mother Prajnaparamita. Machig Labdron combines all of these together. Her Chod practice restrengthened all of the levels of the teaching of the Dharma.

When she was young she was a budding genius, smart, honest, and known for reading extremely well. Her parents saw to it that she received the best possible training, primarily in the *Prajnaparamita*, or "Perfection of Wisdom" sutra tradition.

Cutting Through Ego

She developed clear, perfect realization of the Prajnaparamita, which means perfect understanding of absolute truth, the nature of great emptiness.

What are we doing when we practice Chod? The Tibetan word means "cutting," so we will be cutting something. What are we cutting? First, we're cutting ego-clinging, and second, we're cutting all negative emotions—the five poisons of ignorance, attachment, anger, jealousy, and arrogance. Third, we're cutting the subjects and objects of attachment. Fourth, we're cutting all hope and fear.

Grasping is what we must cut first. That is the essence. So first grasping is cut, demolished, or transcended. Then, we experience negative emotions arising, so we cut them. Next, hopes and fears come up, and we cut them as well. Finally, attachments come up, and we keep cutting and cutting. That is the short answer to the question about the purpose of Chod. Of course, we'll go into this in much more detail later.

If we think about this process, it's none other than the technique of Dzogchen. Dzogchen teaches the essence of Chod. We could also say that Dzogchen practice is absolute Chod practice. Many of us know and practice the Dzogchen approach of Trekcho, which means "cutting thoroughly." In Dzogchen, where are we cutting? We're cutting in the space of the dharmadhatu. What are we cutting? All dualistic conceptions. While we're cutting with this view, there is no cutter, no object to be cut, and no cutting. In other words, our practice is free from grasping on to subject, object, and action. This is the essential view that Dzogchen practitioners use to cut all dualistic conceptions, which is also the essential understanding to maintain during Chod practice.

We can also regard Chod from yet another point of view. Machig Labdron said, "Chod practice is a combination of the view of the Sutras and the skillful means of the

Tantras." The view of the Sutras was taught by the Buddha in the Prajnaparamita Sutras, such as at the beginning of the *Heart Sutra*: "Inconceivable, inexpressible, unborn, unceasing, by nature like the sky." That is the view of the ultimate truth of reality that we discover within the nature of our own mind. Then we deepen this view using the skillful means of the Tantras, such as the ritual implements, chants, visualizations, and meditations that are taught in each specific sadhana. Combining this view with skillful means brings realization quickly.

Khenchen Palden Sherab Rinpoche often quoted from the Samcayagatha Sutra, or the *Three Hundred Stanzas of the Prajnaparamita Sutra*, which is *do du pa* [mdo 'dus pa mdo] in Tibetan. Here Buddha Shakyamuni said, "If a bodhisattva has four powers, he or she cannot be defeated by the four demons." What are these four powers? They are:

Never giving up the understanding of emptiness.
Never giving up compassion towards any sentient being.
Always doing exactly what one promises.
Always receiving the blessings of the buddhas.

These are the "Four Powers of the Bodhisattvas." If bodhisattvas apply these four powers, the four demons cannot disturb them. These are the elements of a Chod practitioner's true practice and they're the four cornerstones of Chod.

The first power—the understanding of emptiness that we must never give up—is the view of the Prajnaparamita. Everything is in the state of great emptiness. This is synonymous with Dzogchen realization in the Nyingma school.

The second power of never giving up on sentient beings is boundless compassion and bodhichitta. When you have true compassion for all living beings, this type of compassion never gives up on any being, regardless of the circumstance. By combining the first and second powers, we find that Chod is a practice of both emptiness and compassion.

The third power is doing exactly what we said we would do in our bodhisattva aspirations and vows. It also means keeping all the instructions and guidelines of the lineage. In action, this means keeping our commitment to the second paramita of maintaining perfect morality and conduct. Therefore, we're doing exactly what we said.

The fourth power of receiving the blessings of the buddhas refers to the lineage blessings, which come from Buddha Shakyamuni and are transmitted to us through the kindness of the great masters of the past up to our own teachers in this lifetime. These four powers are essentials for Chod practice. If a practitioner upholds these four powers as guidelines, she cannot be defeated by the four demons.

So what do we actually mean by the term 'demon?' This term is difficult to translate and is easily misinterpreted since it has such a variety of meanings in different cultures and religions around the world. Usually the term 'demon' points to a substantially existing, even if invisible, force of evil. In Tibetan Buddhism, the term *dud* [bdud] or 'demon' points to a mental or physical obstacle that blocks our spiritual growth. In the Buddha's Sutra teachings, the four demons are named as (1) the demon of the aggregates, (2) the demon of emotions, (3) the demon of distractions, and (4) the demon of death.

For Buddhists, demons do not exist externally. They are phenomena that our minds create when they're clouded by grasping, attachment, and clinging. Our minds fabricate emotional reactions and disturbances all by themselves, without needing any outside help. When we experience this disturbance, we grasp at it, which makes it seem like a "real" thing, which we then think of as a separate, existing threat, or a "demon."

Because this is the way our human minds work, the great master Machig Labdron said that grasping was the root demon: the king of the demons. If we don't have grasping, then there are no demons! When we understand this, "demons" cannot disturb us as bodhisattva practitioners.

In this book, we're following the Chod practice called the *Bellowing Laugh of the Dakini*, which was taught by the great master Jigme Lingpa. This practice is renowned throughout Tibetan Buddhist history. Let's examine the title of this specific sadhana. The text is from the *Longchen Nyingthig* lineage. The term *nyingthig* means "heart essence" or "heart drop." What are some of the meanings of *longchen*? *Longchen* is the "original vastness" or "space." The person Longchenpa was one of the greatest masters of Dzogchen. This great spaciousness is also a reference to the Dzogchen practice of Trekcho. Trekcho opens up spaciousness, a state of awareness where there are no boundaries, no limitations, and no restrictions. Everything is in the original state, totally enlightened.

This state is original and perfect; nothing has to be changed, ever. The Buddha's coming to this world and giving teachings didn't change the original nature. On the other hand, if the Buddha hadn't come to this world and never gave any teachings, the true nature still wouldn't have changed. By teaching or not teaching, by practicing or not practicing—the original nature is never changed in the slightest.

From that original nature, skillful means and wisdom strongly and actively radiate in the form of dakinis. Dakini is a Sanskrit word, which is *khandro* in Tibetan. The literal translation into English is "sky-goer," or maybe "sky dancer." On the absolute level, who or what is this sky-goer? The sky-goer is our awareness—the nature of mind moving freely and joyfully, with skillful means and wisdom naturally in union. There are no fears about anything, and no hopes for something. In the enlightened state, everything is already here. That state is great glowing love. Love is the absolute dakini.

So when we practice Chod, we're bringing out our already present nature of love, free from fears and expectations. There's nothing to gain and nothing to lose. In this way, the title *Bellowing Laugh of the Dakini* gives the essential meaning of the entire teaching.

Once we begin the practice, our fearless love appears in a specific form. In the commentary, the great terton Jigme Lingpa begins by saying, "I prostrate to the queen of space, lady of great bliss Yeshe Tsogyal." Yeshe Tsogyal is the form in which our active, fearless love appears as the dakini. She is blissfulness, fearlessness, and total enlightenment. She abides in the original nature exactly as it is, without increasing or decreasing any aspect. We're practicing Chod to be able to abide in our natural state in the same way.

In general, there are three types of prostrations: outer prostrations, inner prostrations, and absolute prostrations. An outer prostration means we make prostrations with our bodies while our hearts are full of devotion and joy. We clearly see the qualities of an enlightened being like Yeshe Tsogyal, and as a gesture of honor, we offer outer prostrations that come spontaneously from our respect and appreciation. In other words, we're deeply moved by the qualities of realization. An inner prostration is being in a single state with Yeshe Tsogyal, and having the same realization. An absolute prostration is beyond anyone who prostrates, any object to prostrate to, and the activity of prostrating itself. It's simply abiding in the natural state, exactly as it is.

Jigme Lingpa's commentary continues by saying, "The true nature, the Great Perfection, cuts the root of samsara in one stroke. Thus it transcends the cutter and the cut." If we maintain this realization of Dzogchen awareness, all obstacles and hindrances are instantly transcended in the absolute, natural state. This is the perfect view, the essential Chod practice.

Many students ask when they can begin practicing Chod. We can do some forms of Chod practice at any point after we've begun our Ngondro practice. His Holiness Dudjom Rinpoche said that the last section of the short Dudjom Tersar Ngondro is a condensed Chod practice. But no matter when we begin practicing Chod, it's always important to generate bodhichitta to bring meaning to what we're chanting.

Buddha Shakyamuni

Part 1:

Introduction to the Practice of Chod

Ven. Khenchen Palden Sherab Rinpoche

Chapter 1:

Understanding the Place of Chod in Buddhist Practice

There are many different ways that Dharma practices get their names, such as after a buddha or bodhisattva, or by using various poetic images of beauty like garlands or lotuses. Chod practice is named for its central action. In Tibetan, Chod means "cutting"— immediate, complete cutting. What are we intending to cut? We're cutting through our deluded state of mind, which is ego-clinging. Ego-clinging is the root system from which our suffering grows and flourishes. Using this practice, we're going to slice through this very tough root and completely sever its result, which is always suffering.

Buddha Shakyamuni gave different levels of teaching, matching them to the different capabilities and needs of his students. In general, the Chod teachings fall within the category of Mahayana[1] teachings. Chod practice combines the essence of both the Sutra Mahayana[2] and Tantra Mahayana[3] teachings. More specifically, Chod practice is the essence of the emptiness view of the Prajnaparamita Sutras,[4] the perfection of wisdom known as the "Mother of all the Buddhas." Furthermore, it unites the Prajnaparamita teachings with the Dzogchen[5] view. Chod practice also uses the skillful means of tantric practices, and in this way it unites skillful means and wisdom.

Tantra Mahayana teachings can be subdivided into two different levels of meaning: (1) the literal or provisional meaning, and (2) the ultimate or true meaning. The Chod teaching is particularly related to the ultimate level of meaning, which is why it belongs in the Inner Tantras, which provide the most direct methods to reveal our own primordial wisdom nature. Because they're from the Inner Tantras, the particular teachings and practices of Chod belong within the Vajrayana school of Buddhism, as taught by Buddha Shakyamuni and Guru Padmasambhava.[6] The tantric practice aspect of Chod is not included in the Buddha's Sutra Mahayana or Foundational Buddhism teachings.

By practicing these methods, those who have joyful effort, commitment, and devotion can reach enlightenment within one lifetime. That's why this is known as a profound and vast teaching—the fastest way to reach enlightenment.

Developing the Correct Motivation for Practice

In order to undertake the practice of Chod, we must demonstrate that we're serious by seeking and receiving a Chod empowerment and transmission from a qualified master who holds this lineage. Then, in order to truly receive the Chod empowerment, and to study, contemplate, and practice these teachings, it's necessary for each of us to develop and maintain the right motivation. This motivation has two aspects. The first aspect is the motivation of vast bodhichitta. We develop vast love and compassion, united with wisdom, for all sentient beings without any exceptions. This vast, pervasive power of love and compassion arises from the true nature of our mind.

Developing the Correct Motivation for Practice

The second aspect is the skillful means motivation, called purity understanding, or "pure perception." This is our view of the inherent purity of all phenomena, both externally and internally. In the Vajrayana, one way this purity is experienced in how we perceive our environment, which is expressed as the "five perfections:" the teacher is perfect, the teaching is perfect, the time is perfect, the place is perfect, and the assembly is perfect. We'll discuss this in more detail later. When we recognize that these five perfections are the nature of every experience, we have "pure perception." By cultivating this understanding, we're not brainwashing ourselves, pretending to believe in a fantasy. Exactly the opposite is true—we're progressively discovering what is actually true. Most of us haven't recognized this purity yet—the true, inherent qualities of all external and internal phenomena—but the methods and view of the Vajrayana will reveal this purity with practice. Therefore we should develop deep vajra[7] courage, vajra commitment, and vajra confidence so that we can remain in a state of purity understanding without being shaken by doubt and hesitation. Holding the commitment to understand and maintain this realization of inherent purity is the skillful means motivation.

With these two motivations, we can begin to study the teachings of Chod.

THE WISDOM DAKINI

The central deity of the Chod practice is the Wisdom Dakini known as Sangwa Yeshe Khandroma, Troma Nagmo, Yeshe Tsogyal, and many other names. She can be perceived in three different ways: according to beings of (1) the highest capability,

(2) medium capability, and (3) lower capability. In Vajrayana terms, these three forms are known respectively as a dharmakaya buddha, sambhogakaya buddha, and nirmanakaya buddha. Although she is perceived differently by different people, her ultimate nature is always the same.

We shouldn't misunderstand the three kayas[8] by thinking that the dharmakaya, sambhogakaya, and nirmanakaya buddhas are three separate beings in different locations, as if they were living in three different condominium units. It's not that the "dharmakaya" lives in the penthouse, "sambhogakaya" lives on the eighth floor, and the "nirmanakaya" lives in the basement! This would be an incorrect understanding. The three kayas are one buddha, but depending on our own capabilities we perceive this buddha in three different ways. This division doesn't arise due to differences in the realization of various buddhas. The division reflects our own ways of understanding and knowing the qualities of these enlightened beings. Our minds create the division.

To highly capable beings, the wisdom dakini who we call "Yeshe Tsogyal" is beyond all names, all categories, all fabrications, and all labels. Those are all mental limitations, and none of them—no conceptions, rules, or regulations—apply to the ultimate nature of the wisdom dakini. She has completely gone beyond all duality to the unborn and unceasing openness nature, which is beyond all conceptual states of mind. This is the ultimate understanding of the wisdom dakini. If we give a name to this ultimate wisdom dakini, she is known as Prajnaparamita,[9] the "Mother of all the Buddhas." In Tibetan, she is called *Yum Chenmo*, or Buddha Kuntuzangmo, which is Buddha Samantabhadri in Sanskrit.

Beings of medium capability understand the nature of the wisdom dakini Yeshe Tsogyal as a sambhogakaya buddha, the unceasing emanation of wisdom mind. This continuous creative energy arises in five different aspects known as the "five wisdoms." The five wisdoms are (1) mirror-like wisdom, (2) equanimity wisdom, (3) discriminating wisdom, (4) all-pervasive wisdom, and (5) all-accomplishing wisdom.

The five wisdoms are actually the enlightened, essential nature of the "five poisons," which are the unenlightened, negative emotions of sentient beings' deluded mental states.[10] It's not that something changes into something else, or that one form changes into another. Actually, when we simply recognize that the true nature of these five negative emotions is the five wisdoms, they self-reflect as various buddhas.

Within Chod practice, the same five wisdoms can be labeled as various deities, such as the five emanations of Vajrayogini or Vajravarahi, the five Female Dhyani Buddhas, or the five emanations of the wisdom dakini Sangwa Yeshe. These are all ways that the creative energies of the five wisdoms naturally express and reflect. Creative wisdom energies relate to the body, speech, mind, qualities, and activities of the sambhogakaya buddhas. Altogether these arise as five different pure displays of the sambhogakaya aspect of the wisdom dakini.

Sambhogakaya buddhas emanate in order to subdue and transcend all our grasping and dualistic conceptions. They aren't bound by our conceptualizations. Sambhogakaya buddhas appear in many forms: peaceful, semi-wrathful, and wrathful. For example, Guru Padmasambhava describes practicing in a frightful charnel ground where the powerful and mighty Vajravarahi is dancing on top of a corpse, surrounded by many wisdom dakinis, transforming all the limited ideas and duality conceptions of sentient beings. Vajravarahi is a wrathful dakini.

Sambhogakaya buddhas reside in the pure land of Akanishtha,[11] which is not a location, but the domain of the all-pervasive true nature. Sambhogakaya nature pervades all directions, all times, and all places. It's not contained by temporal or spatial boundaries. It is the creative wisdom energy of everything in the universe—the entire expanse of the dharmadhatu. Akanishtha definitely isn't a place that has a geographical location. It is a pure land that's never far away. There's a famous quote by the great master Longchenpa which introduces Akanishtha: "If somebody asks: 'Where is the place of wakefulness? What is the location of wakefulness?' Wherever we wake up, that is the place." Wherever we remove duality and ignorance, that place is Akanishtha. Akanishtha is no further away from us than the instant we completely wake up to our own wisdom awareness.

The third emanation of the wisdom dakini Yeshe Tsogyal's true nature is as a nirmanakaya buddha, who can be experienced by beings with lesser capabilities. Having lesser capabilities is not about being "bad" or "stupid." It just means having a state of mind that's occupied with regular conceptions. This is where we all are—fixated on the level of conceptions, with the constant mental activity of always naming things. Just think of how many names we've already said! Even choosing to name someone as having higher, medium, or lower capabilities is really just conceptual. To the extent that we hold tightly on to our conceptions, our knowledge will be based on grasping, duality, and making rigid distinctions. This type of mentality is known as "lower capability."

Lower capability beings have a wealth of conceptions! Our minds are just crammed with thoughts and opinions. Right now we're too full of this to be able to see the true nature. As lower capability beings, we regard the wisdom dakini Yeshe Tsogyal primarily through a conceptual lens—as a historical figure who was born in Tibet in the middle of the 8th century. We want to learn when and where she was born, who she knew, and what she did so we can try to fit her into a framework of our own limited dualistic system. She grew up, met Guru Padmasambhava, received Vajrayana teachings from him, and became his consort. She did retreat practices with tremendous joyful effort and strength until she reached enlightenment. Then she began transcribing Guru Padmasambhava's teachings into symbolic dakini language. Guru Padmasambhava and Yeshe Tsogyal then hid all these teachings as treasures called *terma*.[12] Yeshe Tsogyal stayed in Tibet for about 212 years.[13] Then she attained the transcendental wisdom rainbow body[14] and dissolved into space without leaving any physical remains. This description tells us "who she was" according to our common level of conceptual ideas. Beyond all of this, she is a fully enlightened being—the perfect embodiment of love, compassion, and wisdom.

Chod Empowerment, Transmission, and Instructions

Every sentient being has innate buddha-nature. Because of this, if we receive an empowerment from a qualified master, then meditation, mantra, and ritual objects become conditions that instantly invoke the power of our inherent buddha-nature. By receiving the samaya substances, the lineage blessings will be connected to our own primordial wisdom, or buddha-nature. These blessings create great opportunities for us to invoke and discover our own buddha-nature. This is the general purpose of empowerment.

Empowerments have different categories and divisions. There are empowerments of body, speech, mind, qualities, and activities, and each of these can be further divided into five categories, which makes twenty-five empowerments altogether. The number of empowerments for a particular lineage practice depends on the nature of the teaching and the instructions of Guru Padmasambhava, or Buddha Samantabhadra. The different categories of empowerments can be summarized into four: outer, inner, secret, and absolute.

How should you receive an empowerment and how should a vajra master give an empowerment? We all have to work together and generate our bodhichitta intention of love, compassion, and wisdom for all beings. Always have strong devotion and appreciation for all the lineage masters, the buddhas and bodhisattvas, and for Guru Padmasambhava. Maintain this state and receive the empowerment while applying the visualization and meditation instructions that we'll go over according to the lineage instructions. We'll do the same. Activating our bodhichitta and feeling strong appreciation and devotion to all the lineage masters means we're mingling our devotion, loving-kindness, and compassion into a single state, which invokes the lineage blessings and our own buddha-nature.

Chod is an extremely powerful practice: it arouses strong and deep energies that can be difficult for us to handle. For this reason, Chod practice should never be attempted by anyone without first receiving empowerment, transmission, and instruction,[15] and without forming and maintaining a close, ongoing connection to a qualified teacher.

All Dharma Practices are Chod

Fundamentally, all of the Buddha's teachings are forms of Chod practice because they're all teaching us how to recognize and remove ego-clinging and its activities. All of the past buddhas taught Chod, the present buddhas are teaching Chod, and all the future buddhas will teach Chod.

About 2,600 years ago, Buddha Shakyamuni turned the Wheel of Dharma three times. All of these teachings were designed directly or indirectly to cut ego-clinging and the sufferings that arise from it. The Buddha taught this profound teaching to many highly capable students, including gods, asuras, gandharvas, and human beings, as well as animals, nagas, and many others. Among the human beings, there were monks, nuns, arhats, siddhas,[16] and bodhisattvas. By receiving these teachings and then applying them in practice, many of these students reached enlightenment.

As we mentioned before, the view of Chod practice is primarily based on the second turning of the Wheel of Dharma, the Prajnaparamita Sutras. When the Buddha entered mahaparinirvana, these teachings were preserved by many great bodhisattvas, including Manjushri, Maitreya, and many great arhats. They preserved, collected, and spread these teachings according to the capabilities of the practitioners who received them, many of whom gained realization. Foremost among these students were the great masters Nagarjuna[17] and Asanga.[18] They analyzed and taught these sutra teachings according to two different methods, giving rise to the Madhyamaka[19] and the Mind Only schools.[20] The methods of both of these schools include the Buddha's instructions on cutting through ego-clinging, and many great practitioners from both philosophical schools fully actualized the results.

In teaching the Prajnaparamita Sutras, Buddha Shakyamuni revealed that all phenomena—all subjects and objects, whether appearing as a display of samsara or nirvana—are within great emptiness. Every possible aspect of grasping and clinging is therefore within this true nature.

This nature is unborn and unceasing, beyond conception. Within this primordial nature, notions like ego-clinging, subject, and object don't even exist. In all the Prajnaparamita Sutras, the Buddha showed again and again that everything is within this primordial nature. The Buddha didn't perform incredible miracles by appearing to transform everything into the primordial nature because everything is *already* the true nature of reality, as it is. By using logic, he revealed his enlightened understanding to his followers as the essence of the Prajnaparamita teachings. Chod is totally based on this view of emptiness.

In his tantra teachings, the Buddha taught the methods of skillful means to Guru Padmasambhava, the Eight Vidyadharas[21] of the Nyingma school, and the Eighty-four Great Mahasiddhas[22] of India. They all received these teachings, practiced them, and achieved enlightenment. This is how these teachings spread through the different Buddhist traditions and lineages, and how they've been preserved and practiced continually up until now.

How do we apply all this to our own experience? Sometimes we feel happy, and other times we're sad. Sometimes we might be famous, and other times we're unknown. Yet all of these apparent "states" are only conceptions, only clinging. They're nothing else—only notions that we grasp on to. The very moment we cut through clinging we discover our primordial nature. That absolute nature is known as "great nirvana," or enlightenment. It's totally relaxed and peaceful.

When we truly want to get rid of our suffering, it doesn't work to focus on external things. If we only look outside, no matter how many times we try to remove our suffering, we'll never achieve our goal. Instead, we should focus inwardly to discover where all our suffering begins.

All Dharma Practices are Chod

Suffering is the result of the unbalanced conditions of our mind. It arises from our duality conceptions.[23] Where do these duality conceptions come from? They come from our minds. Where does the mind come from? It arises from the true nature. In this way, every aspect of duality and all the movements of grasping must be resolved back into their true nature. By recognizing the illusory, empty nature of our conceptions, that very moment our grasping is released, and all the dense, tangled network of delusions completely disappear. We reach the final goal, resting in our primordial nature.

Once more, all of the Buddha's teachings are designed to help us attain just one result: to remove ego-clinging and the suffering it brings. In this way, every teaching of the Buddha is a teaching on Chod.

Guru Padmasambhava

Chapter 2:

History and Lineages of Chod

The Chod practice taught by Buddha Shakyamuni was widely practiced in India. After the Buddha's mahaparinirvana, the great master Nagarjuna and his foremost student Aryadeva[24] were renowned as masters of Chod. Aryadeva popularized the practice of Chod in India and wrote a very famous root text of the Chod practice tantras named *chod kyi chokor* [gcod kyi chos skor] that was translated into Tibetan around the 10th century.

Guru Padmasambhava and the Early Lineages

The primordial Buddha Samantabhadra is the ultimate source of these teachings. He passed the teachings and lineage to Buddha Vajradhara. From there it continued on to Buddha Vajrasattva, and then it was passed through great human masters in India, one after the other. Buddhism first started coming into Tibet from India in the 5th century, and was later firmly established there in the 8th century by Guru Padmasambhava, Khenchen Shantarakshita, and King Trisong Deutsen. When Guru Padmasambhava came to Tibet, he gave these teachings to many students, particularly his nine heart disciples.

In Tibet, there are two famous Chod lineages: the early

and the later. When Guru Padmasambhava brought the early lineage of this teaching to Tibet, it was closely connected to the Vajrayana. Guru Rinpoche gave these teachings to many people, including his twenty-five main students and nine heart-like disciples. The great Khenchen Shantarakshita also gave extensive Prajnaparamita sutra teachings to many students. The Prajnaparamita opens up one's capabilities to practice Chod. In this way, Guru Padmasambhava and Khenchen Shantarakshita included both Vajrayana and Sutra Prajnaparamita teachings, which were incorporated into a single system.

Yeshe Tsogyal became one of the foremost early lineage holders of Chod. Guru Padmasambhava gave her the essential pith instructions, which she fully accomplished. She summarized, transcribed, and hid his instructions throughout Tibet. In later centuries, 108 great tertons rediscovered termas on Chod. Many great tertons in the Nyingma school have discovered Chod teachings.

Padampa Sangye and Machig Labdron: The Later Lineages

The later lineage originates with a great Indian siddha called Dampa Sangye, whose name roughly translates as "true buddhahood," or "excellent buddha." Many Tibetans, however, add one more syllable, calling him Padampa Sangye, expanding the meaning to "Excellent Buddha Father."

Some histories say that Padampa Sangye was a south Indian master who came to Tibet around the late 10th or early 11th century. Padampa Sangye received many teachings from very great masters, including Guru Padmasambhava.

This was during the period of the new translations and the formation of the Sarma[25] schools. The Nyingma

Padampa Sangye and Machig Labdron: The Later Lineages

Padampa Sangye

Cutting Through Ego

tradition goes back much further and links him to Guru Padmasambhava.

It is said that Padampa Sangye lived for about five hundred years. This is difficult to reconcile in the histories because the activity of enlightenment is beyond our conceptual understanding. Padampa Sangye was held to have reached the state beyond death and birth, so over different periods he was known by different names.

Guru Padmasambhava's Lama Dance Above Samye Monastery

Padampa Sangye and Machig Labdron: The Later Lineages

There are many historical traditions according to what the relationship is seen to be between Guru Padmasambhava and Padampa Sangye. Padampa Sangye himself said that when Guru Padmasambhava was the *vajracharya*[26] or *dorje lopon*, [rdo rje slob dpon] conducting the ground-breaking ceremony of Samye Monastery,[27] Padampa Sangye was the chopon taking care of the ritual aspects of the ceremony.[28] During this ceremony it's said that Guru Padmasambhava levitated in the sky and performed a dance. By dancing in different directions, Guru Rinpoche laid out the outlines for Samye Monastery. While Guru Padmasambhava was dancing up in the sky, Padampa Sangye must also have been dancing on the ground! That's one way he was connected with Guru Padmasambhava.

Another aspect of Padampa Sangye's 8th century history is as follows. The Indian master Shantarakshita came to Tibet at the invitation of King Trisong Deutsen, shortly before Guru Padmasambhava. Shantarakshita was a leading scholar who was known as a direct emanation of the bodhisattva Vajrapani.[29] While Abbot of Nalanda Monastery—the greatest of the Indian monastic universities—Shantarakshita had many students from India, Nepal, China, and Tibet. One of his leading students, who later came with him to Tibet, was Kamalashila. Kamalashila's extensive teachings are still preserved and studied in Tibet and elsewhere. He's very well-known for his three volumes of instruction on the practice of meditation,[30] and for his Yogachara Madhyamaka philosophical text, the *Light of Madhyamaka*. He was regarded as an emanation of Padampa Sangye. Kamalashila said of himself, "Kamalashila is none other than Padampa Sangye," meaning they were the same person appearing with different names and at different times.

Padampa Sangye came to Tibet repeatedly by various

routes. He also went to China and then came back through Tibet. During Padampa Sangye's fifth visit to Tibet, as he crossed the Nepalese-Tibetan border at Nyana, he saw eight black birds in the sky flying towards Tibet. At that moment he told his attendants, "Tibet is a truly fortunate country. It has eight great wisdom dakinis." Padampa Sangye was famous for reading signs.

Wisdom dakinis appear in order to preserve the Buddhadharma and benefit all sentient beings. In Tibet, emanations of wisdom dakinis can be found in many different times, places, and forms. To us those birds would just seem like eight crows, but Padampa Sangye saw a subtle meaning in the appearance of these birds. To him, those eight black birds were indications of eight wisdom dakinis. He later identified and glorified these eight wisdom dakinis, one of whom was Machig Labdron. Usually people say that the wisdom dakini Yeshe Tsogyal was the great female master of early times, and Machig Labdron was the later great female master.

Padampa Sangye's fifth visit to Tibet was his longest. First he traveled to western Tibet and then he gradually came back to central Tibet. He eventually settled in an area of southern Tibet called Tingri [ting ri], a region with the Himalayas on the south and the Tsangpo River on the north. It was on an important route for traveling back and forth between Nepal and Tibet. Even now people go to Tibet from Nepal by that route, although it's harder to make that trip now. Padampa Sangye spent many years there, establishing the retreat center of *tingri langkhor*, a place that's still renowned as his residence. He translated Aryadeva's famous Chod text and began to give teachings on Chod. Many students gathered to receive his teachings.

It seems that Padampa Sangye had some difficulty with planning boards and zoning! Most of the Tingri villagers didn't initially feel connected or devoted to him. They had a meeting and decided, "He's a strange old Indian man. He showed up from nowhere! We didn't ask him to come, and now he's attracted all these other outsiders and they're occupying our land. This is *our* area and *our* place, and this is for *our* use. We should ask him to move!" So they went to Padampa Sangye and said to him, "Please, you must move from this place." And Padampa Sangye said, "Why should I move?" They said, "Because this is our place. We were born here, we live here, and this is our public gathering place." Padampa Sangye said, "No! This is *my* land. I have been here longer than any of you. In your grandfather's time I was here. You weren't even born then. I'm staying." Then, to prove his point, he recited the names of their grandfathers and grandmothers, and told them many details about their ancestors. His case was very strong; there wasn't anything they could say. He also told them that he had met Guru Padmasambhava in earlier times—as Kamalashila—and that Guru Rinpoche was one of his great teachers.

Padampa Sangye based every aspect of his teachings on the Prajnaparamita Sutras on emptiness. His own lineage of teachings is named Shije [zhi byed], which means "pacification," or "making peace." The more complete lineage name is *Dugngal Shije* [sdug bsngal zhi byed], which means "pacification of suffering." These teachings were perfectly mingled with the Chod lineage teachings.

He wrote many great volumes of teachings and practices. His *Hundred Verses of Advice to the People of Tingri* [ting ri brgya rtsa] was one of his last. It's concise and to the point: simple heart instructions useful for people who are neither monastics nor scholars. It's become very popular in the English language.

Male and Female Chod Lineages

Many commentaries on the Chod lineages distinguish between the male Chod lineage called *pho chod*, and the female Chod lineage called *mo chod*. The male Chod lineage emphasizes its direct descent from the Indian master Padampa Sangye, who is known as the father of the Shije lineage. The female Chod lineage emphasizes that it comes down from the Tibetan master Machig Labdron. Chod belongs to this Shije lineage.

Although there is a historical distinction between *pho chod* and *mo chod*, Machig Labdron's lineage is essentially the same as Padampa Sangye's lineage. Padampa Sangye met Machig Labdron on his third trip from India to Tibet. On the relative level, Machig Labdron was an emanation of the wisdom dakini Yeshe Tsogyal, and on the absolute level, she was none other than Prajnaparamita. After Padampa Sangye gave her teachings on the meaning of Prajnaparamita according to the great terton Nyangral Nyima Ozer,[31] as well as his own Shije practices and Chod, she merged these teachings in her heart and that very moment she became fully realized. She then spread the complete teaching of Chod according to her realization. This is the source of the female Chod lineage which comes down from the Tibetan master Machig Labdron. Although there is a historical distinction between *pho chod* and *mo chod*, Machig Labdron's lineage is essentially a slightly altered form of Padampa Sangye's lineage.

The Life of Machig Labdron

Machig Labdron was born in 1055. Machig Labdron is a shortened version of her full name, Machig Labchi Dronma. *Machig* [ma gcig] means "only mother." She was born in the

The Life of Machig Labdron

Machig Labdron

Cutting Through Ego

region of Labchi in western Tibet and was recognized as a female "light" or "lamp," *dronma* [sgron ma]. So *labchi dronma* means "the [female] lamp of Labchi." Buddha Shakyamuni and Guru Padmasambhava had both predicted her appearance as a direct emanation of Yum Chenmo, the Great Mother of the Buddhas, and as the wisdom dakini Yeshe Tsogyal. Since she was a wisdom dakini, at birth she was as radiant as the Buddha, like the sun emerging from the clouds, already fully awake. Without obscurations, she could see each of her past births.

Birth and Early Life

Machig Labdron's father was Chokyi Dawa and her mother was Bumcham Dza. They were the village leaders, as well as kind, educated people who were good Dharma practitioners. At the time of conception, Bumcham had a vision of four dakinis dressed in white. They came to her with jars of water and bathed her all night, saying, "You've got to be completely clean—our mother is coming to stay with you." She also saw fourteen semi-wrathful ladies of various colors carrying weapons, who said, "We're here to protect you."

On another night, she dreamt that a dark-blue dakini wearing bone ornaments and carrying a hooked knife appeared. This dakini cut open Bumcham's chest, removed her heart, and she and the other dakinis ate it and drank her blood. Despite how terrifying this dream was, Bumcham awoke with feelings of incomparable happiness. As her pregnancy progressed, Bumcham looked younger and younger, seeming to be the same age as her sixteen-year-old daughter.

Her neighbor also had a dream, and she came over to visit and said, "If you make me a nice place to sit and some nice offerings, I'll tell you this dream." Bumcham told her neighbor,

"I've also been having lots of interesting dreams for many months now." The family arranged the hospitality, and the neighbor and Bumcham shared their dreams with each other.

On the twenty-fifth day of the month,[32] before the baby's birth, Bumcham began to hear mantras from her womb. She heard OM AH HUNG, and sometimes she heard just the syllable, AH, AH, AH, AH.[33] Sometimes she heard the mantra of four syllables HA RI NI SA.[34] Many times she heard the mantra of the *Heart Sutra*, TADYATHA OM GATE GATE PARAGATE PARASAMGATE BODHI SVAHA. Those mantras continued to sound until Machig was born.

In a Tibetan custom for cleansing negative energy, people use a smudge of juniper and gugul[35] tree sap, like we sometimes use in ceremonies. Just before the birth, Bumcham heard a voice from her womb say, "Ama, when I come out, I want to be wrapped in stainless white cloths that have been held over the smoke of gugul and juniper leaves. I want those cloths!"

Machig Labdron was born in the Year of the Sheep, in the third month, on the full moon morning, which is around May in 1055. She was born without causing her mother pain, full of joy and brightness, and gazing up into the sky with a smile. She continued chanting the same mantras that her mother had been hearing from the womb. She was smiling at her mother, moving her arms and legs actively in dancing postures.

Of course, when Bumcham gave birth there weren't any birthing clinics in Tibet, so it was what's called a "home delivery." The birthing assistant was Machig Labdron's elder sister, Bumey, who was about sixteen. Bumey held the stainless, smoke-purified white cloth, and the baby kind of leapt out into the cloth. Bumcham and Bumey saw that on the top of Machig Labdron's head there was a glowing light with the secret syllable, AH. On her forehead they saw a small glowing five-colored light.[36] They also saw glowing light in her heart center.

Cutting Through Ego

In Tibetan tradition, when a baby is born, they place a little piece of special butter on the baby's tongue as his or her first food. They tried to put the butter into Machig's mouth, but she wouldn't take the butter—she just kept looking up into the sky and chanting AH. A little later, she ate the butter and went to sleep.

Soon, the glowing lights dissolved into her head, forehead, heart, and each area of her body. Once the glowing five-colored light dissolved into her forehead, it appeared that a third eye was there.[37] When Bumcham saw her baby girl's third eye, she felt worried and uncomfortable.

Soon after, the baby's father Chokyi Dawa came in. Bumey immediately told her father the good news, "Mother gave birth to a daughter, perfectly, without any pain or trouble. Everything went perfectly beautifully." But the sister was also partly hiding the baby, saying, "She sort of has a third eye. Maybe it's bad, and I don't know what you will think!" Her father said, "Just show her to me. Let me see." So she handed Machig Labdron to her father, who held her up in his palms and looked at her very carefully. Deep in her third eye he could see many very fine white AH syllables. Then he said, "She must be very special. I think this is a wisdom dakini, so we should all be joyful." Then all the family felt relieved.

Gossip spread rapidly through the villages. They were saying that the village leader had a new baby girl who had a third eye. Everybody was talking about it and saying that this baby girl might be a wisdom dakini. Soon after, the family held a big celebration of her birth. Everyone who came to the birthday party to see her thought she was extraordinary, with qualities that they'd never experienced with ordinary babies. They all decided this child must be a great being. Dron Tsema, "Clear Light Lamp" was the name her mother gave her when she was a young girl.

Her family, being committed to the Dharma, had a shrine room with many *pechas*,[38] and both of her parents read and practiced the Dharma sincerely. When Drontse turned five, her mother began to teach her how to read Tibetan characters. The moment that Bumcham told her something, Drontse understood it. Her mother never had to repeat what she was teaching, and soon Drontse could read perfectly.

In Tibet, every family had a small shrine, and if they could afford it they would have texts, even if no one there knew how to read them. They might have sutra teachings or Vajrayana texts, but everyone aspired to have at least twelve volumes of the Prajnaparamita Sutras, which they kept like offerings on the shrine. Periodically they would invite a lama or nun to read those texts aloud. In Drontse's family, there was a nun, or an *ani*, who stayed with them and read the Prajnaparamita texts all the time. One day while she was reading a Prajnaparamita text aloud, young Drontse, who was about eight years old, joined her. The nun started teaching her, but it was clear that the girl already understood, as she was easily reading along with the nun.

While they were reading the Prajnaparamita text together, the nun could read one line, but Drontsema could simultaneously read three lines, each in a separate voice. When the nun heard that, she knew Drontse was definitely a wisdom dakini, just like everybody had been saying. The nun gave Drontse her next name, Sherab Dronme.[39] *Sherab* [Tib.] or *prajna* [Skt.] means "wisdom," and *Dronme* means "burning lamp."

Young Sherab Dronme's reputation was spreading in every direction, and many people started coming to visit her. Even the king of that area in southwestern Tibet heard about her. The kings of that area were descendents of the royal line of Dharma King Trisong Deutsen. After King Trisong Deutsen's death, within a couple of generations his heirs had lost the central power. Yet several of his descendents went to the borderlands and established small kingdoms where the Dharma traditions were maintained.

When Sherab Dronme was ten or eleven, the King sent a letter to Chokyi Dawa, who was his regional minister, saying, "We've heard a wisdom dakini was born into your family. I would like to see and visit with her. Could you and your wife and family all come with her to my palace?" Twenty-one people—including Sherab Dronme and her mother and father—all went to visit the King on his command.

The ruler gave a big welcoming reception, and the family was escorted to the King's own temple. Then he began asking questions of Bumcham. "When and how was this girl born? What dreams did you have? What signs were there when she was born?" Bumcham tried to explain, but she was so nervous her voice became tiny, and she couldn't really answer the King. When Sherab Dronme saw that her mother was too nervous, she began to tell the story herself. Then the King asked her some questions directly, "Can you read letters? Can you read the texts?" Everyone said, "Yes, she definitely knows how to read." Immediately, someone brought out a Prajnaparamita text called the Samcayagatha Sutra.

Usually the Buddha's sutra teachings were in the form of dialogues. Different students would ask questions that the Buddha would then answer. This particular Prajnaparamita sutra is famous because the Buddha spoke it in one session, without dialogue or interruption.

The King asked Sherab Dronme to read for him, and she read the entire teaching quickly, thoroughly, and correctly. Very surprised, the King asked, "Well, you certainly know how to read this really well, but do you know what the text means?" She answered, "Yes, I know all the meanings, too." It was at this point that the King gave her the name we know her by to this day: Machig Labdron. The King felt that his kingdom was blessed by her auspicious presence so he gave a generous offering, including thirty groups of nine different items. Machig Labdron received beautiful new clothes, and the family received bountiful gifts of necessary supplies, as well as luxuries. After that, they went back to their home village.

Over the next several years, Machig Labdron spent her time with her mother and sister, reading, studying, contemplating, and meditating on the Prajnaparamita texts, and her abilities grew greatly. By the time she was thirteen, young intellectuals and scholars were coming to debate her, and then to ask for clarifications on various difficult points in the teaching. They arrived thinking she was so young she probably didn't know much. Yet when she debated them, she left them all speechless.

When she was thirteen, her mother passed away, and later when she was sixteen, her father passed away. From then on her elder sisters took care of her. Both sisters—the oldest sister and the middle sister—decided they should all join a temple in the local area. But the local lama named Lama Aton said to them, "Your youngest sister has brilliant wisdom capabilities that I cannot match. You must take her to central Tibet, where there is a very renowned teacher known as Drapa Ngonshe [grwa pa mngon shes]. He is the teacher for her."

Training

Drapa Ngonshe (1012–1090) was a very renowned Nyingmapa monastic, scholar, and terton. Both Machig Labdron and her elder sister Bumey took ordination from Drapa Ngonshe.[40] After that, Bumey said to her sister, "Now we should really just go on retreat. If we do retreat for three years, we both will go to the pure land without leaving a body behind." But Machig Labdron answered, "No, that's not right for me. I don't want to go to the pure land because I have to fulfill my purpose in coming here.[41] You go on retreat. Then after I finish my purpose and liberate many sentient beings, I will meet you there. But I won't go now." So Bumey went on retreat, and died three years later, leaving no body and going to the pure land of the dakinis.

Drapa Ngonshe requested that Machig Labdron stay for four years as his object of veneration, to practice, and to help him. So she stayed at the Drapa Monastery until about the age of twenty. At that point, an older couple that lived nearby requested that Drapa Ngonshe send her to stay in their house for a year as their reader of the Prajnaparamita texts, with the promise that she would then become their heir. So she lived there for a while.

Machig Labdron asked Drapa Ngonshe for additional empowerments, but he didn't give them to her, and instead sent her to Choton Sonam Lama.[42] Choton Sonam told her that she didn't yet understand the exact meaning of the Prajnaparamita. He said, "*Jo chung*;[43] the meaning is to liberate all. You still grasp at 'good' and 'bad.' When you connect to the original state, all is equanimity." Then he gave her tantric empowerment.

At night, he very secretly conferred the *Guhyagarbha Tantra* empowerment on Machig Labdron and four ngakpas. By early morning, her realization was such that she was dancing in the sky and moving unimpededly through walls. She danced at a secret local spring, which was protected by an irritable naga. The naga lost its power and became her student. She walked back to the others in the full sunlight, naked except for her bone ornaments. The four ngakpas dismissed her as completely crazy. But Choton Sonam corrected them saying, "You four ngakpas only understood the literal meaning of the empowerments. This dakini received the full empowerment."

Even before this time, she had already started having dreams about Padampa Sangye. People had been telling her that he was coming from India to see her. Then he arrived unexpectedly at Drapa Ngonshe's big monastery. Machig Labdron was walking nearby, and people pointed to a man in the street and said, "That is Padampa Sangye." Machig Labdron immediately felt great devotion and she wanted to make prostrations. She prepared herself and began to prostrate, but Padampa Sangye insisted that she stop, and he held her hand and touched her forehead to his own. Machig Labdron said, "Oh, great teacher, I'm so happy! You're so kind to come to Tibet to help the Tibetan people. I revere and respect and honor you." And Padampa Sangye replied, "You are a great wisdom dakini who purposely came to this world and Tibet to help all beings. That is even more wonderful, gracious, and kind."

Then Machig Labdron asked Padampa Sangye, "How should I continue to carry on my beneficial activities so that I can reach every living being?" Padampa Sangye replied, "Even though on the absolute level you already know all of this, on the relative level I'm older than you, so therefore in order to give a good example to future generations, I'll leave you with these words:"

> Give up attachment to one location. Don't stay in one place all the time.

> Whatever difficult situation comes, crush it. Step over it. Don't

> pay attention to it. Don't be sensitive. Whether it's a good or bad situation, don't stop.
>
> Have courage and commitment that is as vast as the sky. Always wear the armor of patience.
>
> Always fill your heart with boundless love and compassion.
>
> Mingle your awareness with the sky all the time.

Those were his parting pith instructions. After he said those few words, they separated and he departed. Around that time she started having dreams about another teacher from India. The voices in her dreams would say, "Topa Bhadra is coming to meet with you. He will be your consort, and you are to live together as a couple. You must stay together in order to accomplish your bodhichitta activity." She had that dream again and again.

In another dream a white dakini appeared, saying, "You must meet with this man." Machig Labdron asked her, "Who is he actually? Where does he come from? What is his story?" The white dakini said, "He comes from Kosala in India. He was born into a family of the warrior caste. He is a very great yogic practitioner who practices the *Chakrasamvara Tantra*. His purpose is to meet you, and you must meet him."

At first, she didn't pay much attention to these dreams. Sometimes dreams are accurate, and sometimes they're not. But the dreams kept coming, repeating the same predictions and instructions. Finally, she decided to ask her lamas Drapa Ngonshe and Terton Choton Sonam Lama if the dreams were true, and to advise her about whether she should do this or not. Both teachers told her that her dreams were correct.

"You should meet this teacher who is coming from India. It will be very beneficial for your teaching now, and for the continued lineage of your teaching in the future."

During the next phase of her life, she went to receive teachings from the renowned teacher Sherab Bum [Shes rab 'bum] who was giving Prajnaparamita teachings to about 300 students. When she arrived, many of the monks present were intensely curious. One of them asked her, "Who you are? Where did you come from? We heard that in this chief's family there is a special young girl who has three eyes, and that now she's become a nun named Jo Chung—the Little Nun. Is that you or not?" She replied, "Yes, I am that nun." They received her with honor and brought her to the teacher, bringing three levels of cushions, seating her on a high throne.

The monks said, "We heard that you're an expert on the Prajnaparamita teachings. What can you tell us?" First, she gave some teachings. Then seven of the best student monks came forward to debate her on subtle points in the Prajnaparamita Sutras. She answered all their questions perfectly so all the monks were completely satisfied. Everyone developed great appreciation for her knowledge, wisdom, and deep understanding of the Prajnaparamita.

After that time, Machig Labdron returned to Lama Drapa. His two patrons had once more requested her as their household Prajnaparamita reader, so she was sent to their home to stay.

Adult Life

Immediately after she started her journey towards their house, she had more dreams in which dakinis appeared, instructing her to make a union with Topa Bhadra.[44] Then she finally met

Topa Bhadra on the road as he was coming from India to meet her. She saw that this teacher was dark skinned, his eyes were very round, and his gaze was looking straightforward.[45] He was a very powerful looking yogi. They continued together, traveling to the family of the patrons.

Machig Labdron and Topa Bhadra were there about seven days together. During those days, they had discussions about the different meanings of the teachings. They also discussed the signs, omens, and conditions, and whether these indicated that they should come together. In Tibet, these factors and conditions are called *tendrel*.[46] Through signs and indications one can foretell the whole pattern of days—whether they are auspicious or inauspicious. If one really knows the systems of divination, some signs can tell you years ahead, or even more. From their discussions on the *tendrel*, they determined that the circumstances were auspicious. As a result, they came together in union. Because of Machig Labdron's realization of the absolute true nature, she wasn't limited by the keeping or breaking of vows. Therefore, her vows were never broken.

After about seven days, Topa Bhadra departed, heading towards southern Tibet. Machig Labdron stayed and finished her commitment to the patrons. On returning to her teachers, both lamas urged her to rejoin with Topa Bhadra in order to start a family lineage. Thus, from about age twenty-three until about age thirty-five she stayed with Topa Bhadra and gave birth to her first son who was named Drubpa—which means "fulfilled," because his birth fulfilled the prophesies—and a second son, Drubse. Then she gave birth to a daughter who was named Drubchungma, "small accomplished girl." Because Machig gave birth to her while they were crossing over a mountain pass, the little girl was also called La Cham, or "Lady of the Mountain Pass."

During these years, Machig Labdron and Topa Bhadra stayed together, practiced together, and raised their children. Then they decided it was time to separate. Topa Bhadra went back to India, and Machig Labdron stayed in Tibet. When they were starting off in different directions, they sang a very wonderful song to each other. In the song, they exchanged their realizations and understandings of their duties in all of the different worlds to benefit all sentient beings.

Over time, all of their children became great yogis and yoginis.[47] Machig Labdron's sons and daughter requested and received all of her teachings, and they became her lineage holders and great teachers.

Machig Labdron continued to periodically receive teachings from Drapa Ngonshe and Sonam Lama. She also reconnected with Padampa Sangye in Tingri. She received many more teachings on Prajnaparamita and Shije from him. Padampa Sangye held a very famous lineage of inner and secret teachings that started from the Buddha and then went to Manjushri. At that time, he passed all those lineage teachings on to Machig Labdron.

After receiving his final instructions, she decided to go to the meditation caves in Zangri Kharmar [Zangs ri mkhar dmar], the Red Copper Castle.[48] In a vision, wisdom dakinis came to her and said, "Let's go! It's an auspicious place, and you can lead all sentient beings to enlightenment." She established her hermitage at the Red Copper Castle when she was about thirty-seven.

Teaching Activities

Zangri Kharmar is still a famous pilgrimage place because that's where she stayed most of the rest of her life. She primarily taught Chod, and thousands of people came from the north, south, and east of Tibet. Many famous Tibetan and Nepali masters also came to receive teachings.

At that time, three Indian panditas[49] came to Tibet to investigate her. They had been hearing rumors in India that in Tibet there was a lady who was a renowned emanation of a wisdom dakini who had three eyes and the other marks. She was giving some "new" teachings called "Chod." The panditas argued that there was no teaching like this in India, and no text about it preserved in Sanskrit. At that time, many scholars—both Indian and Tibetan alike—believed that only teachings with an Indian ancestry, for which the existence of an original Sanskrit text could be demonstrated, could be authentic. They were worried she was teaching something that was not authentic Dharma. So they came to check it out—to "taste" the teachings she was giving.

According to the great master Karma Chagme, Machig Labdron addressed the panditas in beautiful Sanskrit, and discussed the Prajnaparamita with them according to three systems. (1) The first system was the Prajnaparamita oral transmission lineage that came through Buddha Shakyamuni to Brahmin Aryadeva, and then went to Tibet. (2) In the second system, the great wisdom dakini Machig Labdron transmitted Chod teachings according to the Sutras, as well as the Tantras that she received from mother Tara, which she then transmitted to her son Tonyon Samdrup as a Tantra lineage. (3) The third Chod system Machig Labdron directly realized as the inseparable union of Sutra and Tantra, which she transmitted to her fortunate disciple Khugom Chokyi Singe and many others as the Chod lineage of the "Inseparable Union of Sutra and Tantra."

The panditas were fully satisfied and accepted the authenticity of Chod. Machig Labdron's Chod teachings became the first teachings originally written in the Tibetan language that were then translated into Indian languages and accepted in India.[50]

Machig Labdron has had many famous emanations. Relatively recently in Tibet, the great yogini Jetsun Rigdzin Chonyi Zangmo (1852–1953), who was also called Ani Lochen and Shugseb Jetsun Rinpoche, was a recognized incarnation of Machig Labdron and a famous Chod practitioner.[51]

Yeshe Tsogyal

Great Masters of Chod

The Early Terma Lineages of Chod

The early lineage came to Tibet directly with Guru Padmasambhava, and can be divided into two systems: *Kama* and *Terma*. The Kama Chod practices are an unbroken oral transmission lineage, continuing through the centuries. The Terma Chod system was established when Guru Padmasambhava gave these Chod teachings to the wisdom dakini Yeshe Tsogyal, who transcribed them into secret dakini script, then hid them so they could be rediscovered by great tertons when the time was right.

Nyangral Nyima Ozer (1124–1192) is called the "King of the Tertons." He was able to recall his previous lives back to King Trisong Deutsen, and he recovered many termas. Among his many glorious activities, he received the *pho cho* teaching lineage from direct disciples of Padampa Sangye. Then he revealed a terma cycle of dakini teachings at Juniper Ridge of Pearl Crystals, including a very famous Chod practice on Vajravarahi, or Black Troma.[52]

Tsasum Lingpa was also a great Chod practitioner who revealed a very famous Chod text. When he was young he practiced in many frightening and powerful spots. His terma is known as *Sangwa Yeshe*, the "Secret Wisdom Dakini" practice, which is a very beautiful practice.[53]

Somewhat later, Jigme Lingpa revealed the termas of the *Longchen Nyingthig* lineage, which include the practice we're discussing, *Bellowing Laugh of the Dakini*.[54] His wisdom dakini practice became very famous in many of the schools of Tibetan Buddhism.

Most recently, in the late 19th century (1835–1904) another great terton known as Dudjom Lingpa came from

Cutting Through Ego

the Golok region of Tibet. He was the direct predecessor of His Holiness Dudjom Rinpoche, Jigdral Yeshe Dorje. He revealed many great termas in a cycle called the *Dudjom Tersar*, including a very famous Chod practice of Vajravarahi, or Black Troma called "Troma Nagmo: A Practice Cycle for Realization of the Wrathful Black Dakini."[55] All of these Chod lineages are contained within of the terma lineage of Chod practice. This is briefly about how these terma teachings of Chod practice came in the first place.

The Later Lineages of Chod

The later Chod lineages arose in the 11th and 12th centuries. The male lineage started from Padampa Sangye and his main students Chokyi Sherab, So Chungba, Yeshe Gyaltsan, and Machig Labdron who founded the female lineage of Chod. Her foremost disciple was her son Tonyon Samdrup.

In the 12th through 14th centuries, Chod became very popular throughout Tibet. Chod practices became incorporated into every Tibetan Buddhist lineage, and are still practiced in all of them. The Kagyu and Nyingma schools particularly emphasize and actively practice Chod. In the Karma Kagyu school, the third Karmapa Rangjung Dorje was renowned as a Chod master. Other Kagyu schools such as the Drigung and Shangpa are also well known for their Chod practices.

In the 17th century, the great master Karma Chagme[56] brought the early and later Chod lineages together into a single lineage like two great rivers joining. He wrote one of the most revered Chod practices, the *Tsogle Rinchen Trengwa*,[57] or *Precious Garland of Accumulation*. This Chod practice became very popular in Tibet, and is widely practiced around the world today.

Great Masters of Chod

LONGCHENPA

Longchenpa Drime Ozer (1308–1364) was born into a Nyingma practitioner's family in Yoru in central Tibet. Guru Padmasambhava predicted that Longchenpa would be the lord of the Sutra, Tantra, and Dzogchen teachings. Even when he was very young his brilliance was notable. When Longchenpa was nineteen he joined Sangphu Neuthog,[58] the most famous monastic college in Tibet at that time. His wisdom was incomparable, and he became its most famous student. His capabilities were so great that his classmates named him Samye Lungmingpa [bsam yas lung ming pa]: "He who remembers all the Buddha's teachings." Yet Longchenpa realized that his knowledge was mostly based on his intellectual mind. He decided it was time to develop knowledge based on practice.

At the age of twenty-seven he went to meet the great Dzogchen master Rigdzin Kumaradza.[59] Kumaradza had experienced indications and signs that Longchenpa would become his most famous lineage holder, so he gave him every Dzogchen Nyingthig teaching. Longchenpa then meditated for three years in retreat at Samye Chimphu cave.[60] During that time, his realization became equal to that of Guru Padmasambhava, Vimalamitra, and the wisdom dakini Yeshe Tsogyal. In other words, he reached enlightenment within those three years. Longchenpa became one of the most famous Dzogchen masters in history, and was known as the "Second Garab Dorje."

For the benefit of future generations, he wrote famous Dzogchen texts, including the *Seven Treasuries*, the *Trilogy of Comfort and Ease*, and the *Trilogy of Self-Liberation*.[61] Longchenpa combined the Dzogchen teachings of the *Vima Nyingthig* lineage from Vimalamitra with those of the *Khandro Nyingthig* from Guru Padmasambhava, preparing the ground for the fully unified system of teachings that four centuries later became known as the *Longchen Nyingthig*.

Longchenpa's writings are especially beautiful and powerful. This is because they aren't just scholarly teachings based on intellect—he wrote them from the vast realization of his wisdom mind.

Great Masters of Chod

JIGME LINGPA

Jigme Lingpa (1729–1798) was a great meditation master, terton, poet, and scholar in the Nyingma tradition. He was born in central Tibet in 1729. He had little scholarly training—instead, he practiced intensively all his life, spending most of his life in retreat. When he was in his twenties, he did a three year retreat in central Tibet in the same Samye Chimphu cave where Guru Padmasambhava had given teachings and did retreat, and where Longchenpa had attained realization.

During the this retreat at Samye Chimphu, he particularly practiced on Longchenpa. In the first year, he saw the wisdom body of Longchenpa right in front of him. The emanation did not speak to him, but was simply meditating and radiating wisdom light. During the second year, he again saw Longchenpa's wisdom body, and this time he received speech empowerments from him. During the third year, Longchenpa gave him the empowerments, transmissions, and instructions for all of his teachings. Jigme Lingpa received and perfectly understood all of these teachings from Longchenpa simply by seeing him these three times. He had never been in a monastic college or taken formal classes, but when his mind and the wisdom mind of Longchenpa completely mingled, that moment he instantly became a great scholar. After this retreat he also received many visions of Guru Padmasambhava and the wisdom dakini Yeshe Tsogyal, and began revealing terma teachings. Some of his famous works are the *Longchen Nyingthig*, and a nine-volume history of the Nyingma Vajrayana.[62] He taught students from all schools of Tibetan Buddhism.

He became known as the Omniscient Vidyadhara Jigme Lingpa. His speech became so special that he was also known as "Vajra Voice." His teachings were like Milarepa's—every word carried a profound meaning in the form of beautiful poetry.

The Longchen Nyingthig

The Chod practice we're teaching here—*Khandro Gejang* [mkha' 'dro gad rgyang]—comes from the *Longchen Nyingthig* cycle of terma. The *Longchen Nyingthig*, which means "*Heart Essence of Longchenpa*," is very famous in the Nyingma school. Almost every Nyingmapa practices some aspect of the *Longchen Nyingthig* teachings, so its Chod practice became widely practiced. The highest lamas, many thousands of monks, nuns, and wandering yogis and yoginis have all practiced the *Longchen Nyingthig* lineage of Chod. The special masters of this lineage are known as the "Golden Chain of Mountains Lineage Holders" [brgyud 'zin gser ri'a 'khring ba]. This lineage has now also become well-known in the West, and many students have received a lot of teachings from the *Longchen Nyingthig* lineage. It has continued unbroken, and remains one of the most active lineages in the Nyingma school.

Khandro Gejang can be translated as "Joyful Bellowing Laugh of the Wisdom Dakinis." This is the joyful laugh of the wisdom dakinis Yeshe Tsogyal, Machig Labdron, the five wisdom dakinis of the five buddha families, Troma Nagmo, the secret wisdom dakini Sangwa Yeshe, and all of their retinues.

Ven. Khenpo Tsewang Dongyal Rinpoche

Chapter 3:
Essential Elements of Chod Practice

The Proper Practitioner

A Chod practitioner who's going to cut grasping must maintain the four cornerstones that we discussed earlier in the Preface. They are the four powers or qualities of the bodhisattvas.

(1) The first power is a good view and understanding of the true nature. We must recognize and abide in the sky-like view of the nature of our mind without any doubt or hesitation.

(2) The second quality is infinite compassion for all sentient beings without partiality, expanding in every direction to include all beings without exception.

(3) The third power or technique is receiving and maintaining perfect lineage blessings, perfect instructions, and perfect samaya.

(4) The fourth necessary quality is continuous joyful effort and devotion to the teachings. We must have great confidence, great joy, and great joyful effort.

How do we cut? We must have a fearless attitude known as "vajra courage," in addition to good understanding, confidence, wisdom, and compassion. When all of these qualities are activated in our hearts and minds, we're ready to practice Chod. People who have all these qualities are called "perfectly qualified Chod practitioners." If we don't have all of these four qualities right now, it's very important to begin with devotion, confidence, and joyful effort, then courage, wisdom, and the other qualities will grow.

There are four different targets to cut. (1) The self-importance of our ego-clinging is our major target. This is our belief in the real existence of an "I." (2) The second target is our dualistic conceptions. These arise when we make a rigid, deluded separation into subject and object, almost as if we're starting a war between the two. (3) The third target is grasping on to the idea that there is solid existence. Without investigating or analyzing it, we believe that things truly exist as solid objects. This belief manifests as our constant reliance on names and labels. (4) The fourth target is grasping on to notions of identifying characteristics. "This is blue and that is white. This is high and that is low. This is small and that is large." All of these fabrications about different characteristics and identities must be cut.

The fourth target to cut, in which we grasp on to the identity and characteristics of things, is the strongest of these. We really believe in characteristics, on both the relative and absolute levels. We believe that the qualities of samsara and nirvana really exist. We constantly grasp at this. Sometimes we may even think that this kind of clinging is great! But eventually the sense of greatness deceives us, and again we fall down to the other side of our habitual patterns and suffer. All of our grasping on to these notions has to be thoroughly cut.

Where does this cutting take place? It takes place right there on the spot! On our cushion or wherever we may be in the moment. Right here is the spot.

Cutting through ego-clinging is the target of all the Buddha's instructions, without exception. The great masters of the Chod lineage, including Yeshe Tsogyal, Machig Labdron, and Padampa Sangye analyzed ego-clinging and gave the name "demon" to four specific inner and outer challenges of ego-clinging. There are both philosophical and practical ways to understand these four demons.

The Philosophical View of the Four Demons

When we hear about and contemplate different synonyms for "ego-clinging," we get a clearer understanding of what exactly has to be removed or transcended. First we must find the demons and then we begin to cut them.

The four demons are taught in both the Sutrayana and Tantrayana. They are (1) the demon of the aggregates, (2) the demon of death, (3) the demon of negative emotions, and (4) the demon of distraction. Why are these called "demons?" If something always helps us, we believe it's a "god." But if something always obstructs us, we think it's a "demon." In other words, on the relative level of samsara, demons are obstacles that prevent us from succeeding in what we really want, which is attaining realization and the ability to truly help ourselves and others get out of the cycle of suffering.

The Demon of the Aggregates

Maybe you're wondering how the aggregates make obstacles for us. On the simplest level, our own body is made up of the aggregates.[63] This body is one of the major obstacles for our practice. In Tibet there's a village saying: "This body is so small—just the length of one's own arms outstretched. Our mind is also small—so small that we can't even see it. The mouth also is very small. Yet we're always laboring for this small body, invisible mind, and tiny mouth!" So it goes from the time we're born until we die.

Of course, we don't usually describe it that way. Instead we say, "I'm really busy. I have to do this cooking and get my hair done up and go to that entertainment, then play golf. I have so many things to do!" We may think up all sorts of ways to describe what we're so busy doing all the time, but if we look honestly, these three things are what we've been serving, and they're what's kept us so busy all this time. As a result, our spiritual activity gets lost in the shuffle. We may have devotion and good aspirations to benefit other beings, yet even with these good qualities, many times we pass up Dharma opportunities because we're so strongly attached to our aggregates. In the language of Chod, the demon of the aggregates has obstructed us and carried us away from our main goal.

The Demon of Death

Death is an inevitable experience that we will all have to go through. Nobody wants to go through that transition, or *bardo*,[64] but it's definitely going to happen. There's nothing we can do to prevent it. Death is a major obstruction. It prevents us from fulfilling our intentions and wishes in this lifetime. We don't know when, where, or what kind of circumstances will send us on our journey. This unclear, unknowing quality is known as ignorance.

Even if we have a wonderful motivation, are doing

beautiful Dharma activities, and have a strong meditation practice, it's uncertain how long these opportunities to develop will last. Death will eventually interrupt our work. When it comes, it's powerful and urgent, and there's no way to delay the inevitable. We can't say, "Please wait for awhile until I finish this meritorious activity, and then I'll come." Arguing won't help at all! Even if we're on the road to success, we'll still have to leave when we're caught by the demon of death.

THE DEMON OF NEGATIVE EMOTIONS

The third demon is stronger than both the demon of the aggregates and the demon of death. The Buddha called this demon the "three poisons demon," referring to the three fundamental negative emotions of ignorance, attachment, and anger.

Because of the three poisons, when we achieve some kind of success, we tend to develop arrogance and pride. We feel like we're so special. We puff ourselves up like baking powder "puffs up" a cake or biscuit. Once we've developed arrogance, next comes jealousy. Everyone is capable of feeling jealousy, but most of the time it arises from arrogance. If we see that someone else is going to have even a little more success than us, we feel like we're losing, and we feel jealous.

The five negative emotions of ignorance, attachment, anger, pride, and jealousy don't always arise in the same order. Ignorance is definitely the ground, and attachment is second. After that could be anger, pride, or jealousy, or they might arise in different combinations. These negative emotions cause us to feel restless and block us from fulfilling our goals. They prevent us from having even a single moment of peace. They also create obstacles for others, preventing them from feeling peace and joy. They're truly demonic! Because of our negative emotions, we may also carry out negative karmic activities. The combination of our karma and negative emotions creates our whole vision of samsara.

The Demon of Distraction

The demon of distraction is sometimes also called the "demon of beauty." It's very subtle and hard to detect. Even the highest capability practitioners can be deceived by this demon. It arises when we get the feeling that we've achieved something big. We don't recognize that it's is a distraction because it's already distracted us. We may realize it later, but by then it's too late. We've already experienced the result.

The demon of beauty seems so appealing and nice, but its results are not. Outwardly, we get carried away by luxuries and beautiful things. We may become almost entirely uprooted from our spiritual life, and pulled in a direction that's free from hardship and difficulties. Inwardly, we get obsessed with entertaining fantasies and intellectual pastimes, drawn away from cultivating loving-kindness, compassion, and meditation. It's said that even great practitioners can be carried away by this demon, so we always have to be very mindful.

Our target is to chop these four demons into dust with our Chod practice. What weapons will we use? Actually, we don't need any weapons or soldiers to wield them. We don't need missiles, guns, swords, or bows and arrows. We have to cut these demons with love and compassion.

The Buddha said that the wisdom of great emptiness and the skillful means of compassion must be united together.

The Philosophical View of the Four Demons

This is how we can cut all the obstacles we face. Wisdom and compassion are equally important. By uniting them we can cut all of our ego-clinging. There are two ways to do this. We can first meditate on the true nature of great emptiness, and then generate great love and compassion. Or we can first generate great bodhichitta during meditation, and then release all grasping and meditate on great emptiness. Either of these methods will unite compassion and wisdom inseparably.

It's very important to know what will happen if we only work with one or the other. If we only meditate on loving-kindness and compassion, we may fall into emotions, grasping at loving-kindness and compassion. That's why the Buddha and other great masters taught that we should always mingle our bodhichitta, love, and compassion with the recognition of great emptiness. On the other hand, if we only practice the wisdom of emptiness without bringing up bodhichitta, then our emptiness meditation will become very dry. Falling into either of these extremes is incorrect because the true nature is beyond dualistic extremes.

The Chod Practitioner's View of the Four Demons

According to the practical way of working with Chod, the four demons are considered somewhat differently. We're not talking about an entirely different set of four demons, but another way of describing the main cause of all our problems: our own ego-clinging. According to this approach, the four types of demons are (1) tangible demons of obstruction, (2) intangible demons without obstruction or form, (3) the demon of exhilaration, and (4) the demon of arrogance or pride.[65]

Tangible Demons

Tangible demons include all of the external, material obstacles we face. These are phenomena of the four elements of earth, water, fire, and wind, like earthquakes and wildfires. They also include wild animals like tigers, leopards, snakes, and scorpions. Tangible demons are forms we perceive through our five senses, including sights, sounds, smells, tastes, and tactile sensations. This category also includes human beings. These would be, most obviously, our enemies. However, even loving family members and friends can be obstructions to our realization.

Intangible Demons

Intangible demons don't appear externally as objects to our senses. They're mental concepts and emotions. When positive ideas develop in our minds, we experience happiness and want to hold on to that experience. When negative ideas arise, we experience negative emotions like anger and fear, and want to reject those experiences. As our mind moves back and forth between these states of craving and aversion, it becomes afflicted with emotions. Because there is no material existence to these emotions they're called "unobstructed demons." Clinging to any dualistic ideas of accepting or rejecting disturb our mental state and hinder our realization and growth.

Demon of Exhilaration

The demon of exhilaration, or hope and expectation, can create a feeling of great joy. Say we've practiced a bit and have some result. We feel very excited about that, and at the same time we want something more. These experiences can lead to a feeling of importance, of being special, and we might decide that there is no need to do any more practice. We expect the world to recognize our accomplishment, and to praise and honor us. This type of exhilaration really undoes our meditation, weakens our spiritual practice, and leads to pride and arrogance.

Demon of Pride

Once we have pride and jealousy, soon there will be aversion, followed by strong attachment. For example, say we practice Chod and get a sudden small realization of some sort. Feeling that we've become really important, we don't care about others so much. We feel that we're the superior, successful ones. We've become spiritual "one percenters." No matter what beautiful idea or brilliant realization we've experienced, if we start holding and clinging on to it, it's a demon.

We must have a firm understanding that "demons" don't exist outside ourselves. They have no existence by themselves. Don't expect a demon to suddenly appear, like some stranger with one eye looking at you and trying to talk to you. A demon isn't some kind of "darkness" trying to haunt you. It's not like that at all. The only demon we face is the "strangler" of our own ego-clinging, which exists entirely within our own mind. This is exactly what we work to remove by practicing Chod. According to the Buddha's teachings, as long as we have grasping and clinging we'll have demons and obscurations. This is what we need to cut. This is our target.

When we practice Chod, we shouldn't aim at the wrong target. The robes, tents, ritual implements, music, and ceremony are important parts of Chod, but they're only the symbolic aspect. We must not get caught up in these outer symbols, making them into powerful obsessions of grasping. Always be careful not to use the forms of a practice to feed your ego. Your "job" is to remove these four demons of ego-clinging. Cut them right now. We're not going to say "mañana" or next year. Instantly, as they arise, this very moment, use the methods we're given to remove the demons.

How To Cut Ego-clinging

According to Dzogchen, Chod practice is actually a form of *Trekcho* practice. Trekcho [khregs chod] means "cutting thoroughly." The view of Chod is really the Dzogchen view. The key point in both practices is to directly and instantly "cut" without waiting for a "better time" or a second chance. No more procrastination.

In Chod practice, we don't have to hunt down the demons. We don't need radar, sonar, microscopes, or telescopes to find them. The obstacles are right here. If we've been observing our minds, we already know how much ego-clinging we have, where it is, and what activities it's performing. We're already quite familiar with the target we have to remove.

Chod practice is famous for its technique of instantly cutting or subduing. At the very moment when any deluded conception or emotional state arises in our mind, whether it's good or bad, we instantly cut it. For example, in the West, the experience of loneliness is very familiar. It's generally accepted as a valid state to be talked about and acted upon. People experiencing loneliness are often advised to counteract it by doing things like joining groups to make more friends. The Chod approach to this habit is definitely different. When practicing Chod, the instruction is to not allow loneliness to build up within our mind—cut it instantly. The moment it arises, cut it. Every notion, whether joyous, frightening, enraging—whatever it is—has to be cut right now, on the spot. All emotions and conceptualized attitudes must be cut.

If we can cut a mental state the instant it arises, that becomes our Chod offering. The title is named the *Bellowing Laugh of the Dakini* because the dakinis are joyously laughing about our success. They're cheering for us loudly and enthusiastically.

PHET Syllable

In order to cut, we're going to use the method of chanting, or sometimes even shouting, a special Sanskrit syllable PHET. That's our mental laser knife. The syllable is composed of two letters: PHA and a reversed TA syllable, which are joined together to make PHET. These two syllables have profound meanings. PHA is the powerful syllable that symbolizes great compassion, while TA is the secret syllable that symbolizes wisdom. So PHET means wisdom and compassion joined together. The exact moment you chant PHET, you must invoke great compassion and wisdom within your mental state to attain the result. You have to keep them together, not separating compassion to the right side and wisdom to the left, but merging them into a single union. Then you can cut duality or ego-clinging.

Ritual Objects of Chod Practice

To symbolize his or her great compassion and wisdom, a Chod practitioner uses specific ritual objects: a bell and vajra, a big damaru, and a thighbone trumpet. They may also use a hooked knife, a sun visor made out of bear-skin, a skullcup, and a small tent. These ritual objects symbolize different aspects of wisdom and compassion in Chod practice. The ritual objects are important and very advanced practitioners may have and use all of these things. But as beginners, we shouldn't focus too much on the ritual objects. That's not the point. Always focus more on the meaning—not just on the symbols or external objects. While a Chod practitioner should have some of these ritual objects, depending on his or her level of practice, it's much more important to have a clear understanding of Chod practice.

All Chod practitioners also carry and use the essential ritual implements of Vajrayana practice: the vajra or *dorje*, and the bell or *drilbu*. In some chants, the sounding of the bell is paired with the beating of the drum.

Another important ritual object or symbol is the curved knife, called a *kartika* in Sanskrit, and *drigug* [gri gug] in Tibetan. This curved, hooked knife is designed for flaying corpses and cutting them up into chunks. The drigug

Ritual Objects of Chod Practice

appears in the right hand of most images of semi-wrathful and wrathful dakinis. In our tradition, the practitioner only visualizes using this implement.

Some Chod practitioners use a trumpet made from a human thighbone, called a *kangling* in Tibetan. This symbolizes the realization of equanimity. In this case, equanimity means that the notions of "dirty" and "clean" are unified into a single state. In ancient times, masters had thighbone trumpets to show they were beyond clinging to these ideas. If you can't find or can't afford a trumpet made from a human thighbone, that's fine. Trumpets carefully made of wood or plastic are acceptable. What's important is that you're developing this understanding of equanimity. The essential focus of Chod practice is to bring all extremes into "one taste." Samsara and nirvana become equal. Dirty and clean become equal. High and low become equal. Happiness and sorrow are a single state.

The large, round Chod damaru drum is made of two wooden halves with a strong hand strap, and two swinging beaters on strings. It's played in complex rhythms during the Chod ritual. Its two united halves also symbolize the state of equanimity free from distinctions.

We have so many extremes or distinctions in our minds due to our ego-clinging, which is based on the belief in "self" and "other." Over time, grasping on to these dualistic conceptions solidifies the deep habit of these distinctions as distractions. By practicing Chod, we're able to move beyond these divisions. Both the skullcup and the thighbone trumpet symbolize removing barriers, bringing the elements together, and transforming all dualities within great equanimity. This state is also called Great Madhyamaka, Mahamudra, or Dzogchen.

As you begin the Chod practice, first cultivate a firm understanding of compassion and wisdom, and develop indestructible vajra courage. Then as you continue, you'll be capable of practicing the ceremony and using your ritual instruments well.

The Eight Worldly Concerns

There is another way to look at the meaning of Chod practice. As we've said, Chod practitioners are equalizing high and low, dirty and clean—but we're also equalizing the eight worldly concerns, which were taught by Buddha Shakyamuni in his first teachings. The first four worldly concerns—or obsessions—are seemingly wonderful things: (1) comfort and happiness, (2) praise and appreciation, (3) achievement or gain, and (4) good reputation or fame. We are all longing, searching, and hoping for these four things. They're what we work for in everyday mundane life. However, if we actually achieve these, we fear losing them and then we suffer.

The next four worldly concerns are the opposite of the first four. No one likes them, and we're very determined to avoid them. The opposite of comfort and happiness is (5) suffering. The opposite of praise is (6) being blamed or criticized. The opposite of achieving is (7) not achieving, losing, or not getting something. The opposite of having a good reputation or fame is to (8) be unknown or disreputable. In the ordinary world, no one likes these last four unless they're crazy. If someone experiences any of them, they react by getting angry, stubborn, or depressed, and then they suffer.

Everyone in the world is acting under the influence of these eight worldly concerns. People go to jail because their actions were motivated by these concerns. People kill because of these concerns. If we consider this carefully, we'll see that at least one of these concerns is the motivation behind all worldly activities.

The Eight Worldly Concerns

A great Chod practitioner equalizes these eight concerns. No matter what happens, the practitioner doesn't make any distinctions. She doesn't just "react." Whatever comes, that's great. If somebody praises her, that's great; if someone's criticizing, that's great too. She doesn't grasp and become angry, stupid, or ignorant. She understands and accepts that all experiences are in a single state of "one taste." By achieving this result of Chod practice, excellent practitioners can definitely reach realization in a single lifetime. We don't have to wait until our next life or the intermediate bardo state. We can get great realization or even enlightenment in this life.

If we have this attitude of equanimity, we'll always be happy and joyful. We'll never get upset. However, as long as we're driven by the eight worldly fears and concerns, no matter what we do, we're never going to be satisfied. We'll always find something that's not pleasing, or that's unbalanced.

Master Longchenpa said that with these eight worldly concerns, we always experience our lives as uncomfortable, "like a sick person's pillow." No matter how nice and new the pillow is, if it's high, it's too high. If it's low, it's too low. We keep trying to adjust and fix the details of our lives, yet whatever we do, it's never quite right.

Preparing to Practice Chod

When we're ready to offer the Chod feasts, the teachings mention to go to certain areas known as "focal points" or "power spots." We gather what we need, go to a special power spot, and then begin to practice. We go there with the four boundless attitudes of bodhichitta, with understanding, and with the view. We're not just going to casually run out there with our busy mundane thoughts. Every step we take is the walk of wisdom, the walk of compassion, and the walk of realization.

There are many characteristics of a true power spot. Even if we don't know beforehand that a place is a power spot, we'll know when we reach it. When we get there, we'll suddenly feel some kind of reaction, or see something that looks really unusual and powerful, appearing without any obvious causes and conditions, or any external signs. If the reaction is strong enough, maybe our hair will stand up and our hearts will beat faster. We look all around, but don't see or hear anything—it's just happening.

Why would we want to go to such a power spot? In Chod practice, we're crushing both hope and fear. We can use our hope and fear as skillful means; they become great assistants to develop our realization. They're actually the fuel to feed a strong fire of realization. Great masters use hope and fear as the path.

THE CHALLENGES OF CHOD PRACTICE

While doing Chod practice over a period of time, a serious practitioner will go through emotional and mental difficulties known as *lhongtse* [lhong tshad]. *Lhong* means "falling" or "dropping down"—it's like the ground is falling out from underneath us. *Tse* means "stirring" or "bringing up," and it's like being in a whirlwind or wild river rapids. Our hope sinks down, and our fear surges up. In this practice, there are lots of fears that we have to bring up. We always fear that we're going to lose or miss something. Usually we try to avoid or push down our fears, or bring up some lovely, hopeful image to soften them. This time, without hope, we're going to purposefully bring up each fear, and then transcend it. This bringing up or arousing will happen most forcefully at a power spot. It's not likely to happen as strongly in our lovely house with a TV, comfortable sofa, gadgets, and beautiful cars in the garage ready to drive away. For this kind of "bringing up," we seek out the kind of place we always try to avoid. The kind of place that makes our hair stand on end. That is a highly recommended place to practice.

The power of the challenge will really depend on our own level of realization. If we don't have much realization yet, even if we go to a qualified practice spot, it won't bring up much fear. This is because we don't yet have the capability to stir up our inner energy systems. The stirring or arousing sign mostly comes to people who have some realization, because that realization plus their meditation is what really does the stirring.

For example, if you were a beggar without much money, you wouldn't worry about someone trying to rob you. But if you're rich and have lots of diamonds, Rolex watches, and big nuggets of gold and silver, you'll always be worried that robbers are looking for a chance to attack and rob you.

The Buddha said, "Whoever has this precious Dharma realization gets great benefit. It will bring that person to the enlightened state and will benefit other sentient beings." But to achieve this precious Dharma realization, there are some challenges and obstacles that we'll have to go through. The stronger our practice is, the bigger the challenges we should undertake, and the bigger the benefit we'll achieve by overcoming them.

Signs and Obstacles

Whatever level of practice we're doing, we must view all obstacles as part of the practice. This is true for all practices, not only Chod. Guru Padmasambhava said, "See obstacles as signs of auspiciousness and achievement." As our realization grows, the size of our obstacles may grow too.

In Chod practice, try to see whatever comes up, whether comfortable or uncomfortable, as a sign of the growth of our realization. We should never hold the slightest thought that something is good or bad, or worry and wonder why it happens to us. A practitioner might start to complain, "I began to practice, and then I got all these troubles and obstacles." Thinking like this isn't skillful. It weakens our motivation, inspiration, courage, and commitment. Then this attitude itself becomes the real obstacle! We may start thinking, "Maybe I should quit." But if we see our difficulties as signs of our growing realization, then they really push us to the next target, the next level. All of these challenges are signs that you're going to have a small nugget of realization. Be happy and move right on to the next level.

There's an old story about the importance of maintaining this view of obstacles as part of the practice. Once upon a time, there was a highly realized yogi doing Chod in a charnel ground in India. His friend wanted to test the yogi's realization. One night he crept up near him as he practiced in the dark, and made a lot of strange sounds and motions around him. The yogi's view was strong and he didn't waver in his practice at all. The next night, his friend came back and intensified his disturbing behavior; he screamed and threatened and waved a sharp weapon around. Again, the yogi didn't blink an eye, and his mind didn't move from the view for a moment. The third night, his frustrated friend came back and suddenly sliced off the yogi's head. The yogi's hand quietly reached down, picked the head up, and placed it back onto his neck without losing his focus for an instant. His friend was crushed and crept away. The next day, in daylight, he came and apologized to the yogi. The yogi jumped up, exclaiming, "That was you?" That moment his head fell off again because he completely lost his view!

Preparing to Practice Chod

When we practice Chod, we definitely must experience *lhongtse*. If we've been doing Chod meditation and nothing like this is happening, then we have to adjust our practice to bring up something. This is called "arranging the situation to bring up the signs."

When signs come up, they're not necessarily always rough. Sometimes they can be nice. Regardless of what comes up, we shouldn't have hopes, expectations, or judgmental thoughts. The moment a judgment arises, that is grasping and clinging. In fact, if we slip back into duality mind between gaps in our meditation, it will undermine our meditation and our visualization. Therefore we should practice to not have any kind of hope and fear. Completely crushing hope and fear in the wisdom state is the central view and meditation of Chod. If we're able to maintain that state, even for a short time, signs will definitely arise.

For example, maybe we'll see Buddha Shakyamuni or Guru Padmasambhava right in front of us saying, "Next Saturday, you're going to reach enlightenment." If this sign comes up, don't pay any attention to it. Don't get excited by that news. Who knows—maybe next time it will be demons that come with strange voices, saying, "You'll die next Saturday. You'll experience terrible misfortune." If that sign comes, also don't pay any attention. Many times practitioners have said that when they start sessions of Chod practice, there would be frightful noises coming from behind them. They kept their seats and kept on chanting, but their voices almost stopped as if they were being strangled. This has happened to many people. If it happens to you, don't even look around. Don't worry who's at your side. No matter what, maintain the view and meditation.

Chod practitioners have shared lots of experiences. One said that when he was practicing Chod, he and his cushion were often lifted up into the sky. He went up and up, and was sometimes afraid that he was going to fall onto the rocky ground below. If something like this happens, remember the instruction that no matter what the experience is, don't pay any attention to it. Don't count or analyze your experiences. Just remain without distraction in meditation.

Lake Manosarovar is a very famous lake in northwestern Tibet located very near to Mount Kailash. In Tibetan, its name is Mapham Yutso [ma pham g.yu mtsho], and it's a popular spot for Chod practice. Once a lama was practicing on the shore of the lake and suddenly his perceptions completely changed. He saw a beautiful bridge coming from the center of the lake to the shore where he was practicing. Monks and lamas were approaching on the bridge. His own teacher was coming towards him and inviting him, very nicely and politely: "Oh, you're here. Please come with us." The lama was excited to see his teacher and all his old friends from the monastery, so he had the impulse to get up and go with them. A moment later, he regained his visualization and meditation. By that time one of his feet was already wet!

These are a few examples of how signs can come up. There are a lot more stories of these things, some beautiful, some terrifying. Either way, whatever comes up, have no hope and no fear. Whether our signs are good or bad, gods or demons, whether they suit our emotions or not—don't analyze or tally them up. See all these signs and all perceptions as the display of mind. When we become a very skilled Chod practitioner, the signs that arise become smooth and very gentle.

Choosing Practice Places

We can begin to understand why the best place to practice Chod is a very frightening place. Our ego-clinging always becomes very active and sensitive when we're in a frightening place. We can really see, taste, and touch it. In that kind of a spot, our

Preparing to Practice Chod

ego's only wish is to hold on and survive. Ego-clinging becomes really naked and obvious. We can thoroughly unmask it and teach it a good lesson.

Some power places are near very high mountains, in caves, or near big lakes or the ocean. Other places are in wilderness areas, or near rocky crags and boulders. Tibetan yogis and yoginis do Chod practice in places that are known as "locally proven." The place has been proven by previous practitioners to have a strong wrathful energy. It's known to be a good place to cut the four demons. Favorite places in Tibet are cemeteries or charnel grounds, glacial mountains, and along some lakes. Not all power spots are charnel grounds. Still, they're all the kinds of places that people prefer to avoid.

In Tibet, after a practitioner finishes Ngondro, they may then receive Chod teachings and begin to practice Chod. In the old tradition, people wouldn't just practice in one place, but at 108 different power spots. They practiced one night in one location, and then at another place the next night, and so on.

Within Samye Monastery, on the northern side, there is a treasury of precious manuscripts. It is called Pehar Kordzo Ling [dpe har dkor mdzod gling] because it's guarded by the famous dharmapala Gyalpo Pehar. Guru Padmasambhava subdued Pehar then appointed him to defend all the monasteries in Tibet. Pehar is very frightening. Every three years the sealed door to his shrine is opened, offerings are placed inside, and the door is sealed again. The offerings from three years before are always gone. An axe and chopping board are put there as well, and after three years people say that the chopping board has been completely chopped up. We haven't seen this ourselves, but many people have, so it must be true. Many people go there to practice Chod right in front of that door. It's one of the most famous power spots.

Tibetan charnel grounds and cemeteries are very different

from cemeteries here. In a Tibetan cemetery, there are "sky burials," where a corpse is cut up and its parts are left for the scavenging, flesh-eating animals and other beings. There may be bodies and skeletons, or severed limbs and bones with lots of blood on the ground. Charnel grounds don't smell good! There may be mountain lions, hyenas, foxes, and jackals lurking nearby. Vultures fly overhead, waiting. Every kind of being—visible and invisible—hovers around a charnel ground. It's not a peaceful or comfortable place. At nighttime, even the most courageous person will hesitate to go there. Of course, in Tibet, Dharma practice is widely accepted and nobody feels that it's strange to do Chod or other solitary practices in those places.

On the other hand, here in the United States cemeteries are beautiful—they're like parks—neat and clean, planted with many flowers and trees. It's more of an enjoyable place where someone might go to exercise or work on a smartphone. In this country, it's not a good idea to go to a cemetery to practice Chod. If we went there to practice as we did in Tibet, someone might dial 911 and we'd end up in jail. Before we even started practicing, the police might arrive and take us away.

In the USA, we have to look and choose a place that's more practical. Yet we must still pick a spot that has the right vibrations. There are many traditional suggestions. An empty house where ghosts or demons are supposed to live could be good. A Chod practitioner might also use an empty cave. It could also be an old battleground where many people were killed. Lonely places are always good for Chod practice. In the flat lands, if there's a place with only one tree, that could be good. In Tibet, practitioners looked for solitary pointed red cliffs, or mountains that were standing alone. Triangular rock formations with water loudly rushing are also used.

Preparing to Practice Chod

A Warning About Power Spots

We'd like to give you a warning about power spots. When you go to a power spot, examine it closely. First, it's important that it feels like a powerful place. However, if the conditions are fragile or unstable, you should avoid it. For example, the teachings specifically mention that if an empty old house looks like it's almost falling down, even if it has powerful energy, you shouldn't stay or practice there. Even if it looks like a powerful spot, don't stay under a tree that's about to fall down. Don't stay underneath or near rocky cliffs that are unstable. If dangerous wild animals live at the power spot, you shouldn't stay there either.

Summary of Preparations

We have completed our overview, introducing all the general principles of Chod practice. If we've made contact with a lama to receive instructions and permission, and if we can maintain a clear understanding of these instructions, we may begin the actual practice. These preliminary preparations are very important. The *Bellowing Laugh of the Dakini* and its practice is a wisdom mind terma—the highest level of terma teachings. It sees this world from the purity view of enlightenment.

Within the Dzogchen view—which means a yogi or yogini has proper realization of great emptiness—there is no need to perform specific rituals, or to go through all these complex processes we're about to describe. Simply put, since Dzogchen is beyond the conceptual state, Dzogchen practitioners have nothing to do. They already see that all activity is in the primordial nature. So there's nothing that intentionally, conceptually needs to be performed. There is nothing to cut, no demons to destroy.

However, we ourselves don't have that realization yet. We're very busy inside our ordinary conceptual minds. This practice is important for those of us who don't yet have realization of the primordial nature. It's how we actualize Dzogchen realization.

Chod practice is also appropriate for yogis and yoginis who do already have Dzogchen realization and want to perform external beneficial activities, such as healing rituals. They might choose to make a Chod offering when a conceptual practice is called for. Chod is known as the "fearlessness practice." No matter what the situation is, we transform it into the wisdom state of the true nature. When we perfectly understand fearlessness, we don't cling to our own bodies. We'll even give up our body to help other sentient beings. In Tibetan, this is called *pungpo zhen du kyur*, referring to the five aggregates that make up our human embodiment. *Pungpo zhen du kyur* means "giving the body as food for sentient beings."

As we are now, we definitely cling to our bodies. Our body with its five aggregates are the main source or root of our ego-clinging. We look no further than our body for an "I." For example, when someone asks, "Who are you?" we say our name and point our finger at ourselves. In other words, we point to our aggregates. There's nothing more important to us. Every worldly activity we do is to protect, support, and please our body and our aggregates. Ego-clinging is grasping on to our body and aggregates. We work day and night to support the objects of our ego-clinging. This activity of ego-clinging doesn't just apply to humans. Beings in all the realms suffer because of ego-clinging. We can easily observe that animals have grasping and clinging to their bodies as well.

The great master Chandrakirti[66] explained the sequence of how ego-clinging develops. He said that first we develop the notion of ego-clinging. From that we develop relationships or "ownerships" based on ego-clinging. Ego-clinging arises first, followed by everything else related to it: "my" friend, "my" enemy, "my" house, "my" lover, "my" parents, and "my" children. The list goes on and on. Ego-clinging is our central focus. It's the center of our mandala, and everything else becomes a support—the ornamentation, retinue, and palace of ego-clinging.

In Chod practice, we stop trying to improve the palace and outer belongings of ego-clinging. We start by cutting the very root of our clinging and sharing our precious body with other sentient beings. We slice up the demon of ego-clinging.

With some realization of egolessness and fearlessness, a practitioner goes to do their Chod practice in a frightening place. When you arrive at this frightening place, you'll have some sense of hesitation or doubt, with the thought, "How can I do this?" As soon as this slight hesitation arises, understand that this thought itself is a demon. If we can instantly cut that thought by reconnecting with our understanding of the true nature, our realization of egolessness and fearlessness will become a bit stronger. Rely on Dzogchen meditation, the true nature of the Great Perfection. Then remain in that state as much as you can.

Buddha Samantabhadri, Sangwa Yeshe, and Troma Nagmo

Part 2:

Detailed Commentary on the Sadhana *Bellowing Laugh of the Dakini*

Sangwa Yeshe

Chapter 4:
Preparing and Overpowering Practices

At the beginning of every meditation session, we always recite our essential lineage prayers. Chod is no exception. We chant the Seven Line Prayer three times, and then the supplications to the lineage masters and root teacher, followed by refuge and bodhichitta prayers, and the prayer of the four boundless aspirations. After that, we continue to the Chod practice itself.

In general, the *Bellowing Laugh of the Dakini* sadhana alternates between the main text to be chanted in Tibetan and English, and passages of detailed commentary and instructions, which are in italics. This auto-commentary was written by the great terton Rigdzin Jigme Lingpa to provide additional guidance to practitioners. It should be read carefully.

The sadhana begins with Jigme Lingpa's line of homage:

> I prostrate to the queen of space, the lady of great bliss,
>   Yeshe Tsogyal.

This is followed by about two pages of detailed instructions on the preparatory activities, leading up to the actual Chod offering practices.

The chanted text begins on page 9 with:

Then, instantly oneself becomes
Sangwa Yeshe Khandroma, the secret wisdom dakini.
As large as the entire universe,
Her body is generated complete in every aspect.
Loudly blow the human thighbone trumpet.
Forcefully generate the power of realization and
   perform the dance.

Sangwa Yeshe Khandroma

In this section of the Chod practice, we are visualizing the deity Sangwa Yeshe Khandroma [gsang wa ye shes mkha' 'dro ma], whose name means "secret wisdom dakini." A wisdom dakini is beyond conceptions. She is an expression of the primordial, true wisdom nature, which is reflected as her form. Sangwa Yeshe or "secret wisdom" is nothing other than one's own primordial nature of mind. All emanating forms arise from that primordial nature. So our wisdom awareness is emanating its secret wisdom as the dakini, transforming its wisdom energies into innumerable forms of dakinis.

As you recite the syllable PHET, instantly visualize yourself[67] as the secret wisdom dakini with all of her retinue. An "instant visualization" is described "like a fish jumping out of water." Until the moment we visualize, our true nature is hidden, mingled with duality. Yet the instant we visualize, our buddha-nature is completely revealed. True buddha-nature reflects in an infinite variety of ways: both as the variety of dualistic conceptions and appearances, and as the richness of enlightened qualities.

Sangwa Yeshe Khandroma is red in color. She has two arms, two legs, and one face with three eyes. Her hair is a fiery dark red, partly tied up on top, and partly falling to her shoulders on the sides. It's very wild, expanding out into all the formless realms. She wears a crown of five skulls. She is baring her teeth, and has four fangs. Her tongue is red and moving like lightning.

Her body is huge. The upper part completely pervades all the formless realms. The middle part pervades all the form realms, and the lower part of her body fills all the desire realms. She is standing in the dancing posture in the center of a mass of wisdom fire with a corpse under her feet. She is chanting the syllables PHET and PHEM, and her voice is so loud that the entire universe is awakened into the wisdom state. She's naked except for bone ornaments and small bells that make a "ching, ching, ching," sound. This sound is celestial music waking up everyone from ignorance.

The entire universe is visualized as the pure land of the dakini. It's very frightening and fierce—it's definitely not nice and beautiful. However, seen with wisdom, it's a pure land.

In the sky above her head are all the buddhas, bodhisattvas, and lineage masters, from Buddha Samantabhadra, Vajradhara, and Vajrasattva, continuing all the way until now. All the great masters who discovered termas are surrounded by wisdom dakinis. Sangwa Yeshe is also surrounded by masses of peaceful and wrathful deities, dakinis, and dharmapalas, standing or sitting according to their specific postures.

The peaceful deities sit within rainbow light, while wrathful deities stand within blazing wisdom fire. All the buddhas and lineage masters are manifesting enlightened activity. The peaceful deities are smiling and joyful, radiating wisdom light. The wrathful deities are singing and chanting syllables in a terrifying manner. The minds of all of these great enlightened beings are totally relaxed in the dharmadhatu state of the primordial nature.

Sangwa Yeshe Khandroma radiates five colored lights: white light radiates from her forehead, red light from her speech center, blue light from her heart center, yellow light from her navel center, and green light from her secret center. These lights shine in every direction, transforming into her retinue of five different groups of wisdom dakinis.

First is the white retinue with hundreds of thousands of white wisdom dakinis. They are all smiling, beautiful, peaceful, compassionate, and kind looking. Second is the red retinue—hundreds of thousands of red wisdom dakinis. The red dakinis are very kind, compassionate and attractive, but they are especially very passionate in regard to sentient beings. Third are the hundreds of thousands of blue dakinis. They are robust, powerful, and strong, kind and compassionate. They are also very tricky and playful, and dancing very actively. Fourth are the hundreds of thousands of yellow dakinis. Their special quality is that of increasing, nourishing, cherishing, and enriching. The fifth group is hundreds of thousands of green dakinis. They are very wrathful, making cruel gestures out of compassion.

These five groups of dakinis all emanate from Sangwa Yeshe in the following way: white dakinis emanate from her body, red dakinis from her speech, blue dakinis from her heart, yellow dakinis from her qualities, and green dakinis from her activities. They are all none other than Sangwa Yeshe.

From these emanations come countless re-emanations, which fill the whole universe. Some are very beautiful and others are very ugly. Some are very wrathful and some are semi-wrathful. Some are very young and some are very old. Some are very attractive and some are repulsive. The entire universe is the pure land of the dakinis.[68] Meditate on this visualization briefly.

By visualizing oneself as the wisdom dakini Sangwa Yeshe, you become able to invoke all the demons, negative forces, and ghosts, which are none other than the reflection of your own ego-clinging. Summon them to you forcefully, but with the immense love and compassion of the wisdom dakini. Fearlessly summon all of your obstacles.

Sangwa Yeshe is holding a thighbone trumpet in her left hand, and a tiger skin and a fresh human skin in her right hand. She waves these skins around her with a whipping movement. She blows the thighbone trumpet and emanates light from her heart center to summon all the demons. Then all the mighty arrogant ones begin coming to her. They must come to her. Meditate that every demon is coming right in front of her, from every direction, without any choice. They all come to her with a shimmering look as if they're made of light. All of her movements and activities are ferocious and forceful, but she carries them out within the state of compassion and wisdom.

Next, with the sound of PHET, a flaming nine-pointed vajra[69] made of meteoric iron emanates from Sangwa Yeshe's heart center. It shoots to our practice spot like a bolt of lightning. As soon as the vajra lands there, thousands more nine-pointed vajras emanate from it. These form a flaming nine-pointed meteoric iron vajra wall that completely surrounds the area. All of the demons—displays of our ego-clinging—are trapped here. They have no escape route. The flaming vajra fence completely seals them in. They have to stay there and wait for the yogi or yogini.

Now, holding the thighbone trumpet in your right hand, hit the mouthpiece with the flat of your left palm three times. This summons all the demons of the three worlds right here to Sangwa Yeshe's feet. The trumpet's message to the demons says, "Come here, relax, don't be afraid. Don't run away. You can relax." Outshining or overpowering the demons in this way takes away their resistance. The Tibetan term is *zilnon* [zil gnon], which is also translated as "tame" or "awe with splendor."

Sangwa Yeshe picks the demons up and swings them by their feet around her head and throws them down wrathfully. Her inner energy is completely compassionate and wise. She's going to help the demons, but first she has to subdue them. When we're doing this practice with skillful means and compassion, at this point the demons will just be sitting there, somewhat sad at the loss of their arrogant powers, but feeling comfortable and relaxed, appreciating the compassion and wisdom that the yogi or yogini is bringing to them.

In short, as Sangwa Yeshe you are doing three things: (1) invoking and summoning the power of the demons or invisible beings, (2) out-shining the power of those beings, and (3) subduing them all.

We would like to illustrate these actions with a brief story about Buddha Shakyamuni. Initially as an ascetic, the Buddha had five student companions. These five had been among his attendants when he was a prince. After he left the palace, his father's clan sent 300 attendants and his mother's clan sent 200 attendants to care for him. The Buddha sent almost all of them back, allowing only one from each hundred to stay with him. These five attendants became his five students, and lived as ascetics with him.

The Buddha devoted six years to extreme ascetic practice. After he completed that, he began to practice the Middle Way of neither self-denial nor self-indulgence. He began to wear simple clothes and eat healthy food. His five students then said, "Oh, Gautama has lost his vow. He is no longer a good practitioner, and we will leave him." So they went away to Varanasi. The Buddha stayed there, and attained enlightenment under the Bodhi Tree. Months later, when they heard that the Buddha was on his way from Bodhgaya[70] to Varanasi to give his first teaching, they held a meeting. They decided not to greet him, pay any attention to him, or show him any respect. However, as the Buddha approached, the moment they saw him they totally forgot their promises to one another, and sprung up to welcome and praise him. His radiance summoned or magnetized them. He outshone them. They prostrated to him and offered him water. All their previous critical thoughts were dissolved. That is how their duality minds were subdued. The strength of the Buddha's enlightenment removed the strength of the students' ego-clinging.

Returning to the Chod practice, now we hold the thighbone trumpet in our left hand and blow it five times for five mantra syllables, which are depicted on page 40 in the sadhana. These syllables are: OM, HUNG, TRANG, HRI, and AH. The series is sounded in succession, from OM to AH, five times through.

The first sounding of the trumpet is OM. The sound must be rather soft and balanced, pleasant like the sound of bees.

OM *Long and pleasing like the humming of a bee.*

The second sounding is HUNG, which has two joined sounds: one that comes down and then one that rises up, like the neigh of a horse.

HUNG *Powerful and dignified like the neighing of a horse.*

The third is the TRANG music, which is very loud, like a tiger's roar.

Cutting Through Ego

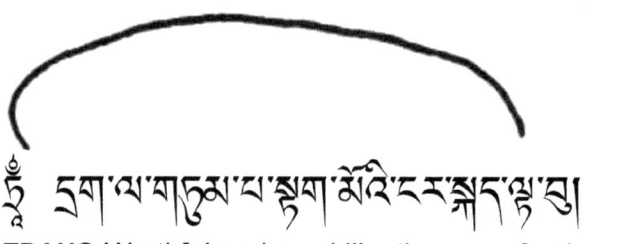

TRANG *Wrathful and cruel like the roar of a tigress.*

The fourth is HRI, which has many bends, ups and downs, and many levels. The metaphor is the song of the gandharvas.

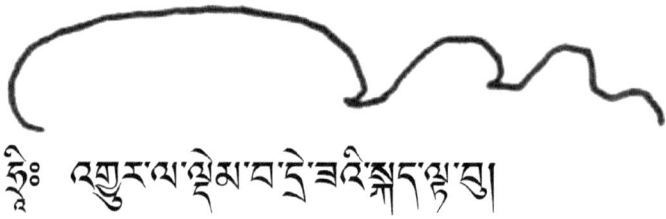

HRI *Moving and vibrating like the voices of gandharvas.*

The fifth is AH, the joyful sound of the dakinis. This is a mild or balanced tone with four joints or knots, which rise into a whistling tune at the end.

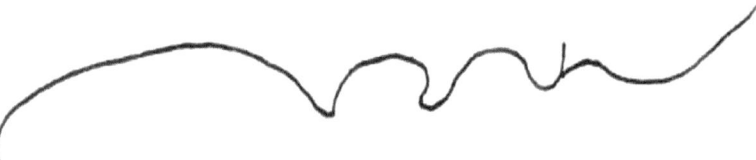

AH *Moving and vibrating like the last one above, but rising up at the end with what is called "the whistle of the dakinis."*

After sounding the trumpet five times, hold the large chod drum in your right hand, while your left hand holds the bell. There are two different systems of playing the damaru: either we start by rotating the drum from inside to outside, or from outside to inside. Either way is correct, but if we're doing this practice in a group everyone should use the same technique.

Various traditions of Chod practice have many different tunes, but we'll use a simple sequence here to begin our practice. First, sound the drum and bell three times, then five times a little faster. Then, sound them twice more a little slower. Then we begin the Chod chant with the syllable PHET on page 10.

The Tibetan verse has nine syllables per line. The chanting rhythm mainly puts two syllables together. For example, the first two syllables are recited together, then the third and fourth together, and the fifth and sixth together. The last three syllables are recited separately. In Tibet, this is called the "flying garuda" tune.

In practical terms, the first skill we need to develop is to be able to visualize and meditate like we just described, while we simultaneously read the chants. Absorb the full meaning of each line in English, or whatever language you understand best. Once your practice develops, you'll begin to use the instruments. Later, you can chant the practice in Tibetan and perform the dance too. At that point, you'll be visualizing, meditating, dancing, and chanting all at the same time. It's not always necessary to physically perform the dance; if we're not able to dance, or if the circumstances aren't conducive, we can visualize it instead. However, at some point we need to memorize the text before we can do the full ritual smoothly and profoundly.[71]

The Chod dance is not simply an external activity of the body. Our aspiration is to integrate the sound of the chant with its profound meaning, our body's movement, our mind, and our meditation states. As we're moving, we're recollecting the meaning. If we're not yet able to do all of that, we can meditate in the state of loving-kindness.

All of this, of course, is quite difficult. Our Chod practice will take time to develop. We'll need to have diligence in both study and practice. Then we will become stable in Chod practice. In its essence, however, the text is playful, the dance is playful, and we become fearless. So all beings can enjoy this!

The Four Styles of Walking

Now it's time to go to the spot we have chosen to offer the Chod feast. We aren't going to run there distracted with busy thoughts, wandering like little old dogs. Don't slouch around or shrug, "I don't care; it doesn't matter much." Don't belittle the power spot or test it: "Let's see what's going to happen. I'm not scared. I'm not afraid." Don't scheme, thinking, "I'm going to pass a test and achieve something. Then I'll go home and tell scary stories to my friends and relatives." Don't plan to brag about your "great experiences." Don't have these kinds of notions! We must appreciate and respect the power of Chod practice.

We must see the mind as sky-like. Both sky and mind are all-pervading and transparent. Bring this vast sky quality into your mental state, and combine this with courage, joy, respect, and appreciation. Someone with wisdom, knowledge, appreciation, and love, who goes to the practice place with the perfect view of sky-like mind is known as a sky yogi or yogini.

Walk to the power spot completely alone, fearlessly, with a "lion's walk." We are without any helpers or guards. The best time to go is in the late afternoon or early evening when the shadows are lengthening on the ground. Don't carry any light or any defense, like a heavy stick or knife. Take just a small

The Four Styles of Walking

meditation cushion and your bell, damaru, and thighbone trumpet. There are four different ways to walk to this spot. They are also part of the dance.

Walking with Great Confidence in the View

The first walk is known as "walking with great confidence in the view." We don't make any separation between our realization and our gestures. We bring up our realization, what we understand, and completely mingle that with our physical movements. The yogi or yogini walks without hesitation, with great dignity and confidence. To completely mingle view, realization, and action, we walk looking up and forward, looking directly into space, and not bending the upper part of the body forward. We gaze into space and walk slowly with awareness. Our movements and our awareness mingle as we walk slowly toward the dancing place.

Dakini Walk

The second walk is the "walk of the dakinis." Keeping our visualization and fearless understanding, this walk consists of small, delicate steps and once in a while a little jump.

Black Snake Walk

The third walk is called the "black snake walk." In Tibetan, the term is *drul nag* [sbrul nag], which literally means "black snake," but really means "cobra." In New Mexico, we'll call it the "rattlesnake walk." In this walk, move smoothly from side to side.

Cutting Through Ego

Crazy Elephant Walk

The fourth walk is known as the "crazy elephant walk." This elephant doesn't only have one way of walking. The crazy or drunk elephant sometimes charges and sometimes slows down. It staggers this way or that. Its walk is completely random.

These four different walks are generally applied according to the situation. The first walk is always a wise choice. We cannot do the last three walks in the city without attracting attention and disturbing people. The first walk doesn't look strange, so it's always good.

Dancing on the Demons of the Five Continents

Maintaining our self-visualization as the wisdom dakini Sangwa Yeshe, we move into the part of the ceremony where we dance. In Tibetan, it's called *dro* [bro]. The venue or "stadium" [dro ra] where we're dancing is the field of the demons, the playground of ego-clinging. By the power of primordial wisdom and our visualization, we trample on the heads of the ego-clinging demons. We crush each conceptual notion, negative emotion, and duality within the state of equanimity.

As the secret wisdom dakini we maintain fearlessness. It is the fearless secret wisdom dakini who dances on, subdues, and transforms all obscurations into the primordial nature.

On page 10, the fearless yogi[72] says:

> PHET I am a fearless yogi who practices crazy wisdom activity.
> Through realization activities which encompass
>   samsara and nirvana as equal,
> I dance and trample on the demons of ego-clinging

And grind samsaric, dualistic thinking into dust.
Vidyadhara lamas of the root lineage, come to the dance!
Ocean of yidams and dakas, come to the dance!
Hosts of dakinis and those who roam everywhere,
   come to the dance!
Grant your blessings for my accomplishing the
   path of crazy wisdom activity.

We are stating our confidence as warrior heroes in our realization, which is beyond the duality of samsara and nirvana. We're "bellowing the laugh" of the dakinis. All Three Roots, come to the dance: (1) lamas of the mind-to-mind, symbolic, and oral transmission lineages, (2) yidams and herukas, and (3) dakinis. Everyone, come to the dance!

Where is our ego-clinging stadium, or nightclub?[73] It is internal, within us. This nightclub is designed with five dance floors: a central floor with four others arranged around it in the four cardinal directions. Each has a different shape and color that matches Buddhist cosmology of the continents.

Five Continents from Above

Cutting Through Ego

Side View of the Five Continents

Dancing on the Demons of the Five Continents

The Three HUNG Syllables

Each dance has four lines of chanting. At the beginning of each verse, we chant the PHET syllable. PHET cuts through running conceptions, provokes realization, knocks out obstacles and hindrances, and transcends negative emotions. The very moment we say PHET, all dualistic notions and conceptions are completely dispelled, returning us to our original true nature, free from duality and conceptions, and radiating the unceasing energy of wisdom, love, and compassion.

At the end of each dance, we chant a set of three HUNG syllables. HUNG[74] is the sound of true awareness, one's own nature of mind. Simply put, it is Prajnaparamita, the perfection of wisdom—the absolute state. We instantly return to our true nature when we chant this syllable. The HUNG syllable is made up of five different segments, which symbolize the five wisdoms. So while you dance, maintain your mind continually in the state of the true nature. As you dance, your movements begin to transmute emotions and conceptions into pure wisdom energy—as displays of the five primordial wisdoms. This is the view to maintain.

In a more formal way, the three HUNGs symbolize the three kayas: dharmakaya, sambhogakaya, and nirmanakaya, which are inherent within our awareness. Our own awareness is their source. In other words, the three HUNGs assert that we're dancing in the three kaya state. Whatever instrument or chant or ornament we're using is in the three kaya state.

Cutting Through Ego

When we chant the triple HUNG, we should also think that we're transforming our three doors into the three vajra states—the original states of our vajra body, vajra speech, and vajra mind. We're also reminding ourselves of the indestructible, three vajra states of all phenomenal existence: vajra form, vajra sound, and vajra space. In addition, the three HUNGs symbolize the three times of the past, present, and future coming together and merging into the fourth time, which is the original, primordial time of the true nature. Perform everything within the timeless state of primordial wisdom. These triple HUNGs remind us of all these different meditations. Chant them over and over to refresh and restrengthen your realization throughout the Chod dance.

First Dance on the Eastern Continent

Page 11:

> PHET While dancing on the eastern continent of Purvavideha,
> On the arena of the dakas and dakinis, which is perfectly round,
> I stomp on the heads of the kings of anger. CHEM SE CHEM
> The trumpet of mirror-like wisdom blows.
> CHU RU RU HUNG HUNG HUNG

As we dance, ego-clinging expresses itself as the five principal kinds of demons related to the five poisons. The demon in the east is a *gyalpo*; a male demon that corresponds to anger, the king demon of the five poisons. Gyalpo means "king" or "lord"—one who has power and authority and likes to strongly control everything. Anger is like that. It likes to conquer everything; it likes to attack. Angry and hateful thoughts are very powerful and explosive. Anger is an eruption like a volcano. It has very cruel ways.

When we dance on the eastern continent, we're crushing and removing anger and its source, ego-clinging. We dance on the form of this male gyalpo demon lying face down on the round eastern continent. The circle represents loving-kindness. So we're subduing anger within loving-kindness. With this dance, we remove, purify, and subdue the king demon of anger.

One of the five wisdoms of the Buddha is mirror-like wisdom, which also corresponds to the eastern direction. Having subdued anger into the state of loving-kindness, we invoke mirror-like wisdom and emanate loving-kindness in every direction in the form of white light. All of the buddhas and all the dancers emanate this white light of loving-kindness as well.

Of course, anger doesn't really exist on the reality level of the true nature. Anger is recognized as mirror-like wisdom. There is no solid structure to this anger. It's just like a reflection in a mirror. The very moment anger arises, see it as transparent and luminous, and it will dissolve back into the original nature.

Now to put it all together: visualize yourself as the secret wisdom dakini surrounded by many lamas and lineage masters, buddhas, bodhisattvas, wrathful and peaceful male and female deities and dharmapalas, as well as the five groups of emanations of the secret wisdom dakini. Everyone comes together dancing with loving-kindness, subduing anger within that state. Smashing anger within the state of loving-kindness is the dance on the eastern continent.

We chant CHU RU RU to symbolize this transformation.

Second Dance on the Southern Continent

Page 12:

> PHET While dancing on the southern continent of Jambudvipa,
> On the arena of the dakas and dakinis, which is a sharp triangle,
> I step on the head of the arrogant Lord of Death,
> CHEM SE CHEM
> The skullcup drum of equanimity wisdom resounds.
> TRO LO LO HUNG HUNG HUNG

Our next action is to dance on the southern continent in the south side of the stadium, which is shaped like a sharp triangle and is colored blue. Here we're dancing on the demon *Shinje* [gshin rje], the Lord of Death. The Sanskrit name is Yama. Yama lies face down on the triangular ground. This means we're dancing on the notion of death, which is the separation of mind or consciousness from the physical body.

Arrogance, or pride, is the poisonous emotion of the southern arena. The Tibetan term is *nga rgyal*, which literally means "self-victorious"—we think we're special, we don't give any kind of appreciation or respect to others, and have an "attitude" towards every other living being. We won't accept that others have any good qualities. In other words, we don't ever learn anything! In a way, we become frozen as our "self," unable to develop any more good qualities because we lack the necessary respect and appreciation of others. That is the danger of real arrogance: it kills off our new growth like a frost. That's why arrogance is the Lord of Death.

Yet in reality there is no solidly existing arrogance. Thinking we're superior is only an illusion. The true nature of arrogance is equanimity wisdom. With this realization, everyone is equal and every being is perfect. No one is higher up or lower down. On the absolute level, enlightened beings and sentient beings like ourselves are also equal. We begin to really understand great equanimity and balance as we practice transforming arrogance into wisdom.

To support our realization of equanimity wisdom, we use the large damaru Chod drum. The drum's sound is TRO LO LO. The drum, with its two identical sides that are connected in perfect balance, symbolizes the two activities of crushing arrogance and actualizing the wisdom of equanimity.

Now, if we smash the Lord of Death—the arrogance demon—what will be the result? [There is a loud clap of thunder, with nervous laughter from the students.] At this point we must principally meditate on compassion. In other words, while we meditate that we're forcefully subduing Yama Raja, we're abiding in compassion. When arrogance completely transforms into equanimity wisdom, we emanate blue light in every direction.

Third Dance on the Western Continent

Page 12:

> PHET While dancing on the western continent of Godaniya,
> On the arena of the dakas and dakinis, which is perfectly
>   semi-circular,
> I tread on the heads of the female cannibal demons
>   of attachment.
> CHEM SE CHEM
> The bells and jingles of discriminating awareness wisdom ring.
> TRO LO LO   HUNG HUNG HUNG

The design of the western stadium is a semi-circle or half

moon, and its color is dark red. Here we're dancing on *sinmo* [srin mo], which are female demons or ghosts. Just as anger is known as the king demon, attachment is the female cannibal ghost. Attachment is one of our ego's very strong emotions. All of our desires and attachments are *sinmo*. "Attachment" is when we continue holding on to desirable objects, grasping at them without wanting to let them go. We don't want to share or offer anything. We're just constantly hanging on. Attachment is greedy, and is often cruel, like a cannibal. It will kill to get and keep what it wants. If we compare anger and aggression, anger is always pushing unwanted objects away, projecting rage outwardly. Attachment is pulling desirable objects in, holding them close in a death grip.

As the secret wisdom dakini Sangwa Yeshe along with her entire retinue, we dance on the heads of these cannibalistic demons, and attachment transforms into the wisdom of discriminating awareness. Discriminating awareness understands every relative object and concept clearly, thoroughly, and in precise detail. Then we emanate the red light of great joy in all directions.

In connection to this view, a Chod practitioner uses a bell. The clear ringing sound of the bell is the echo of discriminating wisdom. While ringing the bell, we transform attachment into wisdom.

Fourth Dance on the Northern Continent

Page 13:

> PHET While dancing on the northern continent of Uttarakuru,
> On the arena of the dakas and dakinis, which is a shimmering square,

I trample the heads of the samaya corruptors of jealousy.
CHEM SE CHEM
The tassels of all-accomplishing wisdom flutter.
PU RU RU   HUNG HUNG HUNG

Next we dance our way into the northern arena, which is square and green. The demon that we see lying face down in the stadium is the *damsi* [dam sri] demon of jealousy. Another translation is "vow breaker"—one who has broken Vajrayana samaya vows.[75] The poison of jealousy, or *tradok* in Tibetan, has the corrupted sense of knowing about positive activities, but then it turns to negative activities like harming beings. As Sangwa Yeshe and her retinue, we dance on and trample *damsi*. By subduing jealousy, we transform it into all-accomplishing wisdom. Then we emanate the green light of equanimity in every direction.

According to the Buddha's teaching, jealousy is a combination of two poisons: attachment and anger. Jealousy is always a kind of expecting, longing feeling that what we have isn't sufficient. It's never enough. Our eyes are always looking around rapidly, even over our shoulders. Our burning gaze constantly checks to see what others are doing. We study the achievements, positive actions, and good lives of others and react by feeling uncomfortable and diminished by their good situations.

Just as with every other negative emotion, when we look directly at jealousy itself we find that it doesn't solidly exist. It's just another illusory troublemaker. It's not solid. The moment we look at jealousy—our own mind is looking directly at itself—jealousy dissolves. Where does it go? It dissolves back into an aspect of the true nature known as all-accomplishing wisdom. In that wisdom state nothing has been lost and nothing remains unaccomplished. Everything is completed. There's no place for discomfort!

With this awareness we can actualize anything. All-accomplishing wisdom awareness is with us in our work, continually assisting and guiding our every activity. Whether we're working for ourselves, for other beings, or both, we're able to fulfill all wishes and attain all goals. That's why this realization is called all-accomplishing wisdom. To arouse it, we swing the tassels or ribbons on the Chod drum, making the sound PU RU RU. As the drum rotates with the chant and dance, this unceasing swinging back and forth symbolizes the poison of jealousy transforming into all-accomplishing wisdom.

Fifth Dance on the Central Continent

Page 14:

> PHET While dancing on the central continent of Mt. Meru,
> On the arena of the dakas and dakinis, which is splendid and charming,
> I crush the heads of the ghosts of ignorance. CHEM SE CHEM
> The melodious HUNG of dharmadhatu wisdom sounds.
> CHU RU RU   HUNG HUNG HUNG   PHET

The fifth dance is done on Mount Sumeru in the center of the stadium. It is a four-sided, blue-green inverted pyramid with four levels. If we were going to draw it from a bird's eye view, it would be a small square in the middle surrounded by three squares of increasing size. If we were going to build it, it's a four sided pyramid turned upside down, with a flat top and three other levels. Here we dance over two types of ghosts.[76] In Tibetan, one is a *shindre* [shi 'dre], the spirit of someone who died with a very negative mind and now won't continue on through the bardo state. It has lost its path, is confused, and is creating obstacles for others. The other type is *sondre* [gson 'dre], which means a living ghost. We see many dead ghosts and living ghosts. Some are lying face down, and some are lying face up. We dance on top of these ghosts, which represent ignorance in its many forms.

This ignorance, or *timug* in Tibetan, is very dark. Often we think we're doing our best, but actually we're not because ignorance obscures the best path. We don't usually see our ignorance—it's in the background, hurting and disturbing us. For example, we don't know where we came from before this life. Why? Because that knowledge is obscured by our ignorance. Similarly, why are we always obsessing about our future? It's the best we can do when we're obscured by ignorance, but it's definitely not the best solution!

By subduing the *shindre* and *sondre* ghosts, we subdue ignorance and invoke dharmadhatu wisdom. Dharmadhatu, or *cho kyi ying* in Tibetan, is the "realm of pure dharmas"—the pristine awareness mind in its luminous, clear state free from obscurations. By transforming ignorance into dharmadhatu wisdom, we emanate the blue-green light of bodhichitta in every direction. Bodhichitta actually means the union of wisdom and compassion, and is not separate from any of the five wisdoms. It unites all of their qualities into a single state.

To summarize the five dances, we can say that these five directions encompass all directions, just as the designs of the stadiums represent all of our mental creations. Whatever arises will come from one of these directions. Similarly, these five designs are the basic ground of mental creation. Even though they may be combined in various ways, the basic designs in the phenomenal world are all based on these five shapes. We also see many different colors, but these five colors are the major colors.

All other colors are reflections, mixtures, or subdivisions of these five. We transform the five poisons into wisdom, or we could say we subdue the five demons and invoke the five wisdom states. Then we emanate the five wisdom lights in every direction.

Conceptual mind is dualistic. From duality mind, obstacles are demons. In Chod practice, it's important to not look externally for substantially existing demons, but to remember that whatever arises is our obscured mind. The principal meaning of Chod practice is that we're subduing the five mental poisons, which only seem to arise externally. When this is fully realized, the entire universe transforms into the five male and female Dhyani Buddhas and the five wisdoms of mirror-like wisdom, equanimity wisdom, discriminating awareness wisdom, all-accomplishing wisdom, and dharmadhatu wisdom.

As we emanate colored lights in every direction, we continue visualizing ourselves as the secret wisdom dakini Sangwa Yeshe with her retinues. Maybe we're actually physically dancing, or maybe we're meditating that we're dancing, but either way, we emanate all these lights. We must have the right attitude when we're subduing: we don't attack the poisons violently, like knocking down five ugly guys in a boxing match [laughter]. We do it by displaying our five beautiful lights: the white light of loving-kindness, the blue light of compassion, the red light of great joy, the green light of all-accomplishing wisdom, and the blue-green light of bodhichitta, the union of compassion and wisdom.

This completes the teachings on the dancing section of Chod. Our concentration on emanating the five lights and subduing the five poisons is important. After we develop good concentration and meditation, then we can also physically dance. The dance must always be done with meditation. There are many styles for this dance. Every region, even every city or village in Tibet has a slightly different form. Yet most practitioners mentally visualize the dance rather than doing it physically.

Staking the Tent

Jigme Lingpa's commentary continues on page 14:

> Then, pitch a small tent on the ground of the cruel demon, who lies on its back with its five limbs extended. Meditate that you pound in stakes of meteoric iron.

After the Chod dance, the practitioner puts up a tent because she's going to stay for awhile and practice. This tent, or *chodgur* [gcod gur], is just for one person. It's small with one center-post and four corners where the stakes go.

While we're putting the tent up, there is a specific meditation. This isn't an ordinary process of setting up a tent, like when we go camping. On the ground where the tent is being placed, we see ego-clinging in the form of a demon, lying down flat and facing up at the sky. Meditate that each corner of the tent is for one of the demon's arms and legs.

The four stakes that pin down the tent's corners are meteoric iron phurbas. The phurba symbolizes immovability in two ways. As a "stake," it means the negative emotions are unable to move. At the same time, our bodhichitta is immovable and unshakeable too. These four stakes are not violent daggers. In reality, they are the four boundless attitudes of infinite love, compassion, rejoicing, and equanimity.

Page 14:

> PHET
> The vajra dakini of the eastern direction
> Carries the stake of great loving-kindness.
> The ratna dakini of the southern direction
> Carries the stake of great compassion.

> The padma dakini of the western direction
> Carries the stake of great rejoicing.
> The karma dakini of the northern direction
> Carries the stake of great equanimity.
> The buddha dakini of the central direction
> Carries the stake of bodhichitta.

The stake for the east corner is boundless loving-kindness. When we set the stake, we meditate that we are the vajra dakini Dorje Khandroma, who is white, very beautiful, and peaceful. She carries the stake of loving-kindness, which is a white phurba with a slightly round or circular shape. The eastern limb of the ego-clinging demon is the right hand, which represents anger. The vajra dakini Dorje Khandroma gloriously stabs the right hand of ego-clinging. She subdues anger and invokes loving-kindness, which radiates freely to every sentient being without any obstacle.

For the south, we meditate that we are the ratna dakini Rinchen Khandroma, yellow with a joyful expression. She carries the meteoric iron phurba of compassion, which is yellow and square shaped. The left hand of the ego-clinging demon represents pride or arrogance. When the dakini steps onto the left hand and sets that stake, that very moment pride and arrogance are subdued, and boundless compassion is invoked. Compassion then freely radiates to every sentient being without obstruction.

For the west, as the red padma dakini, we put a stake in ego-clinging's left leg, which represents attachment. Padma Khandroma is very beautiful and passionate. She carries a semi-circular red phurba of great joy. By subduing attachment, we invoke boundless joy, which radiates unobstructedly to all beings.

The ego-clinging demon's right leg is under the

northern corner of the tent. It is the poison of jealousy. Laychi Khandroma, the green karma dakini, is a little wrathful and has a very powerful expression. She carries the black triangular phurba of equanimity. When she stabs the demon's right leg, all jealousy is subdued and boundless equanimity is invoked. Oath-breaking and samaya obstacles are destroyed, and the attitude of equanimity arises for all sentient beings.

The central buddha dakini is Sangye Khandroma. She is blue and semi-wrathful, and wields the blue phurba of bodhichitta. This phurba combines wishing bodhichitta and action bodhichitta, so it includes all four shapes: circle, square, semi-circle, and triangle. With this stake, the buddha dakini pierces the head of ego-clinging, which represents ignorance. That very moment we strongly invoke the state of bodhichitta, which is the union of compassion and wisdom, radiating primordial awareness in every direction.

It is also taught that these five phurbas are the five activities of enlightened beings. They are (1) the phurba of pacifying, (2) the phurba of increasing, (3) the phurba of overpowering, and (4) the phurba of subjugation. The union of all of these is known as (5) the phurba of bodhichitta, which is the central phurba that stakes the head of ego-clinging.

Page 16:

> By piercing the head
> And four limbs of the demon of ego-clinging,
> It is transfixed, unable to move. PHET

When we put the center stake through ego-clinging's head, we've finished the job. We have subdued the negative emotions of the five directions. Now ego-clinging can never rise up.

We should strongly feel that this is firmly established, and that we have completely subdued the ego.

Dissolution Stage Practice

Now the dakinis of the four corner directions dissolve into the syllables HA RI NI SA, which symbolize the dakinis of the four directions. The syllables then dissolve into the central dakini, and she dissolves back into Sangwa Yeshe Khandroma, who then dissolves into ourselves.

Sitting in our tent on the power spot, release all of your everyday attitudes like, "I'm Khenpo Palden Sherab sitting here," or "I'm [use your name] sitting here." Totally understand your nature as the secret wisdom dakini. You're not just 80% dakini nature—you are 100% Sangwa Yeshe Khandroma. Completely hold the view that where you're sitting is the pure land of the dakinis, which is known as the "frightful charnel ground," and that this is not some temporary hallucination. This is the original nature. From the beginning of time, everything has always been in this state, but we didn't realize it until today. Today we realize that we are Sangwa Yeshe Khandroma, and that the entire universe is the pure land of the dakinis. We have regained our original realization. We have awakened and see everything clearly. Feel great compassion for all sentient beings who don't realize this nature, and who are still clinging to dream-like states.

This primordial nature of boundless love, compassion, joy, equanimity, and bodhichitta is the true, natural quality of mind. Until now, due to so many different conditions, ego-clinging has been in control. With the assistance of the five great mother dakinis, we're now able to subdue these blocking conditions and return to the original, primordial nature of our mind. There's no way ego-clinging will come up. We have discovered that ego-clinging is a temporary condition. We can subdue it. We can return to the primordially natural state. At this moment, rest in the state of great awareness.

We have gone to the stadium and danced. We've put the tent up. Now we have to settle down and move in. We're not going to be wandering yogis and yoginis right now. This will be our address and zip code for a while [laughter].

Orgyen Vajradhara

Chapter 5:

Preliminary Ngondro Practices

We now begin the portion of the Chod ritual in which we offer the generosity of our body, or *lujin* [lus sbyin]. There are special preliminary prayers and meditations that follow the traditional pattern of the Ngondro foundational practices in Tibetan Buddhism. First, establish the perfect objects of refuge, then go for refuge, generate bodhichitta, and make a mandala offering to the objects of refuge. Next do Guru Yoga practice, and then dissolve the meditation.

Visualizing the Objects of Refuge

Page 16:

> PHET   Perception itself is the luminous space of great bliss.
> In the sky, which is free from contrived effort,
> Is the root lama as Vajradhara, the lord of the six families,
> And the gurus and yidams of the mind-to-mind, symbolic,
>   and oral transmission lineages,
> Along with the dakinis, dharmapalas, and protectors.
> They gather like clouds,
> Unobstructed and clear, in a vast, circular rainbow.

To begin this visualization, chant the syllable PHET. That very moment we return to the primordial nature, and the entire universe is transformed into the pure land of the dakinis. It is great blissfulness beyond any effort and fabrication, known as the luminous blissful palace of space.

The refuge field is visualized as follows. In the center of this space, one's own root guru is seen as Guru Padmasambhava, who appears in the form of Vajradhara. This manifestation is called Orgyen Vajradhara. He is surrounded by all the masters of the three lineages seated in space. The first lineage is called the mind-to-mind transmission lineage of the victorious ones, or buddhas. The next lineage is the symbolic transmission lineage of the vidyadharas, and the third is the oral transmission lineage of all the great practitioners. The masters of the three lineages are sitting in rainbow spheres of light above the head of Orgyen Vajradhara. At the very top is Buddha Samantabhadra with his consort Buddha Samantabhadri. Below is Vajradhara, then Vajrasattva, followed by Garab Dorje,[77] Manjushrimitra, Shri Singha, Vimalamitra, and Guru Padmasambhava. The twenty-five main students of Guru Padmasambhava and the 108 great tertons are also present. There are wrathful deities, peaceful deities, and all the dharmapalas right in front of you, unceasingly clear and vivid. Yet they do not exist as solid objects. Everyone has his or her own circle of rainbow light.

Vajradhara has one face, two arms, two legs, and is blue in color. His arms are crossed in front of him. In his right hand he holds a vajra, and his left hand holds a bell. He is in union with his consort who is holding a curved knife and skullcup.

Take refuge in front of these objects of refuge, thinking that you and all sentient beings are taking refuge. Particularly include all the demons and ghosts. See and feel that everyone is joining together with you to take refuge.

This way of taking refuge is according to the Dzogchen style.

With this view, we have always had primordial buddha-nature with us from beginningless time. It's not something newly arrived or something we had lost. Guru Padmasambhava taught, "This primordial nature is always with every sentient being, but they never recognize it. How strange." It's like living with someone for a hundred years, yet never recognizing them. Our primordial nature is even closer than this, and we still don't recognize it.

Jigme Lingpa said, "This primordial nature is always with us. The power of Chod practice provokes that knowledge and understanding." So here we take refuge in the self-existing primordial nature by recognizing it as it is.

Taking Refuge and Developing Bodhichitta

On page 17, the refuge prayer says:

> PHET Because this unfabricated, self-existing awareness
> Is not recognized as the essence of the objects of refuge,
> Beings are drowning in the ocean of suffering.
> May the wisdom mind of the three kayas protect us.

Recite this three times, then generate bodhichitta.

This bodhichitta aspiration is coming more from the absolute level. Our bodhichitta attitude isn't connected with hopes and fears. We go beyond hope and fear, not paying any attention to ego-clinging or dualistic conceptual notions.

Page 18:

> PHET The mind that clings to appearances as solidly existing
> Is severed by the activities of crazy wisdom.

Cutting Through Ego

> So that the perfectly pure nature may be realized,
> I generate bodhichitta free from hope and fear.

Recite this verse three times in the presence of the objects of refuge, then make a mandala offering in front of the refuge tree.

Mandala Offering

With the mandala offering we're making offerings to the beings of the entire universe. Our "illusory body" can represent the subdivisions of the cosmology of the traditional mandala. For example, our back or spine is Mount Sumeru. Our four limbs are the four continents. Our fingers and toes are subcontinents and islands. Our head represents the god realms, or Tushita Heaven. Our two eyes are the sun and moon. In our body there are six organs that represent the luxuries and treasures of all these realms. The hairs of our body represent grass and plants. These are the desirable objects and wealth of all sentient beings, including gods and humans. Our body is also our most cherished possession, so offering it in this way is very powerful.

We make these offerings as a practice to accumulate merit. There are two merits, roughly translated as "accumulation merit" and "wisdom merit." These two terms refer to the relative and absolute ways in which we make offerings. When accumulation is performed with concepts of a "giver," an "object being given," and an activity of "giving," the result is accumulation merit. When we offer with the absolute Dzogchen realization that there is no subject, object, or activity, the result is wisdom merit.

In this way, we meditate that we're offering our body and the entire universe to the refuge tree. In the sadhana on page 19, it says:

Visualizing the Objects of Refuge

PHET   This illusory body, this cherished aggregate,
Is arranged as the offering substance of the mandala.
Without expectations, I offer it to the assembly of the deities.
May the root of ego-clinging be cut.   PHET

Guru Yoga and the Dissolution Stage

Next, with the Guru Yoga practice we reconnect with the Guru, who encourages us on the path to enlightenment. Meditating in the stainless dharmakaya state, radiate vibrating, clear light energy of wisdom like nets of light.

In the center of that, our only father of all of our lifetimes—the omniscient buddha of the three times, Orgyen Vajradhara Padmakara—appears in the form of a heruka surrounded by many mother wisdom dakinis. He has one face, two arms, two legs, and three eyes that are somewhat wide-open or semi-round. Padmakara is a rich white color, or white with a slightly red tint. He is wearing a crown of skullcups and skulls. His hair is partly tied up, with many locks of hair falling down around his shoulders, like a yogi. He wears all the bone ornaments, including earrings, necklaces, armlets, bracelets, and anklets, and he has a tiger skin skirt. His right hand holds a damaru up in the sky, and his left hand holds a bell towards his chest, with his left elbow holding a khatvanga.[78] The sounds of TA LA LA, shimmering and radiant, and U RU RU, ceaselessly sounding, fill the entirety of space. His speech tames all concepts and negative emotions, all hope and fear and ego-clinging. Until now, due to our projections and dualistic clinging, unfortunate conditions have appeared. Because of hope and fear, we have imbalances in our body, speech, and mind. This taming activity brings joy—we begin to see how precious life is, and how precious other beings are.

Cutting Through Ego

Page 19:

> PHET In the stainless space of the dharmakaya,
> Amid a brilliant, circular mass of rainbow light,
> Is Padmakara, the father who knows all the three times,
> In the style of a heruka performing crazy wisdom activity.
> He is accompanied by the mothers, a vast assembly of dakinis.
> His body is radiant with the major and minor marks of
>   a buddha. TA LA LA
> His speech is the sound of the Dharma, taming beings
>   according to their needs. U RU RU
> His mind is the state of luminosity, the indestructible essence.
> I, your child, supplicate you with strong devotion.

All the deities are beautiful, gloriously glowing, singing songs of Dharma and chanting mantras. Their minds are totally in the absolute state of clear light blissfulness.

Now we practitioners name ourselves as their children. We devoted children pray to be able to subdue all external demons, which are the reflections of ego-clinging. Hope, fear, and grasping are inner demons.

Page 21:

> Outwardly, concepts have arisen as enemies; these are
>   the demons' form.
> Inwardly, dualistic clinging is their mind of hope and fear.
> In between, all sorts of unfortunate conditions appear.

Up until now, we've been very patient with our demons. Now we proclaim that they will be destroyed. We will take the royal seat, regain our own dominion, and become an heir of our true royal parents, Guru Padmasambhava and Yeshe Tsogyal.

Visualizing the Objects of Refuge

Our aspiration must be blessed by our father, Lord Guru Padmasambhava. Pray to him:

Page 21:

> May the profound practice of Chod
> Destroy these demons right now, on this very seat.
> So that I may hold the royal seat of the space of dharmakaya,
> Father, Jetsun Lama,[79] please grant your blessings.
> PHET PHET PHET

The three PHET syllables remind us to invoke or establish our understanding of the three kayas: dharmakaya, sambhogakaya, and nirmanakaya. The first PHET here is the destruction of all concepts, the second PHET is the recognition of our own true nature, and the third PHET is regaining the state of Mother Prajnaparamita.

Complete this Guru Yoga practice by dissolving all the objects of refuge into yourself in the following way. The retinues and dakinis dissolve into Orgyen Vajradhara. Orgyen Vajradhara dissolves into five lights, and the lights dissolve into you. This dissolution completes everything within your own awareness. Then meditate in the nondual state in which your own awareness is inseparable from the Lama or Guru Padmasambhava, your root teacher. Meditating in this way is the absolute Guru Yoga.

Troma Nagmo

Chapter 6:

The Main Practice

The main part of the Chod practice is the offering of the "four great feasts." These four great feasts are offered with the skillful means of compassion and the wisdom of emptiness, united together. In the Mahayana teachings, we meditate that there is no truly existent self, ego, or subject. Neither are there any solidly existing, permanent objects. At first, we meditate on this intellectually or theoretically. Yet Chod practice takes us beyond the theoretical stage. The special quality of Chod is that we're no longer just quietly meditating or making an intellectual analysis. Instead, we're bringing our realization into action.

Three Stages of Bodhichitta

We must establish a very strong understanding of both bodhichitta and emptiness in order to perform the actualizing bodhichitta practices of the Chod feasts. First practice equalizing bodhichitta, or *dag zhen nyam pe*, in which we see all sentient beings and ourselves as equal. "I am an equal with them and they are equals with me. We are all the same, with no distinctions. We have similar intentions and similar situations. I want happiness, and they want happiness. I don't want suffering, and they don't want suffering either." These understandings bring us to a more balanced state. Meditating on this equalizing bodhichitta is the first point.

Equalizing bodhichitta is not an exaggeration or distortion. In reality, everyone truly is equal. Every sentient being has the same intention of wanting happiness, joy, and peace. "As I do, you do too. As you do, so do I." There are no distinctions at all. With this realization, feel great compassion for all sentient beings, seeing them as a reminder of your commitment of love, compassion, and wisdom. Don't only try to imagine this, but really feel it from your heart and through every cell and bone in your body. Extend that to all sentient beings. Your whole being is transformed into the state of love, compassion, and wisdom. This process is actualizing our equalizing bodhichitta.

After abiding in this state for a little while, begin the next stage of exchanging bodhichitta, or exchanging our position, called *dag zhen je wa*. An example often used in Tibet for this type of bodhichitta is seeing a person who is cold and giving them your own blanket. The meditation of *Tonglen* is an exchanging bodhichitta practice. Give your joy, peace, and happiness—whatever good there is—to other sentient beings. Then take in whatever negativities others are experiencing, including their sadness, suffering, and misery, so they're freed from that suffering. You don't have to start by exchanging the biggest things—you don't have to be rich Wall Street philanthropists right from the start. Start with very small portions, in a manageable way. Once you succeed with that, you'll discover that you're able to do more and more.

After exchanging bodhichitta, the third stage of bodhichitta practice is meditating that others are even more important than yourself. The Chod feast is exchanging

Three Stages of Bodhichitta

bodhichitta. You see others as more important, so you give them this big feast. What you're giving is yourself. Don't even think of paying any attention to yourself, or of holding anything back for yourself. The feast of yourself is visualized and offered in many ways because of the different needs and desires of your guests.

Having summoned, overpowered, and subdued all of your powerful guests, you then provoke their strength. You're going to use their energies to challenge your view, meditation, and realization of the union of compassion and wisdom—to see how strong and powerful it really is. You're training for the Olympics! Energies that arise externally and internally become the path, and using them skillfully increases your realization. If you have enough strength, compassion, and a stable wisdom-emptiness meditation, challenging events will instantly spark your realization. Obstacles will transform into causes to increase your realization. The strongest fire will burn anything if it's hot enough, even water. That's why in Chod practice, arising obstacles called *lhongtse* are a big bonus. Don't be upset when they come.

These four feasts are highly skillful means. For example, if you simply gave your body to someone, that would certainly be a great generosity and very meritorious. But it's still just one body, so it would only help a limited number of beings. But in these four feasts, you're inviting all the guests of the three thousand-fold universe, including all of the buddhas, bodhisattvas, and sentient beings. You purify, multiply, and transform your body so that you can serve everyone. This is much more beneficial than giving your single small body to one person.

At this point in the sadhana, Jigme Lingpa's instructions mention that you should meditate in nondual equanimity, beyond all conceptions of "I," "you," and "demons." Relax in the primordial nature of Prajnaparamita, the "Mother of All the Buddhas." While relaxing in the nondual state, there are no notions of an existing "I" or "other." The invisible beings and ghosts don't exist either. They have never existed since beginningless time. The *Heart Sutra* describes this state: "No path, no wisdom, no attainment, and no nonattainment." This is our heart goal: to abide in the true nature. Meditating in this state is how you conclude your preparations and enter into the main offering ceremony.

Looking back, recall the sections of the sadhana we discussed in the preparation part of the Chod ceremony. We walked to the stadium, danced, and then put up our tent. Other larger Chod texts, such as Dudjom Lingpa's *Troma Nagmo* [khros ma nag mo] and Karma Chagme's *Tsogle Rinchen Trengwa* [tshogs las rinchen 'phreng ba] have more extensive and detailed Chod instructions. Our preparations here include *zilnon*, the meditation on the complete awesome splendor of subduing the demons of ego-clinging. If we climb up a mountain, we can go by many different trails to arrive at the same spot.

Yet the awesome splendor practices are only preparations—they're not our final goal. We did the awesome splendor practice to subdue the demons of ego-clinging. Now that the demons are subdued, we want to make them happy by giving them a very generous gift. In Tibetan, this giving is called *je* ['gyed]. *Je* means "endless giving," "limitless generosity," "limitless sharing," or "something that you keep giving."

When we say "generosity," what do we really mean? Used in the ordinary, worldly way, generosity means giving food, clothing, money, or some valuable object. Yet as Dharma practitioners, we give love, compassion, and wisdom. And with the practice of Chod, we give our visualized body. Our body is the number one focus of our clinging and attachment.

Three Stages of Bodhichitta

To break this habit, we practice by giving our most desirable possession away to others. We're going to use this precious body of ours for a great purpose.

As Vajrayana practitioners, how should we view our body? It is the essence of the Four Noble Truths and samsara. It's impermanent and illusory. It is made up of the five elements and five aggregates, but these elements and aggregates themselves are empty—they come from the emptiness of our parents' elements and aggregates, and so forth. We're only borrowing this body comprised of the five elements. It's on temporary loan. But in the meantime, by using our awareness, we can make the best use of this chubby, illusory body to benefit ourselves and others. This body—which is so precious, important, and dear to us—is still just an illusion. Or we could say it's a delusion. Therefore it's known as an "illusion body," a temporary combination of the elements of fire, wind, water, and earth. While we have a precious human situation, if we use it to benefit ourselves and others, it's a win-win situation. Truly, we are making a difference. This is the understanding with which we offer our body. Here Jigme Lingpa says:

Page 22:

> Then see your gross body, which is obscured
> > by habitual tendencies,
> As big and fat and greasy.

It is beautiful! [Laughter]. We have all the beautiful grease and all the chubbiness we need. We need it all for the feast! It's so beautiful. And what resides within this beautiful chubby body? Our essential awareness resides here, taking care of us. Now we're going to use this "I."

CREATION STAGE: TROMA PREPARES THE OFFERING

Page 22:

> PHET Then see your gross body, which is obscured
>   by habitual tendencies,
> As big and fat and greasy.
> From within that, the essential awareness
> In the form of Troma, separates upward by the sound of PHET.

We start this section of the practice by visualizing our habitual body becoming very youthful, and very heavy and gigantic—bigger than a mountain. In this meditation, our body looks like us except that it becomes so big and delicious.

The essence of our awareness resides in our heart center. The moment we chant PHET, our own awareness arises from our heart center in the form of Black Troma, who is none other than Sangwa Yeshe. The deity is now appearing in her most wrathful form as Troma Nagmo [khros ma nag mo], which means the "black wrathful one." Our awareness shoots up our central channel and into the sky. Now it's out of our body, up in space, instantly transformed into the form of Troma Nagmo.

The teachings also say that we can visualize Black Troma in our heart center, and then when we say PHET, she shoots up roughly and powerfully through our central channel into the sky.

Page 22:

> She has one face and two arms, and holds a hooked
>   knife and skullcup.
> She slices the skull from one's body.

Creation Stage: Troma Prepares the Offering

> Encompassing the entire universe, this human head
> Is placed on a hearth of three skulls.

Troma Nagmo is a dakini, black in color, with a very wrathful face, two arms, and two legs. She is also a form of Vajravarahi,[80] and for that reason there's a grunting pig's head on top of her head. She has three eyes. In her right hand she holds a flaming curved knife and her left hand holds a skullcup.

Our primordial awareness appears as Troma Nagmo— it is completely separate from our ordinary body. She is dancing up in the sky, and is very joyful, dominant, majestic, and firm. Of course, because she is the essence of our own wisdom mind, her nature is love, compassion, and wisdom. She dominates both samsara and nirvana, and all perceptions are subjugated by her power.

At that very moment, your ordinary body becomes a corpse. In the normal, regular world, since our consciousness has left our body, we would be pronounced dead. To use a traditional metaphor, we'd say this rented house that we called "our" body is now empty of its tenant. The lease is up. We're out, and our "landlord"—our awareness as Troma –is now in control of it.

The next moment, Troma points the tip of her curved knife over the corpse, and the top of its skull is sliced off evenly and turned upside down like a cooking pot. In Tibet, nomads and pilgrims don't use fancy stoves with metal legs or gas grills. They'd just arrange three rocks as a tripod, build a fire, and set a pot on those rocks. Just like that, our skullcup is placed on top of a tripod made of three fresh heads. The three skulls represent the three kayas.

Now the skullcup becomes as huge as the three worlds, "encompassing the entire universe." Troma Nagmo cuts up the gigantic corpse and arranges the pieces of blood, flesh, and bones inside the skullcup. With her activity and that of many other great wisdom dakinis, the body, which is red, completely fills the skullcup, which is as vast as the universe.

Page 23:

> This body made of the elements is arranged
>   as the feast offering.
> With the light of the three syllables it blazes
>   as the nectar of amrita.

That very moment, wisdom fire appears beneath the skullcup and cooks the body very nicely. It's so tender that we wouldn't need a fork and knife to cut it up [laughter]. The moment the fire begins, blessing nectar of amrita descends from Troma's body into the skullcup, and the corpse is completely transformed into wisdom nectar.

Troma Offering Mantra

As the offering boils, vapors rise from the wisdom substances in the form of the syllables OM, AH, and HUNG.

In other teachings, sometimes it's a little different. They say that as the vapors rise, the three syllables OM, AH, and HUNG appear in the sky and shower down, merging with the boiling offerings. OM comes in the form of white light, and has the action of purifying the offering. AH comes in the form of red light, and has the action of increasing or multiplying the offering. HUNG appears in the form of blue light, and has the action of transforming the offering. These three syllables are also blessings from all the buddhas and bodhisattvas of all directions. The buddhas' body blessings

Creation Stage: Troma Prepares the Offering

come in the form of OM, their speech blessings come in the form of AH, and their wisdom mind blessings come in the form of HUNG. OM is the nirmanakaya, AH is the sambhogakaya, and HUNG is the dharmakaya. So what's boiling in the skullcup is no longer flesh and grease and all that: it has been transformed into wisdom nectar. It is now the absolute wisdom feast of kindness, compassion, wisdom, and perfect enlightenment. The mantra also contains the syllables HA, HO, and HRI. HA and HO indicate enjoyment. HRI means accomplishment. The mantra is:

Page 23:

    OM AH HUNG dang HA HO HRI

Blow the thighbone trumpet three times if you have one and if the situation is appropriate, and recite the syllables OM AH HUNG dang HA HO HRI as many times as possible with this view and meditation. Thus these wisdom substances become infinite and perfectly pure desirable pleasure objects of all the six senses, as well as the accomplishments of wisdom and enlightenment. The offering becomes everything our guests need or desire.

With our recitation of the mantra,[81] the purified, multiplied, and transformed offering substances become feast substances that have the nature of amrita, although they can take on an infinite variety of appearances to give satisfaction to all of our different guests.

From Troma Nagmo's heart center, many hundreds of millions of wisdom dakinis of the five colors emanate. They're all chanting OM AH HUNG HA HO HRI. These wisdom dakinis will serve the feast, distributing our offering objects to all of the buddhas, as well as to all the other guests.

Cutting Through Ego

After the dismemberment, cooking, and transformation of our precious body, what's left that we can hold on to? Really—what is there to be afraid of? Our body is now within the wisdom state, our awareness is always within the wisdom nature state, and the causes and conditions of our karma and habitual patterns have been transformed into wisdom.

Preparing the Four Feasts

We offer four feasts because we have special "menus" for each of the four types of guests. (1) The first feast is the white generosity, or the white gift *karje* [dkar 'gyed]. (2) The second is the striped feast, or the "zebra gift" [laughter]. Actually, it's not zebra-striped—it's black and white all together. The Tibetan word is *traje* [khra 'gyed], which means "mixed" or "multi-colored." Next is (3) the red gift *marje* [dmar 'gyed], followed by (4) the last offering of the black gift, which is *nagje* [nag 'gyed].

Larger Chod sadhanas have sections for all of the four feasts. This sadhana, which is smaller, emphasizes two feasts—the white feast and the red feast—but in the commentary by Jigme Lingpa, all four feasts are described.

White Feast

Why make distinctions between different feasts? Some masters specifically connect these different feasts to different levels of the teachings. Some great masters said that the white feast is mainly connected to the Vajrayana teachings, and the red feast is mainly connected to the Sutra Mahayana teachings, while the striped feast is not connected to any particular teachings. It is for all the beings of the six realms, including the habitually karmically connected obstructers. The black feast is mainly focused on beings who are experiencing suffering, troubles, and karmic debt.

Now we'll briefly describe these "menus," or gifts. In general, during all four feasts we meditate that our own cut up, illusory body has become blessing nectar and different wisdom elements.

For the white feast, the wisdom substances appear as prized wholesome foods like yogurt, milkshakes, fruit, honey, molasses, and cheese—all vegetarian foods, and everything that's beautiful. From those appearances emanate all desirable objects. Nothing is restricted. The power of your samadhi visualization expands without limits. This is what we're giving especially to our highly honored guests, but no one is excluded from taking part. Beginning practitioners should always do this first.

Red Feast

The red feast involves visualizing the wisdom nectar offering as your bones, flesh, muscles, blood, and fat—all of your organs and every other body part as they usually are. It's all raw and dripping with juices.

Next, Jigme Lingpa explains the sequence of the visualization: from your heart center, Troma appears in the sky. While your body is on the ground, Troma again points the curved knife at the body, but this time the entire skin comes off the body and is laid out flat. This skin then expands until it becomes as big as the universe. Troma puts a huge heap of all the parts of your multiplied bodies, flesh, and bones, and chops it all up as an endless red feast. The red feast is definitely non-vegetarian [laughter], and as rough and raw as a slaughterhouse. Visualize your body as infinite and inexhaustible, then feed it to everyone. For those beings who like only bones, you have endless bones to offer. For beings who only want blood, you offer endless blood. For beings who like flesh, you give endless flesh. And for beings who like all of these substances, give them everything they want, which still appears as recognizable parts of your body.

Again the three syllables instantly appear as we chant OM, AH, HUNG. The syllables descend as a shower, and they absorb into the red feast. Even though the feast's appearance is bone, grease, and red, bloody flesh, its nature is absolute wisdom. In reality, it's all transformed nectar.

Your guests are already there, but still you re-invite them. Restrengthen your visualization of Troma Nagmo, and welcome all the guests again. This red feast is particularly designated for invisible beings who are highly negative, or very emotional, and ones who do cruel activities.

Yes, you're really giving offerings to cruel and violent beings so that they're completely satisfied and won't continue acting that way. Once they're satisfied, their violent emotions become completely pacified, and their negative energies are transcended into wisdom.

Offer this feast to beings "in the world and beyond the world," which refers to the fact that many of our guests are invisible beings. There's a story about this. In Buddha Shakyamuni's lifetime there was a powerful, invisible worldly being named Trama, or "Robber Lady," who had 500 children to feed. One time, when the Buddha was staying with the Sangha in Rajagriha at Vulture Peak, the neighboring villagers came to him because they were losing all their babies. The villagers were doing everything they could think of to guard their children, but babies kept inexplicably vanishing one by one. The parents told the Buddha that they were sure a spirit or demon was responsible.

With the Buddha's omniscience, he could see the spirit

Creation Stage: Troma Prepares the Offering

Trama and where she was living, so he went to her place. She wasn't there, but her own youngest baby was there. The Buddha gently set his begging bowl upside down over the baby, hiding him. Trama soon returned, and in a panic began looking for her baby, calling and calling his name. She went around the entire universe crying, "Where's my young one, my dear, my love?" Returning home, trembling, she asked the Buddha for help. He asked her, "How many babies do you have?" "I have 500 babies, Lord." "So why do you care so much about just one?" "He's my love, a piece of my heart," she answered. The Buddha asked her, "Do you think you're the only one who cares about your babies?" "Well, I guess other beings care too," she admitted. "So why do you kill other people's babies?" Reluctantly, she said, "Because I need to. I need food for my children and myself." The Buddha then replied, "If you promise never to hurt or kill another being, I will help you get your child back." "Oh, that would be wonderful," she said. "But how can I feed my family if I stop this? How will we survive?" The Buddha said, "As long as the Dharma survives, the Sangha will make offerings to you. You will never need to commit unvirtuous, evil karmas again." The Buddha then gave her teachings, and put her under oath as a powerful black protector or dharmapala. Once she had taken the vow, the Buddha turned his begging bowl back over, and her little boy came out. Trama and her child embraced and were happy again. This is why in fulfillment of the Buddha's promise to Trama, there is a ceremony in the Vinaya teachings to make offerings to Troma.

In some of the larger, more detailed versions of Chod practice, the red feast is slightly different. It's mentioned particularly that the red feast includes a visualization of all the five dakini families: the buddha dakinis, vajra dakinis, ratna dakinis, padma dakinis, and karma dakinis. The red feast highlights that you're making offerings to all of these wisdom dakinis, as well as all

Cutting Through Ego

of those karmically connected obstructer guests. The offerings you're making this time are the five poisons—the causes of every trouble. Ego-clinging is the root cause, which reflects as the five poisons. From the five poisons originate all troubles, including famine, poverty, war, disease, and every unwanted thing.

When you make the red feast in this way, the offering gathers all of the emotions and negativities, which merge with the red feast, transforming it into wisdom nectar which is then blessed by the three syllables OM, AH, HUNG. First you make offerings to the vajra dakinis. Vajra dakinis are a brilliant white. They could be big or small, youthful or aged, but they all have the same nature of wisdom and compassion, and are totally enlightened beings. All of the troubles and misfortunes related with the emotion of anger are consumed by the vajra dakinis and other guests. Of course, you're not offering them negativity—anger has been completely transformed into wisdom amrita by the power of the three syllables OM, AH, and HUNG.

Then, in the same way, make the next offering to the ratna dakinis and all the guests. All diseases and troubles caused by arrogance and pride are consumed with that offering. Then you offer the padma dakinis all of the emotions of attachment and their related troubles and difficulties, which are all consumed. You offer the karma dakinis jealousy with all of its troubles and suffering, and you offer the buddha dakinis all forms of ignorance and its sufferings and difficulties. All of these are completely consumed. So this is a slightly different visualization for the red feast.

Striped Feast

One way of understanding the striped feast is as a variety feast: the ultimate smorgasbord of wisdom nectar transformed into all

Creation Stage: Troma Prepares the Offering

sorts of luxuries. To those who like horses, give them horses. Or sports cars, limousines, land, mansions, food, drinks, precious metals, jewels, clothes, and so on. It includes beautiful gardens, medicine, gold, silver, jacuzzis, swimming pools, private planes, yachts, golf resorts, everything! And there are multiples of all the gifts too, not just one of each. These gifts offer beautiful forms, sounds, fragrances, tastes, and body sensations. You're offering everything you can possibly imagine that's desirable, from both samsara and nirvana. Because your body is now vast and inexhaustible, there are no limits, so give all the guests as much as they need or want. In Tibet, the list for the striped feast always includes favorite things like yak butter tea and cheese—lots of rich foods! Choices, endless choices—that's what you're offering.

Black Feast

The black feast deals with karmic debt and karmic habitual patterns. Every sentient being has these. The signs of a big karmic debt, or *lenchag*, could be that someone has profound depression, crushing poverty, mortal illness, or crippling disabilities. We have innumerable karmic creditors, and maybe it's payback time. If they're prepared to make a big disturbance, we have to feed them or give back to them. That's why the black feast takes all the karmic experiences of sadness, suffering, sickness, evil deeds, and so on, and transforms them into black liquids and black solids—all types of food—to offer to those who are habitually connected to you from the past and have great expectations to get something from you.

For the black distribution, you need great compassion. Think that whatever obstacles and troubles you experience this lifetime are reflections of your previous lifetimes' negative karma. While generating great compassion and loving-kindness for all beings, meditate to remove all disease, sickness, and negative thoughts by the power of Vajravarahi, Troma, and all the wisdom dakinis. Maintain this vajra courage without any hesitation or doubt. Throughout your Chod practice, never lose your compassion and bodhichitta. Bodhichitta is the essence of both the Mahayana and Vajrayana.

According to the Buddha's teachings, although we have taken countless lives, we still hold onto our body very dearly. Yet even though we cling to this body we'll still have to leave it. Now we are reversing this clinging attitude. We're giving our body to our guests for the sake of all sentient beings, asking them to enjoy it.

The black feast is more rough or "crazy" than the other gifts, even the red feast. The great master Jigme Lingpa mentioned that we should visualize the black feast in the late evening, or just before dawn.

Visualize yourself as Troma Nagmo in one of two ways. Either Troma Nagmo instantly appears from your heart center, or your consciousness instantly goes up your central channel and out into space, becoming Troma Nagmo. Either way, your ordinary body falls to the ground as a corpse.

This time you contemplate all the negativities that you've accumulated since beginningless time. All of your negative habitual patterns, obstacles, and diseases, plus all the negativities of limitless sentient beings, gather together as a great black cloud, which is magnetized or absorbed into the body that's left on the ground. The body then becomes immensely heavy, dense, and dark because of all the negativity that has gathered into it. Then chant the three syllables OM, AH, HUNG, visualizing them showering down all the blessings of the buddhas' body, speech, and mind. Although the offering's appearance remains the same, it's now the wisdom nectar of amrita. That is the true nature of

Creation Stage: Troma Prepares the Offering

the black feast. You're sharing this with all the guests, particularly those demons who long to take the lives and life-force of others. They accept your offering eagerly because it looks just like what they want. Yet because they're actually receiving wisdom nectar, they completely transcend their negative emotions into a calm and peaceful state, and eventually they attain enlightenment.

A black feast can be further divided into (1) smooth and (2) rough black feasts. The rough feast is something that looks terrible to you. For example, if you're karmically indebted to pigs and have to feed them, you might think to put that food in beautiful golden dishes, but they'd rather that you just throw it on the ground! We have to do it their way, not "our way." For some karmically connected beings, the rough black feast is best.

Other karmically connected guests may appear as refined, arrogant beings. You give them the smooth black feast if they prefer a pleasing and attractive gift. You can even transform it into a very beautiful display of wisdom to offer. The central idea is that coming from yourself, you offer both types of black feasts to feed others.

Because the black gift is mainly practiced to purify the sickness and miserable conditions of yourself and other sentient beings, it has always been very popular for healing in Tibet. If lamas and doctors came to treat a sick person, and they couldn't cure them with medicines or other remedies, they would perform the black feast Chod ceremony.

Definitely visualize these feasts according to the guests' desires. Many of your guests may go for the delights of the white feast, or the luxuries of the striped feast, or even the fresh raw flesh of the red feast. They may be coming to the feast as scavengers like vultures, hyenas, maggots, or microbes. If their preference is something dirty and unclean—if they'll enjoy it—prepare it and offer it to them. "Those of little strength," invisible beings of all kinds, and even bacteria are here because they need something. Even though you can't see them with your naked eyes, because of your generosity they'll finally get what they need and stop causing trouble. The minds of sentient beings have various desires and necessities. Something may look nasty to us, but another sentient being might really enjoy it. For example, pigs enjoy mud baths and cool ground to lie on. If we bring a pig into a palace and offer it a warm jacuzzi and a nice soft Turkish carpet, the pig may prefer to go somewhere else! The main idea is always to give a suitable gift to each guest.

Four Groups of Guests

We need to sharpen our focus so that we can fully visualize all of the guests with whom we're going to share this body that is so precious to us.

Honored Guests

First are the honored guests, or *kon chog si zhu-i dron* [dkon mchog sri zhu'i mgron.] This group includes all of the buddhas, bodhisattvas, and noble sangha, as well as all the gurus, devas, and dakinis. All of these realized beings are known as the highly realized "honored guests."

Qualified Guests

The second group includes "qualified guests"—dharmapalas who actively bring good qualities or goodness to sentient

Creation Stage: Troma Prepares the Offering

beings. They can be male, female, or *ma ning*, who are neither male nor female. These *gon po yonten gyi dron* [mgon po yon tan gyi mgron] are called "dharma protectors." They include Mahakala, Mamo Ekajati, Rahula, Dorje Legpa, and many others. All dharmapalas are qualified guests. Some are enlightened beings, and some are worldly beings. Some enlightened ones even appear as king-like worldly beings. Their appearance can vary from very beautiful to extremely wrathful. Actually, Mamo Ekajati is none other than Sangwa Yeshe—the red dakini with three eyes who we meditate on during Chod practice. When we see Sangwa Yeshe as Mamo Ekajati, it's because she wants to be more active in the world, so she is wearing her regular dharma protector uniform [laughter].

Guests of Compassion of the Six Realms

The third group is known as "guests of compassion of the six realms," or *rig drug nying je dron* [rigs drug snying rje mgron]. These are all the ordinary unenlightened beings of the six realms, including gods, asuras, humans, animals, pretas, and hell beings. Because all of these beings—including ourselves—are caught in the samsaric cycle of rebirth, they receive our compassion and are given whatever they need or want to be happy.

Obstructing Guests

The fourth group of guests includes demons and those who make obstacles—those who cling to us due to habitual patterns, and those who expect something from us like the repayment of a karmic debt. In Tibetan, they're called *don geg len chag kyi dron* [gdon bgegs lan chags kyi mgron]. Repayment may be requested directly or indirectly, visibly or invisibly. For example, if we fall ill, it might be that some being has come here that really wants something from us, perhaps a *sha 'khon*, or "killing debt." We are karmically in debt to them because of non-virtuous actions we performed in this or previous lives. We have debts to them, and they hold our loan and will keep making trouble until they're fully repaid. We took out a big loan and now we have to make a balloon payment to erase the record. These guests are not at all polite—they're urgent and very insistent.

Maybe they recently passed away, and since they were clinging so tightly to belongings or people, they couldn't move forward and got stuck wandering in the intermediate bardo state. Or maybe they passed away a long time ago, but still hold a strong expectation or obsession. Their emotions are so completely disturbed they can't find a moment of comfort and peace. So we have great compassion for these guests that are invisibly carrying heavy burdens of habitual patterns. We pray that they receive everything they wish for so they can finally be happy.

You gathered all of these four types of guests earlier during the four different "walks." You asked them to come because you're going to give this feast. When you blew the thighbone trumpet, you asked them, "Gather and come here right now." We also said, "Please stay calmly and peacefully and receive the feast."

These are your guests: you invited them, they are innumerable, and they have every possible sort of want and need. Reconnect with your understanding and

Creation Stage: Troma Prepares the Offering

realization of the true nature, and maintain that state. It is from within the true nature that, as a good host, you give boundless love, compassion, and wisdom, together with your body.

Inviting the Guests

Now you're going to invite your guests to "come to the table." This is a general invitation or invocation. Visualize guests of the four types assembling, along with hundreds of thousands of wisdom dakinis of the five families ready to serve them. They distribute your offerings to these inconceivable numbers of guests, giving each one what they want, as they want it, without missing anyone. Every offering is well-prepared and transcendent.

Page 24:

> PHET
> You who are the objects of offering, beginning
>   with the Three Roots and samaya protectors,
> And you who are the objects of generosity,
>   principally the eight classes of spirits,
> As well as the karmically-connected demons and obstructers,
> Come to this place of crazy wisdom activity.
> Today I, the fearless yogi,
> Offer this illusory body that differentiates
>   between samsara and nirvana.

Once again say PHET, and then, "You who are the objects of offering, beginning with the Three Roots and the samaya protectors." This line identifies the honored guests and the qualified guests.

Then the guests of compassion are highlighted: "You who are the objects of generosity, principally the eight classes of spirits," which emphasizes the invisible beings. The text mentions eight classes: *gyalpo* (king-like), *lu* (nagas), *senmo*, *tsen*, *sinpo* (rakshasas), *lha* (gods), *mu*, and *jungpo* (ghosts). *Gyalpo* are king-like spirits, the manifesting power of anger. *Lu* are mainly reflections of ignorance. *Senmo* are mainly reflections of attachment, and *sinpo* are a combination of jealousy and short temper.

Then give your "address," saying, "Come to this place of crazy wisdom activity." This is the place where "I, the fearless yogi, offer this illusory body that differentiates between samsara and nirvana."

This is the defining moment of realization. If there is grasping to this body—that is samsara. If there is no grasping—that is the nirvana of fearlessness. As a fearless yogi, this vast body becomes a ganachakra offering. If this body, which is an illusion, is experienced in the normal regular way, the experience of samsara will be constantly reaffirmed. If this illusory body is seen with the right view, the experience is beyond samsara.

Page 25:

> In the skullcup as vast as the three thousand worlds,
> The corpse is arranged as the ganachakra offering
> And transformed into the nectar of stainless wisdom.
> With a magical display in which all desirable
>   things have arisen
> I make this offering without holding it dear.
> Please come as guests to this great party.
> The drum of a supreme skullcup beats brightly.

Creation Stage: Troma Prepares the Offering

> The supreme skin is magnificent.
> The thighbone trumpet blows melodiously.
> The bells, tinkling bells, and tassels swing joyfully.
> Just like vultures landing on flesh,
> Please come here this very instant. PHET

"The skullcup is as big as this three-thousand-fold world," or "trichiliocosm." According to the Buddha's teachings, this equals a universe of a billion world systems (3,000 to the 3rd power). The nature of the ganachakra offering is that the corpse is transformed into the "nectar of stainless wisdom," which is also multiplied as infinite offerings—the "magical display in which all desirable things arise." The appearance of the ganachakra depends on which of the feasts we're offering.

We don't keep anything at all for ourselves. "Today I make this offering and generously give it to you without holding it dear." Don't hold anything back. The phrase "holding it dear" suggests that we might still be thinking, "This offering is valuable and I want something in exchange." So don't have any expectations of personal benefit from this offering. Really mean for your guests to take it all.

The party setting is inviting with the melodious music of an orchestra. "The drum of the supreme skullcup beats brightly" and "the thighbone trumpet blows melodiously." There are lavish decorations like "bells, tinkling bells, and tassels swinging joyfully." Remember that you're visualizing your awareness as Troma Nagmo while you play the drum, thighbone trumpet, and bell. In another part of Jigme Lingpa's commentary, it also says that Troma calls everyone to the feast by waving the "magnificent, supreme skin."

How do you ask the guests to arrive and park? Just like circling vultures quickly drop down like arrows out of the sky, and land on a corpse. "Come like that. Come instantly and receive this blessing." By reciting this, feel certain that everyone is arriving right now, particularly those highlighted guests of habitual patterns and karmic connections.

Offering and Distributing the Feasts

Reconnect your mind with complete fearlessness. This is your vajra courage: absolute, immovable, and indestructible. Continually maintain and restrengthen this vajra courage. Along with this, we need very clear minds, great devotion, commitment, and compassion to offer these feasts.

Now, referring to the honorific guests and the qualified guests who bless us and assist us, chant:

Page 26:

> PHET
> To all of you—down from the primordial protector
> And up to the root lama
> And the vidyadhara lamas of the three lineages,
> As well as the yidams, dakinis, and dharmapalas—
> I offer the amrita of the great corpse.

"To all of you, down from the primordial protector, and up to the root lama and the vidyadhara lamas of the three lineages," means the entire lineage from Buddha Samantabhadra to Buddha Shakyamuni to Guru Padmasambhava, as well as all the other deities and great masters in between, up until now. These are the vidyadhara lamas of the three lineages. As we already mentioned, the yidams, dakinis, and dharmapalas are also qualified guests. To all of the qualified guests we make an offering of the "amrita of the great corpse," which is our expanded, magnified corpse transformed into wisdom nectar.

Next, we pray to the guests to fulfill the aspirations of ourselves and all beings:

Page 27:

> May I and others, and particularly the demons,
> Perfect the two accumulations and purify the two obscurations.
> Having perfected crazy wisdom activity and
>   the benefit of beings,
> May appearance be accomplished as illusory clear light,
> And fear and anxiety be liberated in the dharmakaya.
> Please bless me to become a heruka.

You're doing this practice with great bodhichitta aspirations for all sentient beings, especially the karmically connected guests. May everyone "perfect the two accumulations and purify the two obscurations." The two accumulations are the accumulation of merit and the accumulation of wisdom. Because of the power of accumulating merit and wisdom, the two great obscurations of knowledge and ego-clinging will be completely removed.

Then pray to the buddhas, lamas, and the other honorific and qualified guests for their help in attaining several accomplishments. "May I immediately fulfill all the crazy wisdom activities." This means that each of our negativities and all of our habitual patterns are instantly transformed into wisdom. We are wishing to achieve supreme accomplishment and to be able to benefit all beings without any hindrance. And then, "May everything that I see, all my appearances or perceptions, be accomplished as illusory clear light." Here you are praying for the attainment of seeing things as they truly are: illusory magical displays of wisdom inseparable from the dharmakaya state. Finally chant, "May fear and anxiety be liberated in the dharmakaya." Fear, anxiety, worry, and all of our illusions are ultimately none other than the magical displays of our primordial nature.

When you attain these realizations, how do you want to be changed? Wish, "May I become a heruka," which is the same as saying, "May I become exactly the same as Guru Padmasambhava."

Then, referring once more to the compassionate guests, karmic creditors, and demons receiving heaps of bodies, flesh, blood, and bones, continue:

Page 28:

> PHET To those in the world and beyond the world,
> The eight classes of spirits and the non-humans,
> And to the hosts of flesh-eating demons
>   who lead beings astray,
> On a human skin the size of the three thousand worlds
> I offer heaps of flesh, blood, and bones.
> If I cling to this self, I am being weak.
> If you cannot use this, you are being lazy.
> If you are in a hurry, swallow the raw flesh whole.
> If you have time, cut it into pieces and cook it.
> Don't leave even one morsel uneaten.
>
> PHET For those who, from beginningless time in samsara,
> Have had resentment and other habitual tendencies,
> And those who have suddenly arrived, all the guests
>   of my compassion,
> Including those with little strength, who always listen to others,

Creation Stage: Troma Prepares the Offering

> As whatever each individual wants
> I dedicate this inexhaustible treasure of desirable things.
> May whoever is connected with this feast attain
>   unobstructed enlightenment
> And be cleansed of all karmic debts and
>   habitual tendencies. PHET

The Buddha taught that we have taken the lives of countless beings, yet hold on to our own body and life very dearly. This is the ego-clinging of selfishly holding on to oneself as more important than others. Still no matter how fiercely we cling to this body, we will still have to leave it. In Chod practice, we fearlessly reverse our normal attitude. We freely give our body and invite our guests to enjoy "us." This is the bodhisattva mahasattva's attitude of exchanging bodhichitta—of holding others more dearly than ourselves. Today, you have cut through your clinging.

Dedicate the feast for "whoever is connected with this feast," which means every sentient being—every single one—because you invited them all. The benefit for all sentient beings, including yourself, is being cleansed of all karmic debts and habitual tendencies, and attaining unobstructed enlightenment.

If Chod is your main practice, or if you're doing a Chod retreat, you should offer each feast distribution according to the time of day. In the morning session do the white feast offering, and at midday make the striped feast offering. In the evening, do the red feast offering, and late at night offer the black feast.

In these busy modern times, if you only have time to do two feast distributions, it's highly suggested that you offer the white feast and the striped feast.

Dissolution Stage: Dzogchen Meditation

After the four distributions are complete, meditate that the entire visualization dissolves into the state of the primordial nature. Then abide in that state of the Great Perfection.

The great master Mipham Rinpoche spoke of "unshakeable vajra samadhi," which refers to the Dzogchen state of Trekcho, or "cutting thoroughly." What is the state of Trekcho? Look to your own mind. Whatever you perceive happening is really the display of your own mind, and that display is empty of substantial existence. Trekcho meditation leads us to the ultimate realization that mind itself is empty. Bring up that realization courageously, firmly, and strongly. That is the vajra samadhi. Our view and meditation are completely unshaken by any turbulence we experience. No matter how we're tested, remain strongly and beautifully in that state.

Mipham Rinpoche also said, "Relax in magical meditation." Magical meditation is the union of emptiness and compassion, which is also known as Dzogchen or absolute bodhichitta. Externally, everything is an illusory magical display. Internally, our mind is the illusory magic of loving-kindness, compassion, and wisdom. Bring up this realization and relax. That is magical meditation, or *gyuma tabu tingngedzin* in Tibetan.

With this realization, we'll never be shaken or moved in our conduct or morality. We will maintain our conduct exactly as we said we would. We will receive the buddhas' blessings and absorb them with devotion.

Provocations and Challenges

Jigme Lingpa's auto-commentary now instructs us on the arising of challenging experiences and how to successfully handle them.

Provocations and Challenges

Challenges may arise at any point during your Chod practice, but they can be particularly powerful and difficult when they arise during meditation.

The key point to remember is this: provocations must happen. If they don't happen, your practice isn't correct in some way. Without them, you won't have any challenges to work with, and there may be no signs of accomplishment. Difficulties arise according to your capacities as a practitioner and what you can work with. What might seem like a huge challenge to a beginning practitioner doesn't seem big at all to an experienced practitioner. Seasoned yogis and yoginis need much stronger challenges to continue boosting their realization.

So up to this point you've done the practice in sequence: you went to a scary place, overpowered your ego, and visualized yourself as Sangwa Yeshe to subdue the area and all the invisible beings you summoned. Then you did the Ngondro preparation practices on that spot. Afterwards as Troma Nagmo, you made the invocation, prepared and offered the feast to all of your guests, and dissolved the visualization, relaxing in meditation. Now what? You need to experience *lhongtse*, which we translated earlier as "provoking," "coming up," or "arising." This arising energy is not bad. It's good. It means you're on track.

The full experience of energetic, provoking displays manifest in stages. In general, (1) the arising point is the *lhongtse* itself, when you're first aware of the provocation. (2) The second is the *chotrul* [cho 'phrul] display, or "magic trick." (3) The third stage is *tsartse* [tshar tshad], which means "completing," "exhausting," or "nearly finished." And finally (4) the fourth stage is *chodtse* [chod tshad], which means "finished," "concluded," or "stopped."

The teachings say that if you're not ready you really don't

Cutting Through Ego

have to go to some horrible place to do your visualizations, meditations, and practices. You should always do every practice according to your capabilities. Therefore, if you're personally not ready for that, you shouldn't try to go. Maybe when you go there, you find that you can't handle everything that arises and you run away. If that happens and you really leave the practice spot, you must go back to that same spot again. Try that spot again and again. The teachings say that if you run away from a practice spot nine times, you shouldn't try any more since you don't yet have the achievement to practice there.

These arisings happen because they're activated by our minds. In general, we go through many different emotions during practice times. These experiences are all reflections of our ego-clinging and are by no means only restricted to formal practice sessions. So many times in our lives we go through powerful emotions. Chod practice in particular will provoke these powerful experiences of *lhongtse*.

When Guru Padmasambhava was traveling into Tibet, there were many invisible beings who tried their hardest to prevent him from getting there. When he would first arrive to a mountain range, river valley, or power spot, his presence would stir up the *lhongtse* energy of the invisible beings residing there, causing them to exert their malevolent powers over everyone who lived nearby. Enraged and afraid, they manifested all sorts of displays (*chotrul*), like rock slides, thunderbolts, hailstones, and all that, which we can read in the life story of Guru Rinpoche. Yet after having done their worst, they would see that they weren't able to stop Guru Padmasambhava, and their energy was exhausted or weak, which is *tsartse*. Inevitably, the invisible beings surrendered. They came to Guru Padmasambhava saying, "I take refuge in you. I will never make any more obstacles." Guru imprison us. So when will we finally remove that? When we will stop swinging back and forth in the chains and nets of hope and fear? When we smash free of that, we'll rule the queen's realm of Mother Prajnaparamita, and the king's realm of Father Samantabhadra and all the enlightened ones. Nothing more is needed. Everything is already in the luxury state of sambhogakaya. By offering ourselves as the feast, the tremendous power of Chod practice brings out the realization needed to finally go beyond hope and fear, and return to our original nature.

The commentary says, "Give without holding anything back and meditate within the state of emptiness," together with bodhichitta. The great master Machig Labdron said, "You should think that your body is a corpse. And now that you've become a corpse, why are you holding back? What are you afraid of?" And then she said, "Keep the mind like the sky. Don't think anything. Does the sky have hope and fear? No. Therefore, let go of hope and fear. Does the sky have ego-clinging? No. Let go of ego-clinging and grasping." When we release ego and grasping, there isn't any fear. Anything can arise, but nothing is happening. We become fearless yogis and yoginis.

Meditate in the great emptiness-openness state. Regardless of what happens in the sky—thunderstorms, lightning, hail, or tornados—nothing actually changes the sky. It's all just a temporary display. Jigme Lingpa continues, "At that time, if you hold your body dear, or fear and hesitation arise in your mind, remember that your body doesn't exist. It's already been given to the guests." And also recall, "Your mind is groundless and rootless; it can't be found by the demons." Even the Buddha, a totally enlightened being, free from all obstacles and endowed with all powers couldn't find this emptiness mind even if he wanted to. So why are we worried about mere demons? Maintain fearless courage as perceptions and conceptions arise. Don't hold them. Let them go. If we hold *lhongtse*, we're grasping. Due to our habitual patterns, even if we think we're doing something useful by analyzing all this, what we're actually doing is still grasping. We have to release it. All these displays must eventually be handled by mingling them with our realization of emptiness.

There are three ways to handle *lhongtse*. (1) First, for great practitioners who already have a lot of realization, the moment a challenge arises, it's recognized as display. We're constantly in the midst of the display of samsara. All displays are reflected by our six empty senses, so they are all emptiness: emptiness form, emptiness sound, emptiness smell, emptiness taste, emptiness touch, and emptiness imagination. Displays are inseparable from emptiness. Abiding in that undisturbed realization, highly realized beings release *chotrul* displays right there on the spot.

(2) Medium or moderately realized beings will be somewhat disturbed. Yet they'll respond skillfully by trying to immediately remember and apply the instruction to "look to their mind." When you look to your mind, that very moment think to yourself, "Who is experiencing?" It's none other than mind. Mind is experiencing that. And as Jigme Lingpa said, "Mind is groundless, mind is total emptiness." Remembering these instructions, a medium-level practitioner will continue their Chod practice with devotion, courage, and confidence.

(3) A less accomplished practitioner's emotions may be very strong and turbulent. She should try to apply an analytical approach by using intellectual strategies like saying, "It's all mind. I read that the Buddha taught that, and my teachers are always saying that, and other great

Cutting Through Ego

masters said that too. I'm going to move forward with confidence that these ideas are true. It's just mind." We can also try to remember stories of great masters and how they acted in those circumstances. Finally, by one technique or another, we come back to the mind, look to the mind, and relax. That's how we can handle these situations and then eventually, realization will come.

The excitement demon can be a big factor in *lhongtse*. Tangible excitement includes nice things we can really see or hear. If we obsess about that, it can become a deep obstacle to maintaining meditation. Intangible excitement demons may be visions or dreams. Maybe we have a vision of Machig Labdron or the Buddha. Of course, that kind of vision might be a sign of achievement, but if we grasp on to it, act conceited and start boasting, our practice is really in trouble. For that reason, when *lhongtse* such as lovely visions come, recognize them, but remain humble and committed, and restrengthen your realization of inseparable bodhichitta and emptiness. Just be normal. There's a particular instruction to use when we cling to something exciting: "Shout PHET, and then immediately sever that clinging into the space of dharmadhatu."

There are many famous stories about the experiences of the great yogi Milarepa who spent many years as a solitary hermit in a rocky cave. One time, after he had stepped outside for a minute, he came back in and there were seven *atsara*[82] harmful spirits in his cave threatening to kill him. At first, he was scared and he prayed to his lama and the deities, but that didn't help. The atsaras didn't budge—they just shrieked and laughed. Then he remembered his teacher Marpa's instruction that everything is mind, and mind itself is emptiness. The very moment

Provocations and Challenges

he restrengthened this view, the atsaras merged with space and disappeared.

Another time, Milarepa was visited and harassed by a female ghost. When he threatened her, she said, "If you do anything to get rid of me, many more ghosts will come in my place. I'm not the end—I'm just the beginning! But if you realize the nature of mind as great emptiness, not only will you subdue me, but I will become your obedient servant." In response, Milarepa sang her a song of realization, and she became subdued and peaceful. In this way, when we realize that everything is a display of the nature of mind—the union of emptiness and compassion—it can be a big, positive benefit to other beings as well.

Some practitioners may go to a hermitage or secret spot to perform Chod and don't get any provocations. There are two possible reasons for this. (1) Perhaps that yogi or yogini has stable realization that everything is in the dharmakaya state, which is unmoving and unchanging. (2) On the other hand, perhaps that practitioner doesn't yet have very stable meditation, can't visualize very well, and doesn't have much realization. Invisible beings may think, "This one is so small it's not worthwhile to provoke. I don't want to waste my time. Why bother? [Laughter.] A stone or an animal would be just as much fun, so why bother with this one?" In other words, the practitioner is too weak to arouse the beings in that area, so he needs to go somewhere else.

We need provocations because that's how we train ourselves. If we handle our demons skillfully with meditation, it will boost our realization. At any time, in those crucial moments when suddenly something really challenging happens, if we look immediately to our mind it brings awareness vividly to the front. We momentarily remove all the mists of conceptions and look to the nature of infinite openness. Vivid displays handled skillfully introduce the nature of mind. Then all these arising energies and displays won't disturb us and soon subside. As we continue in meditation, it's over. Invisible beings may come and say, "I'll take refuge," and maybe they'll even ask to become our disciples, receive teachings, and begin to practice the Dharma.

This is similar to dream practice. At the beginning of a dream, the displays are unusual and turbulent, tumbling one after another. If we don't become disturbed but stay relaxed in the dream—as the Buddha's Dream Yoga teachings say—then the calming down or finishing stage comes. In that type of a dream, we may be climbing up beautiful glacier mountains in the sunshine, wearing white clothes, and lots of people are coming to greet us, pay their respects, and offer things to us. Then, dreams of building bridges and crossing rivers may be signs of completing.

We may not have exactly these dreams, but if we have a positive dream and feel comfortable, peaceful, and present when we wake up, it suggests subsiding. On the other hand, if we had auspicious dreams, but when we wake up we continue to feel strange like we're still in the display, then it's good, but it doesn't indicate finishing. Therefore, restrengthen your practice. Always remember the four powers of the bodhisattvas, and use them as a point of reference.

We translated *chodtse* as "finished" or "completed." Many teachings say that these types of dreams might include drinking an ocean of nectar without any hesitation; we're not shy and we even ask for more. Or many girls may come offering lots of strange foods and we have no hesitation or doubt—we eat everything they give and we want to have more. These are dream signs of the completed state. In reality, we feel infinite love and compassion for all living beings. And our devotion to the Buddha, Dharma, and Sangha is overwhelming, and is blended with a perfect realization of great emptiness. We feel calm and peaceful, and maintain our practice with courage and strong joyful effort.

Buddha Shakyamuni Teaching His Five First Students

Chapter 7:

Concluding Dedication and Aspiration Prayers

On page 33, the dedication prayers begin with the syllable AH:

AH All thoughts, whether virtuous or unvirtuous,
   are self-liberated.
The characteristics of hope and fear cannot be found.
However, since interdependent appearances inevitably
   continue as the accumulation of virtue,
Dedicate this within the undefiled dharmadhatu.

AH is the secret syllable of *Kadak* Trekcho in Dzogchen. The term *kadak* means "pure from the beginning." On the absolute level, there are no notions of virtue and non-virtue. Virtue and non-virtue are self-liberated. This is ultimate reality. Everything is free, and nothing substantially, solidly exists. But on the relative level, there are causes and conditions that reflect unceasingly. Because of interdependence, there are trillions of conceptions that support one other in virtuous and unvirtuous ways. We must strive to perform only virtuous activities. On the relative level, merit is accumulated as the fruit of interdependent coordination.

Dedicate the merit of your crazy wisdom activities and good conduct for all sentient beings without any discrimination, so that they reach the dharmadhatu and fully

realize the true nature.
Now, the aspiration prayer:

Page 34:

> PHET By giving this body of relative truth
> May karmic debts and habitual tendencies, accumulated
>   for aeons, be purified.
> When my being has been liberated by the Dharma
>   of absolute truth
> May these demons be born as my first disciples.
> Whenever the unfabricated, self-existing, innate truth
> Arises in the mindstreams of the wild demons,
> Without following after confused ego-clinging
> May their mindstreams be saturated with love and compassion.
> For myself, having perfected the yogic activity of crazy wisdom,
> May happiness and sadness be one equal taste, and may
>   samsara and nirvana be accomplished as the dharmakaya.
> Victorious in all directions, may I have
>   a meaningful connection with everyone,
> Accomplish buddha activity, and attain
>   the rainbow body. PHET

This body we offered, the act of giving, and the guests receiving the feast all exist only on the relative level. Similarly, karmic debts only exist relatively. Here, in the second line, the Tibetan phrase *bulon lenchag* refers to the karmic debt and the karmic creditor. We wish that all karmic debts be purified and that all creditors are totally satisfied. And, beyond this point—which in a way is just "breaking even"—we wish for the minds of the demons to be completely filled with love and compassion. Even if these beings have done bad things to us, we aspire for their realization.

Concluding Dedication and Aspiration Prayers

There is a Jataka tale that teaches us about the power of aspiration. Once, long before his enlightenment, when the Buddha was a bodhisattva, he was born as Gyalpo Jampe Tob [rgyal po byams pa'i stobs], King Maitribala, or "King with the Power of Love." At that time, five yaksha cannibal demons came to him and requested some humans to eat. This king thought, "I shouldn't give any of my subjects to these demons. But since they asked me, why should I give them someone else? I will give my life to them." There was some negotiation, and the King gave his blood first. He thought, "Accumulations will scatter, high will become low, and gatherings will separate." So he willingly gave his own body to these five cannibal demons. Before he died, he made the wish: "Just as I feed you now, when I reach enlightenment may I share my first teachings with you, and may you all achieve realization." Due to this connection and these aspiration prayers, in the future these five cannibal demons became none other than the Buddha's first five students. They were reborn as the five ascetics who received the first teachings on the Four Noble Truths from Buddha Shakyamuni in Sarnath, practiced them, and then reached arhathood. This story points to the essence of Chod: the practice of bodhichitta. We should never give up bodhichitta. This is the heart of Chod practice.

In another one of the Buddha's previous lives, he was a giant sea turtle. At that time, 500 merchants were crossing the sea in a loaded ship returning from a jewel island. In those days there were plenty of jewels just lying about on many islands. They had filled their boat very full, and when a big typhoon came up, their vessel was swamped with water and it started to sink. The turtle said to himself, "Now is the time to save these people," so he swam down under the ship, lifted it up, and carried it all the way to shore. When the turtle finally got to shore, he was very

Cutting Through Ego

tired so he slept there for awhile. When he woke up, his body was completely covered with ants and flies sucking his blood. At first he thought to go back into the sea so they couldn't bite him. But then he thought, "I just saved 500 people, and now I'm thinking about drowning all these insects. Why do that? If I go into the sea I'm only protecting my ego. I'm not caring for these insects." So he made this great aspiration: "These insects who are connected to me now and are drinking my blood, may they become my first students when I reach enlightenment. Just as I am feeding them now with my blood, at that time may I be able to feed them with the nectar of Dharma."

Many lifetimes later, when Buddha Shakyamuni reached enlightenment, his first teachings were given not only to five human students, but also to 80,000 celestial beings. The Buddha said that these 80,000 celestial beings were the rebirths of the ants and flies who drank the turtle's blood in the distant past. When we chant this aspiration prayer at the conclusion of our Chod practice, we're directly following Buddha Shakyamuni in our practice.

Complete your Chod practice by reciting prayers for auspiciousness to Mother Prajnaparamita, Buddha Shakyamuni, Yeshe Tsogyal, and Guru Padmasambhava.

Page 35:

> Inconceivable, inexpressible Prajnaparamita,
> Unborn, unceasing, by nature like the sky,
> Experienced by self-reflexive awareness'
>   discerning pristine cognition,
> Mother of the Victorious Ones of the three times,
> Please bring forth auspiciousness.

Concluding Dedication and Aspiration Prayers

Born through skillful means and compassion
 in the Shakya family,
You vanquished the forces of evil that others could not subdue.
Your body is resplendent like a golden mountain.
King of the Shakyas, please bring forth auspiciousness.

Most Excellent Lady Samantabhadri—Prajnaparamita,
Queen of Space, Mother of the Buddhas—Vajrayogini,
Goddess of Eloquence, Sarasvati—Yeshe Tsogyal,
Three Kaya Guru Dakini, please bring forth auspiciousness.

Great Indian pandita so kind to Tibet,
Pema Jungne, unborn and undying,
You now tame the rakshasas in the southwest.
Orgyen Rinpoche, please bring forth auspiciousness.

Then we recite the Interdependent Coordination mantra in Tibetan and English:

OM YE DHARMA HETU PRABAWA HETUNTESHAN TATHAGATO HAYAWADAT TESHANCHA YO NIRODA EWAM WADI MAHA SHRAMA NAYE SWAHA

Page 38:

Of all things which proceed from a cause
The Tathagata has explained their cause
And likewise their cessation.
This is the doctrine of the Great Ascetic.

And, follow that with:

Do not engage in any negative activity.
Practice virtue perfectly.

> Completely tame your own mind.
> This is the teaching of the Buddha.

Then finish with:

Page 39:

> May the elemental spirits who are living here or visiting,
> Living on the earth, under it, in the sky, or wherever,
> Always be loving towards beings
> And practice the Dharma day and night.

As we said in the beginning, there are three generosities: (1) material generosity, (2) wisdom teaching generosity, and (3) protection generosity. This Chod practice itself is clearly the generosity of material necessities. These concluding prayers are the generosity of words of wisdom, or the teaching generosity. These last few lines are really the heart teaching of the Buddha, and we are saying it here to all the compassionate guests and karmically, habitually connected guests. Essentially it means, "Be kind. Be compassionate. Always do virtuous activities day and night. Recognize the nature of your own mind. These are the words of the Buddha." Every Chod practitioner should conclude like this.

Then, as always, complete your practice with prayers for the swift rebirth of our precious teachers who passed away, and for the long and healthy lives of those who are blessing us with their presence in this lifetime. At the end, recite the lineage prayers of dedication and aspiration from the PBC "Daily Prayers" sadhana, The *Treasury of Precious Mantras and Prayers of Supplication, Dedication, and Aspiration*.

Special Instructions for Concluding Retreat

Traditionally, advanced Chod practitioners are instructed to go and practice in 108 different secret spots instead of settling in one secret spot or hermitage. The instructions say that at each place we stop, we should stay either three days, five days, or up to a maximum of nine days according to our time. After a few days, leave that spot and move on.

The first instructions we went through on visualizing nine-pointed vajras, preparing the tent, and all those things, were for when you arrive to the secret spot and begin your practice. The following instructions are for when conclude your practice and are about to leave a spot. You shouldn't just casually leave—you should go with mindfulness in meditation.

On the exact spot where you stayed, you should put an object of veneration that represents the Buddha's body, speech, and mind. In Tibet, pilgrims pile up stones, or build cairns as symbolic stupas. Japanese Zen gardens have those too. Secretly, you can put some sacred syllables or mantras in the stone pile as the speech blessing. You also invoke mind-blessings and merge them into the stupa. With all this, the cairn becomes a representation of the Buddha's body, speech, and mind, or of the Buddha, Dharma, and Sangha. Then chant that all the invisible beings of that area, and those who came during your Chod practice, now stay and circumambulate, practice, and meditate in a Buddhist way with love, compassion, and wisdom.

Machig Labdron also said to chant, "Don't follow me. Don't come after me." If you don't conclude your Chod practice correctly, the invisible beings you summoned and fed could follow you. She explained that even if you gave good gifts, some beings will just keep longing for more and will follow you. This is why you should do this nice way of concluding. So you should say, "Use this special place as your object of veneration. Stay here, practice, and meditate. Don't go anywhere—just enjoy this spot." There are also some short prayers that we should chant, which we'll go into in the next chapter. Then walk away by taking seven steps, then pause, turn, and walk back to the stupa. Check that everyone is going to stay there and not go anywhere. Then walk away about seventy steps and visualize that there's a gigantic red garuda that flies in every direction to secure the boundaries.

Conclude your Chod practice by abiding in Dzogchen meditation with mindfulness, and by feeling the presence of the Great Mother Prajnaparamita, Troma, and Sangwa Yeshe.

This completes our teachings on Chod from the *Longchen Nyingthig* terma, the *Bellowing Laugh of the Dakini*, which was revealed and taught by the great master Jigme Lingpa. This condensed practice, which is very famous in Tibet and elsewhere, is based on Dzogchen. It is a very secret and profound teaching—the heart treasure of all the wisdom dakinis. We have given these teachings to you just as we received them. This is an authentic, fresh, lineage teaching.

Prajnaparamita, Sangwa Yeshe,
Padampa Sangye, and Machig Labdron

Part 3:

Practical Advice for Beginning Chöd Practitioners

Chapter 8:
Brief Overview of Chod Practice

When you begin Chod, it's always important to base your practice on wisdom and compassion. From this, your primordial awareness, which is bodhichitta, is transformed instantly into the red dakini, Sangwa Yeshe Khandroma and her dakini retinues. She is red and so vast that her body pervades the three universes. Visualize yourself in that state.

Then you summon the five demons, which are the reflection of your own ego-clinging. Dance on and subdue these demons, or negative emotions, and transform them into the five wisdoms. Then you put up the tent while meditating that you emanate the five wisdom dakinis, who stake down the ego-clinging demon's four limbs and head. The stakes are phurbas, like in Vajrakilaya practice. When you place the phurbas, you're puncturing your own ego-clinging. Meditate that ego-clinging is completely destroyed at its root—it will never have any potential to arise again. This courageous understanding is very important.

After these outer preparations, you start the Chod ceremony itself. First, you do a Ngondro practice. You invoke all the lineage masters, buddhas, and bodhisattvas, including your own root teacher as Guru Padmasambhava. In front of them you take refuge and generate bodhichitta, make mandala offerings and practice Guru Yoga.

After finishing the preliminaries, you then perform

the main Chod ceremony. To begin, visualize that your primordial, innate awareness rises like a shooting star up through your crown chakra into the sky, transforming into the black wisdom dakini Troma Nagmo. Other than being black in color, she is the same as Sangwa Yeshe. Troma Nagmo is the primordial wisdom of your own mind. Your ordinary body is just left behind on the ground. It's a corpse.

Troma Nagmo then points her sharp, flaming curved knife at the corpse and the top of the skull separates from the rest of the body. This skullcup is put on a tripod of three heads. She cuts up the rest of the body and puts it into the skullcup. The body is transformed by wisdom fire into wisdom nectar. Offerings are then made to the four kinds of guests, first making offerings to the higher guests, and then to the equal and lower guests. These are called "feasts," "generosities," or "gifts." After you finish the white feast, the second is the striped feast, the third is the red feast, and the fourth is the black feast. Perform these according to your lama's instructions, as well as your time and capabilities.

After meditating, make dedication and aspiration prayers. In particular, dedicate the merit for all those demons you invoked. Think, "Today I have fed my body to all these demons who are my guests. When I reach enlightenment, may I share my first Dharma teaching with these demons. Then, may they instantly develop bodhichitta and enter the path of enlightenment." In this way, dedicate the merit and perform aspiration prayers.

Chapter 9:
Frequently Asked Questions about Chod Practice

Question: Khenpo Rinpoche, could you please explain the four powers of the bodhisattvas a bit more?

Answer: Buddha Shakyamuni taught the wisdom aspect of Chod in the Prajnaparamita teachings, which come from the second turning of the Wheel of Dharma. To this, he added teachings on buddha-nature as the Third Turning, followed by the skillful means of the Vajrayana. The foundation of accomplishment in Chod practice is taught in Prajnaparamita Sutras such as the Samcayagatha, the *Three Hundred Stanzas of the Prajnaparamita Sutra*, or *do du pa* [mdo 'dus pa mdo].

There the Buddha said, "If bodhisattvas are skilled in the four powers, the four demons cannot disturb them. What are these four powers? (1) The power of maintaining the realization of emptiness, (2) the power of never giving up on sentient beings, (3) the power of doing exactly what we made a commitment to do, and (4) the power of receiving the blessings of the sugatas." If we establish these four as causes and conditions in our hearts, we become very powerful practitioners. Then demons or obstacles—which are the same—cannot attack us or stop us. This is why the four powers of a bodhisattva are the four cornerstones of Chod.

According to the great master Longchenpa's instructions,

we should always plan and carry out our practice within the "three frames" of a noble beginning, noble middle, and noble conclusion. We begin with the preliminary or foundation practices, followed by the middle main or essential practices, which are then completed with the concluding practices of dedication and aspiration prayers. We also call these the "three excellent ones," or the "three perfections" of a practice.

What is the first frame of Chod practice? It includes several practices: going for refuge, developing bodhichitta, generating devotion, and Guru Yoga, with which we activate the sizzling, shining, glorious qualities of our hearts and minds. We receive the blessings of the buddhas, and merge with the great power of the buddhas and bodhisattvas. This is related to the power of the fourth cornerstone of a bodhisattva.

On the level of absolute reality, there's no separation or difference, high or low, between buddhas and the rest of us. We're all the same. Yet on the relative level, there are some temporary differences caused by our habitual clinging to ego and duality. By the power of the blessings—our refuge, bodhichitta, and devotion—we're able to expel our grasping on to duality, which is the great blessing. This is the first noble frame.

When we look ahead to the concluding practices of Chod, we perform the activity of the third noble frame by dedicating the merit for the happiness and enlightenment of all living beings. We're following in the footsteps of the Buddha, doing exactly what the buddhas and bodhisattvas did. We don't say, "Oh, I'll leave it to the buddhas to do that. They have higher realization than I do. They're more capable to help beings." We don't use that excuse! No, we have received the blessings. We're performing this activity and dedicating the merit just like the buddhas and bodhisattvas do. We're sharing with all sentient beings. What are we sharing? As the great teacher His Holiness Dudjom Rinpoche said in the last section of the Dudjom Tersar Ngondro sadhana,

Frequently Asked Questions about Chod Practice

"Now, my body, possessions, and the source of virtue, all together, I give without clinging to all beings who have been my parents. May I accomplish great benefits, unobstructedly, for all beings."

If we begin our Chod practice by receiving the blessings, and end it by both receiving and dedicating the blessings and merit, we have made a "perfect frame of our practice." We have a perfect foundation and perfect conclusion. The beginning is excellent and the end is excellent.

Now we must think about the middle frame, the main part of Chod practice. During that time we practice the other three powers of the bodhisattvas. The first cornerstone is maintaining meditation on emptiness; the second is never giving up on sentient beings; and the third is doing exactly what we said we'd do. Together, these form the middle excellence of our practice.

Regarding the first of these powers, Ven. Khenchen Palden Sherab Rinpoche mentioned many times that our meditation on emptiness is known as "vajra-like samadhi." This means a meditation that is indestructible, immovable, undefeatable, and fearless, just like Jigme Lingpa said. We carry this fearless understanding of emptiness as we perform the main feast offerings.

The unshakeable vajra samadhi is Dzogchen Trekcho or Mahamudra meditation. From samsara to nirvana, there's nothing solidly or substantially existing at all. That's what the teachings say and we can use our own intelligence to verify this. We can look carefully, investigate, and analyze this closely. We look through our eye of wisdom to sharpen our intelligence. Then we bring up a vivid understanding, free from any doubt or hesitation. This is our view—the beginning of the vajra samadhi.

It's all display. There's no substantial, solidly existing compassion, and there's no substantial, solidly existing emptiness either. They're both magic. Yet we arouse unceasing great compassion and loving-kindness for all living beings without discrimination. This is known as the magic-like samadhi meditation.

Then what? We're going to put that view into practice and action, which is exactly what we mean by "meditation." Meditation is practice. Practice is meditation. They are the same. There's no separation.

With this type of meditation we are able to transcend our demons. Basically, these demons are metaphors for the various types of suffering of samsaric existence. Of course, suffering like this doesn't only happen to Chod practitioners or to Buddhists in general. In different traditions people may call them various names, but we all have these troubles: external, tangible troubles and internal, intangible troubles. Basically, they're attachment troubles and ego-clinging troubles.

Machig Labdron highlighted each of these for us, just like road signs. On modern roads there are plenty of warning signs: signs for sharp curves, signs for bumps, signs for construction ahead, maybe even big red signs saying, "Bridge closed ahead." Why do they put these signs up? To make our travel safer and smoother. Similarly, Machig Labdron highlighted the most dangerous "demons" or obstacles for practitioners to look out for so that our road—our journey to enlightenment—and the growth of our beneficial activities for all sentient beings will be smooth and rewarding, and so we don't get sidetracked or accidentally drive into any deep ravines.

We've learned that our path is made up of "view, meditation, and conduct." Conduct is maintaining all of our activities according to the vows of morality that we've taken. Doing what we promised to do and keeping our word is morality. If we maintain perfect conduct and combine it with our view and meditation, our journey will be heroic and adventurous, and we'll always move forward. We'll keep seeing beautiful things happening around us and we'll continue getting closer to our goal. The moral conduct of Chod practitioners includes keeping up our Vinaya or Pratimoksha vows, bodhisattva vows, and Vajrayana vows, plus the special instructions for Chod practitioners.

The special conduct of Chod practitioners is trying to activate spiritual "adventures" by going to frightening places. They're always trying to activate stronger troubles and obstacles so they can learn to deal with and take care of more and more. Afterwards, when they experience the normal samsaric troubles that we all go through, they can feel, "I've dealt with much bigger things than this already. This little challenge is like a child's game. What a piece of cake!" So this is our moral conduct—it's what we said we would do, and we keep that promise. When we keep our word, we're known as "ladies and gentlemen."

This is how the entire Chod practice includes the four powers of a bodhisattva and the Three Noble Frames. We must receive this essential meaning with joy, respect, and appreciation, and keep it in our hearts. If we use our precious human lives to benefit ourselves and all sentient beings, our lives will be meaningful and beautiful because we're benefitting other beings.

Our journey doesn't end with this life—we're continually moving. If we keep these instructions alive in our hearts and minds, wherever we go throughout the succession of our lives will be bright, beautiful, and rewarding, just like the great master Shantideva said. Moving forward, we will be free from misery because our bodhichitta will continue to spread joy and happiness, and our realization of emptiness will liberate all difficulties. In this way, everything we experience will bring growth, deepening and beautifying our path until we reach enlightenment. This is truly what it means to be bodhisattvas, yogis, and yoginis.

Question: Would you be willing to tell us about how Chod was practiced in your family, and in your area of Tibet?

Answer: In Tibet, Chod was mainly practiced by Nyingma and Kagyu practitioners, and I think Sakya too. Chod is especially practiced when people are on pilgrimage. Of course in our area of Tibet, there were no hotels or restaurants yet, or anything for the needs of travelers. The tradition was that if you had a damaru and bell and did Chod practice, when you needed something you would go to a village family's home, and stand in front of their door and start practicing Chod very forcefully, so the family heard you. Sometimes you'd do this very familiar chant:[83]

> Of all things which proceed from a cause
> The Tathagata has explained their cause
> And likewise their cessation.
> This is the doctrine of the Great Ascetic.

You'd blow your thighbone trumpet and chant this verse with a beautiful melody. Next you'd immediately pick up your drum and chant the next verse:[84]

> Do not engage in any negative activity.
> Practice virtue perfectly.
> Completely tame your own mind.
> This is the teaching of the Buddha.

Then, in thanks for the family's offerings, you'd do another chant, which is in the *Riwo Sang Chod* fire puja sadhana revealed by the great terton Lhatsun Namkha Jigme:[85]

> Through the power of this vast and great generosity,
> May we become self-arisen buddhas for the benefit of beings.
> May all beings who were not liberated by previous buddhas
> Be liberated through this generosity.

Frequently Asked Questions about Chod Practice

Our father, Lama Chimed Namgyal, had a very strong hermit's nature. When he was young, he traveled a lot. He didn't like being settled in one place. When I was around six or seven years old, the situation in Tibet was becoming very unsettled. I remember Father talking about how he'd like to make pilgrimages to Pemako, Lhasa, and other sacred places. At that time, Khenchen Rinpoche was still at home—he hadn't yet gone to shedra at Riwoche Monastery that season. Father told the two of us: "You have to learn the Chod practices." Father urged Khen Rinpoche to learn the Tsasum Lingpa *Sangwa Yeshe* by memory, plus this *Khandro Gejang Bellowing Laugh of the Dakini*—which is so short—and so those were memorized. But conditions weren't right at that time, so Father was unable to go on pilgrimage, and Khenchen Rinpoche departed for the Riwoche shedra.

A couple of years later, the times had really gotten worse, with turbulence in Tibet and the Communists invading. Father was now insistently urging everybody to go to Pemako. This time Father told me, "You need to memorize Chod. You will use this if it's necessary to go to different villages and chant." He specifically asked me to memorize several Chod practices by the great master Karma Chagme. I did memorize the *Tengzungma*, but now I've forgotten it.

Father didn't do any of those Chod practices himself very much. He did do the Tsasum Lingpa *Sangwa Yeshe* practice, but he didn't go on a traditional Chod retreat, traveling from place to place.

I think we left Tibet in 1959. There's one incident I remember about my cousin on my mother's side. He was really "yogi style." He had a mass of twisted hair like an eagle's nest, and he carried a bell, two drums, and his thighbone trumpet. He also carried a skullcup. He drank from his skullcup and used it as an eating bowl. Not too many Tibetans did Chod practice like that, but he did. We met our cousin on the road out of Tibet, and Father asked him about his practice. After that, Father said to me, "You must go with him and do Chod." So I went with him to a village, just once. Of course, I was quite small, and I was also very, very shy. I just stood there—I didn't have a damaru and all those things—and my cousin started playing his bell and damaru, blowing his trumpet and chanting prayers in front of a house. The mother of the family brought out yogurt or buttermilk and some dried cheese. He received the buttermilk in his skullcup because that's what he normally did—it wasn't just for show—and he drank it right from there. So that is my small, personal Chod experience.

I will tell one more Chod story. There was a Nyingma or Kagyu practitioner from our area doing Chod practice while going to Lhasa as a pilgrim. This is a true story—when he came back he told us this. He stopped near a big monastery called Sog Tsenden Gonpa—one of the great Gelugpa strongholds—and he was just starting his next Chod practice session. Most Gelugpas don't do Chod practice. I think he had done just a couple of verses when a big Gelugpa monk suddenly appeared at his camp. The monk grabbed him and stopped him, saying, "I don't want you chanting this kind of thing! What do you mean, saying this, 'PHET! I am a fearless yogi who practices crazy wisdom activity?' I don't want to hear any more of your chanting. Just tell me the meaning of this one sentence, that's enough." And the monk kept his hold on him. The yogi was so shocked he couldn't tell him anything! But when he came back, he told all of us about that experience. He said that it had inspired him to study the meaning of Chod instead of just playing the drum and singing tunes, so he could become a better practitioner himself!

Question: Khenpo Rinpoche, I'm confused about when we do the various visualizations, or rather when one is dissolved and we practice the next one. Could you please help me get clearer on the sequence?

Frequently Asked Questions about Chod Practice

Answer: Yes, of course. There are three major visualizations that we create and then dissolve while performing this Chod sadhana. In the beginning, starting on page 9, while referring to ourselves as fearless yogis and yoginis, we visualize ourselves as the red wisdom dakini Sangwa Yeshe. Maintaining that visualization, we summon all the guests to the dance, we dance in the five directions, and we use the five phurbas or stakes to transfix the demon of ego-clinging. Then we dissolve that visualization at the end of page 16, and rest in equanimity.

Next, for the preliminary practices beginning on page 16, we visualize the field of merit in the sky in front of us, while we are in our ordinary form. The root lama appears as Orgyen Vajradhara, surrounded by all the gurus and yidams of the Dzogchen lineage in the pure land of Guru Padmasambhava. We maintain this visualization through the refuge, bodhichitta, mandala offering, and Guru Yoga prayers. This section is completed with the bottom line on page 21. Then we dissolve this visualization back into ourselves, and meditate in nondual equanimity once more.

Then, for the main practice that begins on page 22, we generate the visualization of our essential awareness emerging from our body as Troma Nagmo, the wrathful black dakini, with her retinue of innumerable dakinis of five colors. Our awareness, as Troma Nagmo, then prepares the corpse of our body as wisdom substances and directs the offering of the four feasts. When all the guests have been served, this visualization is dissolved back into great emptiness on page 33.

Question: Rinpoche, are the tunes we use in this practice also terma revealed by Jigme Lingpa?

Answer: These tunes are very special. In the teaching, it says that when you chant with tunes it brings out the splendor and clarity of the mind. They're pleasing to hear, and they invoke devotion, meditation, joy, and peace. That's why the tunes are very important. Most of these melodies come from visions experienced by Jigme Lingpa, or other great tertons such as Dudjom Lingpa, Tsasum Lingpa, and Machig Labdron. But the tunes don't necessarily have special meanings. Sometimes it's said that they are like dakinis' songs, or the music of some aspect of the god realms. However, they're mostly the visionary tunes of great masters.

Question: Why are there so many different tunes?

Answer: Having many tunes is good. The tunes have different qualities and don't all sound the same. It's not that, "Today it all sounds the same, tomorrow it sounds the same, and the next day it all sounds the same." I think that variety and richness are really good. Those great masters used their wisdom to reveal these tunes. They taught them to others, and the tradition has continued until now.

But it's true, there are a lot of chants. If it's too difficult to chant all the different tunes, you can chant one or any of them. But using all of the chants in our practice is better. They really provoke different states of devotion and understanding, and bring out the splendor of your realization, which is very important. They also connect to the blessings of all the great lineage masters who have chanted in the exact same way, one after another.

Question: Thank you. Rinpoche, I just had a question about when we're preparing the feasts. When do we generate the feasts by repeating the syllables OM, AH, HUNG and HA, HO, HRIH?

Answer: Yes, you will repeat the syllables OM, AH, HUNG and HA, HO, HRIH. [Khenpo Tsewang Dongyal Rinpoche chants

Frequently Asked Questions about Chod Practice

several continuous repetitions to illustrate]. OM, AH, and HUNG are the blessings of all the buddhas coming in the forms of the three syllables and merging into the offering of the feast. This is a short Chod practice, but larger Chod sadhanas also have three PHET syllables, which mean "invoked," "received," and "satisfied." Although this time we're not chanting PHET here, the mantra is still doing all of those activities.

Question: Rinpoche, as we have been learning this practice by doing it with you, I notice that sometimes the mantra is said OM AH HUNG HA HO HRIH, and sometimes it has a DANG syllable in the middle. Could you please talk about the difference?

Answer: The main mantra is the six syllables OM AH HUNG HA HO HRIH. But when you're chanting slowly with drumming, you can add a DANG syllable and a brief pause after HRIH, to keep the meter: OM AH HUNG *DANG* HA HO HRIH, then pause.
    DANG means "and." Of course, HA and HO mean "enjoyment." Like, HA HA! HO HO! And we all know that when we say HO three times, Father Christmas is here! [Laughter.] Lastly, HRIH means "accomplishment."

Question: Rinpoche, when we chant PHET, we've been saying it in a very subdued way. But on page 32 it says that when the displays come, to shout PHET. Would you comment on the different intentions, behind the soft "PHET" and the strong "PHET?"

Answer: When we chant the Chod practice we don't have to chant too strongly—just standard chanting. Whatever tune we're using we can adjust it that way. But here, on page 32, the teachings say we should chant strongly because at that time we're uprooting or transcending our conceptions. So we say PHET a little loudly, and that very moment we look to our minds.

Similarly, in certain Dzogchen instructions by the great master Patrul Rinpoche, he said to "suddenly shoot the PHET syllable" like lightning or thunder, and instantly look to one's own awareness.

Question: Do we chant a strong PHET on page 30 at the very bottom line that begins with *bulon lenchag*, referring to cleansing all karmic debts?

Answer: That particular one we don't have to chant loudly. Nothing has to be emphasized. Just use your regular chanting volume. The loud PHET is on page 32 where it says, "Shout PHET." Once again, that is for when demons are arising in our mind. Our meditation and visualization become unstable when doubt and hesitation arise. Doubt and hesitation make us shaky. Doubt is a demon and an obstacle that has to be removed. For this reason, we shout "PHET," and instantly those conceptions are smashed in the space of emptiness. At the same time, look to your mind.

We don't shout this PHET while we're chanting, but after we've stopped, when we're meditating after the ceremonies and feast distributions. We've completed the whole ritual once and now we're resting in meditation. But while we're meditating, various strange conceptions might start arising. When this happens, strongly shout PHET. Shout it loudly, firmly, and instantaneously like a flash of lightning. With that, all the turbulence and chaotic conceptions in your mind will instantly be cleared. That same instant, look directly to your mind and relax in Dzogchen awareness. This will reaffirm your meditation and realization.

Frequently Asked Questions about Chod Practice

Question: In other sadhanas, those of us who don't know Tibetan will chant the Tibetan and then the English for each section. But this practice is so beautiful with all the different melodies. What should we do if we want to chant in English also? Should we go through it once in Tibetan, and then once in English?

Answer: I think this depends on the individual. But I will say that the tunes are very beautiful—a kind of melodious sound—so if you already roughly know the meaning of the Tibetan, then you don't have to chant it in English as well. Just connect each section to its meaning. You don't have to bring up the meaning word for word. Just bring up the essence of the section. So maybe chant the Tibetan with the tunes. Then if you have time and would like to do it, you can also chant it in English as well.

Question: Early on in the sadhana, when we're dancing in the different directions on the different continents, is that to purify negative emotions? Then later we're offering the mandala in the Ngondro section. Is the dancing actually a way of purifying that offering, or are these two separate things?

Answer: Both aspects definitely purify negative emotions and habitual patterns—they purify or transcend hopes and fears into the dharmakaya. The activity of that first section is what I translated as "overpowering" or "harmonizing." What are we really overpowering? We're overpowering ego-clinging, the source of hope and fear. Who made the four different continents and the center? We did. We're dancing on that. While we're dancing, we're not thinking much about the body. Our focus is on transcending all the different emotions into wisdom.

Later, during the mandala offering, we're focusing on using our body as a mandala offering. Yet we even go beyond that because this body isn't just our small body. It becomes the universe and all its contents, including those continents. Our body becomes the container of everything. This is what we offer in order to attain the two merits.

Question: When you were describing Guru Yoga—how we merge our three doors with the three doors and blessings of wisdom beings—is that the goal of all the aspects of Ngondro?

Answer: Yes, that's our ultimate goal: merging our three doors with the state of the enlightened ones. In Ngondro practice, however, there is a slightly different view compared to the view of Chod. Even though we have the same ultimate goal, what we do in Ngondro practice more strongly emphasizes the view of relative truth, with subjects and objects.

In Ngondro, we develop devotion with confidence, meaning that we—the subjects—feel closeness and connection to the guru and all the enlightened beings in the refuge tree: the objects. Then we take refuge with prostrations. We're strengthening positive attitudes—our feelings of devotion and gratitude. With that foundation, our bodhichitta practice develops our love, kindness, and compassion for all sentient beings, sincerely wishing for everyone to be free of all suffering. We make the aspiration to attain buddhahood in order to bring them all to the state of peace and happiness. Then, with the mandala offering, we again visualize the refuge tree and offer the mandala of Mt. Meru and the four continents, and so forth. We do this to accumulate the two merits and to purify our two obscurations. So we make the mandala offering for a purpose: to restrengthen our merit and remove our negativities.

With the foundation of refuge, bodhichitta, and the generosity of the mandala offering, we then practice Vajrasattva to cleanse and purify our negativities. Again, we want to benefit all living beings—that's why we want to purify our obscurations. Right now, we know that we don't have the capability to help all beings very much. Even though we want to, we can't. What's blocking and preventing us? Our obscurations. That's why we're asking for the blessing of purification, saying, "Vajrasattva, will you please purify this?"

In addition, we practice Guru Yoga, again inviting the blessings of enlightened beings. We sincerely wish, "I'd like to benefit all beings, so I'm practicing on Guru Padmasambhava with strong devotion in order to become exactly like him and all the buddhas."

Question: Following up on the last question, when we're talking about refuge, then it's devotion between subject and object. And when we're practicing Guru Yoga, it's bringing up all that devotion and moving towards completely merging our three doors with theirs?

Answer: Yes, in Guru Yoga we highlight devotion with appreciation. All of that energy adds up. First, we are just ourselves when we receive the guru's blessings:

> The blessings and empowerments of body, speech, and mind are completely and perfectly obtained.[86]

Then we become inseparable with the Guru. As it says:

> Behold your own nature of mind, which is the absolute lama.[87]

That's the point when we really merge beyond all duality.

Question: I have another question that relates to the Dudjom Tersar Ngondro practices. After the Guru Yoga section, we recite the prayer to Amitabha. Then, in conclusion, we offer our body. Is Chod the same thought as that prayer, or is it the expansion of those three lines? When we do that part of Ngondro practice, can we bring up this Chod teaching in our mind and use it?

Answer: Yes, the *Bellowing Laugh of the Dakini* Chod practice is a more expansive and detailed expression of that last prayer in our Ngondro practice:

> Now, my body, possessions, and the source of my virtue,
>   all together
> I give without clinging to all beings who have been my parents.
> May I accomplish great benefits, unobstructedly,
>   for all beings.[88]

Three gifts are mentioned here: (1) my body, (2) my wealth, and (3) my virtues. These three cover everything that the "I" or ego holds dear. There's nothing else. In this prayer it says, "*da ni lu dang long cho ge tsa che*." That's pointing out what we hold on to. We grasp on to our body, we grasp on to our belongings and wealth, and we grasp on to our merit or good deeds. The term *getsa* also means our reputation as someone good or renowned. These are the points in samsara where we're grasping, attached, and stuck. So in this prayer, we're giving it all away—everything that we could hold on to. His Holiness Dudjom Rinpoche says that this is the essence of Chod practice. So yes, you can bring up these Chod teachings in your mind. It is the essence. That's it!

Question: Khenpo Rinpoche, on page 24 in the instructions about the four different feasts, I don't understand the part about the black feast when Jigme Lingpa mentions, "Amassed like a big black cloud," and "Think that the demons' bodies become like charcoal." Could you please clarify that section a little?

Answer: Jigme Lingpa means that the demons become so dense because they received and ate all the negativity, which had been transformed into wisdom. The great master used this terminology in the black feast, but it doesn't mean that the demons are changed for the worse. All negativity—theirs, ours, and that of all sentient beings—is transformed into an offering of wisdom. It appears as heavy and dark, but it is still wisdom.

Question: Thank you, Rinpoche. You said that sometimes after we complete our practice, invisible beings are still there wanting more? And that we should say some prayers to appease them? Could you please say a little more about that?

Answer: Our offering must be made very thoroughly. As the great master Machig Labdron said, if we don't make nice enough preparations, our guests may leave the feast unfinished and still hungry, and come following after us, sort of like "following the wealth." The invisible beings that came to our feast are still in that area. We want them to stay where they are and not follow after us or anyone else. They have good things to enjoy as well as the object of veneration—whatever we left as a monument of the Buddha's body, speech, and mind. They have the opportunity to understand the nature of love, kindness, and compassion. So we're wishing that they stay there to enjoy and benefit from all that.

While we're meditating, conceptions such as scary thoughts, hopes, and fears disturb our meditation. We shout the PHET syllable and they subside. But these thoughts are probably not going to stop coming just by shouting PHET once. When they come back, we must reaffirm our realization by applying the same technique or by using different ones. Nevertheless, we must realize that deep down, all of these provocations are our mind.

The great masters Machig Labdron and Jigme Lingpa said that we should think, "Why am I worried? Why am I scared? I already gave my body to the guests. And my mind—even the Buddha can't do anything to the mind." Machig Labdron also said, as I quoted before, "The body is a corpse, and a corpse has nothing to hold back. The mind is like the sky, and we can't hold on to the sky. The sky has no hope and fear, no expectations." If we look carefully, it's true. This isn't blind faith, just following "what the Buddha says," or "what Machig Labdron says." We don't need to just believe it because they said it. It's not just a belief. It's true. Mind is empty. Where could we find it? Nobody can find it. We have to confirm this for ourselves. Mind doesn't solidly, substantially exist at all. When we have firmly refreshed our understanding of the way things are, we rest in meditation.

Question: If conditions don't permit us to use our drums and bells at a particular time—for instance if we're in a plane or driving—is it still good to chant the sadhana all the way through? Perhaps we can practice along with the nuns of PBC Orgyen Samye Chokhor Ling as they chant using their bells and drums? Is that still helpful in affecting the environment and the practitioner?

Answer: Yes, definitely. Chod is a teaching that's very powerfully connected to our heart. Even if we can't use a drum and ritual implements, whenever we chant, practice, and restrengthen Chod, it will be beneficial for us and those around us. Remember the "four demon experiences" that we discussed? All of us go through these at times, whether we're Chod practitioners or not.

Frequently Asked Questions about Chod Practice

If we can remember this, we'll become more understanding, more mindful, and more courageous.

Question: My question is a more general one on dharmapalas. I wanted to ask if you could briefly explain why Ekajati, Rahula, and Dorje Legpa are the primary dharmapalas in our lineage. Why are they special? And why do we chant the dharmapala practice every day?

Answer: There are many dharmapalas, but in the Nyingma lineage these three are the principal ones, together with Mahakala. The great master Jigme Lingpa said that Rahula represents all the appearance aspects of the true nature, Ekajati represents all the emptiness aspects, and Dorje Legpa represents the union of appearance and emptiness.

Ekajati is a direct emanation of Buddha Samantabhadri, and therefore Buddha Samantabhadri entrusted all the Dzogchen Tantra teachings to Ekajati to be their great protector. Rahula is an emanation of Vajrapani. In the teachings, it's said that Dorje Legpa is an emanation of Buddha Shakyamuni, and also that Dorje Legpa first received refuge vows from Buddha Shakyamuni. When Guru Padmasambhava arrived in Tibet, Dorje Legpa was the only one who had already received the teachings. Often, Dorje Legpa is named *genyen* in Tibetan, or *upasaka* in Sanskrit.

So that's a little bit about these dharmapalas on the external level. Yet on the deeper reality level, many great masters say that these three dharmapalas are appearance, emptiness, and their union.

Question: Khenpo Rinpoche, if we're doing this Chod as a main practice, and doing these cycles four times a day, how would we insert the dharmapala practice into that?

Answer: If you're stretching out this practice all day, insert the dharmapala practice before you conclude the entire day's practice with dedication and aspiration prayers. Or if you're doing a single session practice, insert the dharmapala practice on page 33 before you conclude with dedication and aspiration prayers. You don't have to recite the Sanskrit vowels and consonants, Vajrasattva mantra, and the mantra of Dependent Origination here. Simply visualize yourself as Vajravarahi or Troma, and do the dharmapala practice.

Question: Rinpoche, along with the visualized feast we're offering, is there any kind of outer feast we also have to prepare with actual food or tormas?

Answer: Not unless you're making a ganachakra tsok offering. But this sadhana doesn't have a tsok section because it's so short. It's not like the larger Chod sadhanas that have tsok offering sections. Sometimes they also prepare tormas that look like human figures and those are offered too. But in general, a tsok offering is enough even in the larger Chod sadhanas.

Question: Khenpo Rinpoche, if we're practicing in a wild place where there are bandits and wild animals, and a wild animal really does come and cause trouble, or maybe there's a landslide, a fire, or whatever, what should we do? If our realization is good, should we just keep practicing?

Answer: First of all, as the teachings mentioned, we should carefully examine a spot before we decide to practice there. If we go to a wild place, we should be able to tell if something dangerous is likely to happen. If a practitioner isn't highly realized, she should avoid that spot. But if a practitioner is already a highly realized being, then she really won't care. If

Frequently Asked Questions about Chod Practice

a wild animal or any of those threats come, she's not going to run away. She'll stay. The teachings say that even though those phenomena may happen in relative reality, due to the power of a great practitioner's meditation and practice, the wildest animals will become really calm and peaceful. The elements may appear to be tornados and floods, but they won't disturb great practitioners.

That's why the teachings said that before we choose a practice spot, we must first look for tangible demons. For instance, if there's a split tree that's could easily fall over, or a mountainside where rocks might fall or there might be a mudslide, beginning practitioners should avoid practicing there—even if it looks appealing. We have to be very careful and thoughtful.

It's different with intangible demons. They follow us wherever we go. Again, whether we're Chod practitioners or not, we all have the same intangible demons that disturb us. Continually restrengthening your meditation practice is the best way to deal with that.

Question: Khenpo Rinpoche, we've been practicing this together as a group this week, but as I understand it, when you go to a secret spot, it's usually as a solitary practitioner. Could you explain how it works—we've practiced together to learn it, but is this a practice one primarily does alone?

Answer: Both are genuine ways to practice—it's not that one is better or worse than the other. When we practice Chod alone, it may be a bit more intense. However, the Buddha always emphasized doing sadhana practice together in a group with beautiful harmony, respect, and appreciation for the whole mandala. The great secret wisdom dakini Troma Nagmo isn't alone! She's performing Chod with a huge retinue. She enjoys being with a big group—why can't we? Buddhism never says that individual or group practice is higher and the other is lower. They're equal on the basic level of reality. In the short term, maybe there's some distinction. But that is all illusion.

Question: Khenpo Rinpoche, thinking into the future, after someone has done this sadhana for quite a while and gotten familiar with it, if they wanted to do a longer Chod practice, is there one in particular you'd recommend?

Answer: I'm preparing to translate the *Sangwa Yeshe* Chod practice of Tsasum Lingpa, so in our lineage we should really aspire to practice *Sangwa Yeshe*. It's rather long and we can find quite a lot to work with there! Of course, the Troma practice of His Holiness Dudjom Rinpoche is really wonderful too.

Khenchen Palden Sherab Rinpoche and I have received and uphold many different lineage teachings. However, nowadays the lineage of Tsasum Lingpa is a little bit small. Khenchen Rinpoche repeatedly said how important it is to activate and strengthen it. Of course, we're not doing this just to popularize Tsasum Lingpa's lineage—we're trying to activate Tsasum Lingpa's vision. His terma teaching is perfectly in harmony with the other Chod lineages I just mentioned. *Sangwa Yeshe*, just like the other Chod practices, is very powerful when practiced according to his teaching. Many practitioners have achieved high realization within Tsasum Lingpa's lineage. That's why I would like to make that available and encourage its use in the future.

Dedication of Merit

*May the victory banner of the fearless teachings
of the Ancient Tradition be raised.*

*May the victorious drum of the teaching and practice of Dharma
resound in the ten directions.*

*May the lion's roar of reasoning pervade the three places.
May the light of unequalled virtues increase.*

* * *

*Dharmapalas who made commitments
to the lamas of the three lineages,*

*Dharmapalas of the three groups,
summon up your superior mighty powers.*

*Help quickly disseminate throughout the three worlds,
The treasure of the pure Dharma lineages
of the three enlightened beings.*

* * *

*May all the temples and monasteries,
All the readings and recitations of the Dharma flourish.
May the Sangha always be in harmony,
And may their aspirations be achieved.*

* * *

*At this very moment, for the peoples and nations of the earth,
May not even the names disease, famine, war, and suffering be heard.
But rather may pure conduct, merit, wealth, and prosperity increase,
And may supreme good fortune and well-being always arise.*

Appendices

ༀ༔ ཀློང་ཆེན་སྙིང་གི་ཐིག་ལེ་ལས༔

FROM THE HEART ESSENCE OF LONGCHENPA

གཅོད་ཡུལ་མཁའ་འགྲོའི་གད་རྒྱངས་བཞུགས༔

THE CHOD PRACTICE
BELLOWING LAUGH OF THE DAKINI

Revealed by
Rigdzin Jigme Lingpa

**By practicing on this may all sentient beings
achieve the perfect true-nature state of the lama.
May their highest aspirations be fulfilled
for the benefit of all sentient beings.**

© 2019 by Dharma Samudra

All rights reserved

All rights reserved. No part of this material may be reproduced in any form or by any means, electronic or mechanical, including photocopying, recording, or by any information storage and retrieval systems, without prior permission from the authors.

Published by Dharma Samudra

Padmasambhava Buddhist Center
Palden Padma Samye Ling
618 Buddha Highway
Sidney Center, NY 13839
(607) 865-8068

padmasambhava.org

Seven Line Prayer

HUNG
HUNG

OR JEN YÜL JI NUB JANG TSAM
On the northwest border of the country of Oddiyana,

PE MA GE SAR DONG PO LA
On the pistil of a lotus,

YA TSEN CHOG GI NGÖ DRUB NYE
You have attained the most marvelous, supreme siddhis.

PE MA JUNG NE ZHE SU DRAG
You are renowned as the Lotus Born,

KHOR DU KHAN DRO MANG PÖ KOR
Surrounded by your retinue of many dakinis.

CHE CHI JE SU DAG DRUB CHI
Following you in my practice,

JIN JI LOB CHIR SHEG SU SÖL
I pray you will come to confer your blessings.

GURU PEMA SIDDHI HUNG

Dharma Samudra   Lineage Prayers

Prayers to the Lamas of the Lineage

KÜN ZANG DOR SEM GA RAB SHI RI SING
Samantabhadra, Vajrasattva, Pramodavajra, Shri Singha,

PE MA KA RA JE BANG NYI SHU NGA
Padmakara, the Twenty-five, King and subjects,

SO ZUR NUB NYAG TER TÖN JA TSA SOG
So, Zur, Nub, Nyag, the hundred tertons and others,

KA TER LA MA NAM LA SÖL WA DEB
The lamas of Kama and Terma lineages, to you I pray.

DZAM LING DZE PE JEN DRUG CHOG NYI DANG
You equal the Six Ornaments and Two Supreme Ones of Jambudvipa

THUG JE LUNG TOG NYAM PE THU NGA YANG
In your compassion, knowledge, and realization,

NAG TRÖ DAM PAR BE PE TÜL ZHUG CHI
By practicing yogic discipline in the depths of sacred forests,

འཁོར་འདས་ཆོས་སྐུར་རྫོགས་པའི་ཀློང་ཆེན་པ།

KHOR DE CHÖ KUR DZOG PE LONG CHEN PA
You perfected the realization of samsara and nirvana as the dharmakaya.

དྲི་མེད་འོད་ཟེར་ཞབས་ལ་གསོལ་བ་འདེབས།

DRI ME Ö ZER ZHAB LA SÖL WA DEB
Longchenpa Drime Ozer, I supplicate you.

ཤེས་བྱ་ཀུན་མཁྱེན་འགྲོ་ལ་བརྩེས་བཅེའི་གཏེར།

SHE JA KÜN CHEN DRO LA JE TSE TER
Knower of all phenomena, you are a treasure of loving care for all beings,

དྲི་མེད་འོད་ཟེར་ཡང་སྤྲུལ་ཐུགས་གཏེར་མཛོད།

DRI ME Ö ZER YANG TRUL THUG TER DZÖ
An emanation of Longchenpa, with a treasury of mind terma,

འོད་གསལ་ཀློང་ཆེན་ནམ་མཁའི་རྣལ་འབྱོར་པ།

Ö SAL LONG CHEN NAM KHE NAL JOR PA
You are a yogi of the vast, expansive sky of luminosity.

འཇིགས་མེད་གླིང་པའི་ཞབས་ལ་གསོལ་བ་འདེབས།

JIG ME LING PE ZHAB LA SOL WA DEB
Vidyadhara Jigme Lingpa, to you I pray.

སྔོན་ཚེ་རིག་འཛིན་ནུས་ལྡན་རྡོ་རྗེ་རྩལ། །

NGÖN TSE RIG DZIN NU DEN DOR JE TSAL
In the past you were the Vidyadhara Nuden Dorje Tsal.

མ་འོངས་བདེ་གཤེགས་མོས་པ་མཐའ་ཡས་ཞབས། །

MA ONG DE SHEG MÖ PA THA YE ZHAB
In the future you will be the Buddha Möpa Thaye.

ད་ལྟ་པད་འབྱུང་རྒྱལ་ཚབ་འབྲོག་བན་དངོས། །

DA TA PE JUNG JAL TSAB DROG BEN NGÖ
Now you are the regent of Padmasambhava, the actual presence of Drokben Lotsawa.

འཇིགས་བྲལ་ཡེ་ཤེས་རྡོ་རྗེ་ལ་གསོལ་བ་འདེབས། །

JIG DRAL YE SHE DOR JE LA SOL WA DEB
Jigdral Yeshe Dorje, to you I pray.

འདོད་ཆུང་ཆོག་ཤེས་བསླབ་གསུམ་ནོར་གྱིས་ཕྱུག །

DÖ CHUNG CHOG SHE LAB SUM NOR JI CHUG
Happy with little, content, and rich in jewels of the Three Trainings,

བྱམས་དང་སྙིང་རྗེས་འགྲོ་ཀུན་ཕ་མར་ཤེས། །

JAM DANG NYING JE DRO KÜN PHA MAR SHE
With loving compassion, seeing all beings as parents,

སྒོ་གསུམ་རྡོ་རྗེ་གསུམ་རྟོགས་སུམ་ལྡན་ཆེ། །

GO SUM DOR JE SUM TOG SUM DEN CHE
Through threefold realization, you made three doors three vajras.

དགེ་སློང་པདྨ་ཚུལ་ཁྲིམས་ལ་གསོལ་བ་འདེབས། །

GE LONG PE MA TSUL TRIM LA SÖL WA DEB
Virtuous monk, Pema Tsultrim, to you I pray.

དཔལ་ལྡན་སངས་རྒྱས་པདྨའི་རིང་ལུགས་མཆོག

PAL DEN SANG JE PE ME RING LUG CHOG
The supreme tradition of the glorious buddha Padmasambhava,

སྔ་འགྱུར་རྡོ་རྗེ་སྙིང་པོའི་ལྟ་གྲུབ་ཆེ

NGAL JUR DOR JE NYING PÖ TA DRUB CHE
Which is the essential, extraordinary view and doctrine of the Early Translation school,

སྲོལ་འབྱེད་ཤེས་རབ་སྣང་བ་རབ་རྒྱས་པའི

SÖL JE SHE RAB NANG WA RAB JE PE
You keep alive and spread by the light of wisdom.

མཁན་ཆེན་ཆོས་རྗེའི་ཞབས་ལ་གསོལ་བ་འདེབས

KHEN CHEN CHÖ JE ZHAB LA SÖL WA DEB
Lord of Dharma, Great Khenpo, I pray at your lotus feet.

འོག་མིན་ཆོས་ཀྱི་དབྱིངས་ཀྱི་ཕོ་བྲང་ན

OG MIN CHÖ CHI YING CHI PHO DRANG NA
In the palace of the Ogmin dharmadhatu,

དུས་གསུམ་སངས་རྒྱས་ཀུན་གྱི་ངོ་བོ་ཉིད

DÜ SUM SANG JE KÜN JI NGO WO NYI
The essence of all the buddhas of the three times,

རང་སེམས་ཆོས་སྐུ་མངོན་སུམ་སྟོན་མཛད་པའི

RANG SEM CHÖ KU NGÖN SUM TÖN DZE PE
The one who shows clearly the dharmakaya of my own mind,

TSA WE LA ME ZHAB LA SÖL WA DEB
We pray to the honorable root guru.

PAL DEN TSA WE LA MA RIN PO CHE
Glorious root teacher, precious one,

DAG GI CHI WOR PE ME DEN ZHUG LA
Dwelling on the lotus seat on the crown of my head,

KA DRIN CHEN PÖ GO NE JE ZUNG TE
Hold me with your great kindness,

KU SUNG THUG CHI NGÖ DRUB TSAL DU SÖL
Bestow the accomplishments of body, speech, and mind.

༄༅། །ཀློང་ཆེན་སྙིང་གི་ཐིག་ལེ་ལས༔

FROM THE HEART ESSENCE OF LONGCHENPA

གཅོད་ཡུལ་མཁའ་འགྲོའི་གད་རྒྱངས་བཞུགས༔

THE CHOD PRACTICE
BELLOWING LAUGH OF THE DAKINI

དབྱིངས་ཕྱུག་བདེ་ཆེན་མཚོ་རྒྱལ་མ་ལ་ཕྱག་འཚལ་ལོ༔ རང་བཞིན་དྭོགས་པ་ཆེན་པོའི༔ ཉག་གཅིག་རྩལ་ནས་གཅོད་པའི་ཕྱིར༔ གཅོད་དུ་གཅོད་བྱེད་ལས་འདས་ཀྱང་༔ སློབ་པ་ཅན་གྱི་གང་ཟག་དང་༔ བཏུལ་ཞུགས་སྤྱོད་པ་ལམ་སློང་ཕྱིར༔ ཕུང་པོ་གཞན་བསྐྱུར་མན་ངག་བསྟན༔ དེ་ལ་མཁོ་བའི་ཡོ་བྱད་ནི༔ དྲེགས་པ་ཟིལ་གྱིས་གནོན་པའི་ཕྱིར༔ སྟེར་བཞིན་ཉམས་གཅུན་གཟན་ཕྱུགས༔ ལྟ་བ་ཡས་འབབས་ཆོག་ཏུ་དང་༔ སྤྱོད་པ་མས་འཛེགས་ཁྡོ་ག༔ ལྟ་འདི་དབང་སྲྱིད་མཆོག་ཆེན་ཅན༔ སྣང་བ་ཟིལ་གནོན་ཏུ་མ་རུ༔ མ་ཚོགས་དབང་སྒྱུར་དིལ་གཡེར་དང་༔ ཕག་གཞིག་རས་མ་སྣའི་ཅོད་པན༔ མདོར་ན་བཏུལ་ཞུགས་སྤྱོད་པ་ལ༔ འོས་པའི་ཆས་རྣམས་སྣ་གོན་བྱ༔ དེ་ནས་ས་གནད་གཉན་དམིགས་སུ༔ ཕོ་ཙོང་ལྷ་འདྲེ་བཏུལ་སེམས་དང་༔ ཆོས་བརྒྱད་བསམ་པས་མ་ཡིན་པར༔ ཆད་མེད་བཞི་ཡིས་དཔའ་གདིང་བསྐྱེད༔ སྣང་བ་གར་ཤར་ཐོག་བརྫིས་བྱ༔ དེ་ཙོ་ཞིག་གནོན་དམིགས་པ་ཡིས༔ མ་གཅུན་དགྲ་ལ་བུ་ཧོར་མཆུང་༔ དེ་ཕྱིར་རིག་པ་བཏུལ་ཞུགས་དང་༔ ཡང་༔ ཅེས་རང་གི་སྙིང་ག་ནས༔ གནམ་ལྕགས་རྡོ་རྗེ་རྩེ་དགུ་པ༔ སྐུ་བཞིན་ཕྱི་ཞིང་འཕྲས་པ་ལས༔ འོད་ཟེར་མེ་དཔུང་འབར་བ་ཞིག༔ གང་དམིགས་གཉན་སར་ཕོག་ལྷར་ཕོབ༔ དེ་གནས་ལྷ་འདྲེ་དཔུང་དཔུང་བཅས༔ འགྲོས་ཤིང་འབྱིར་བའི་དབང་མེད་པར༔ དཔའ་ཞིག་ཆག་སྟེ་གནས་པར་བསམ༔ དེ་ནས་ཚུལ་འཆོས་དོར་སོགས༔ ཕ་མལ་འཕྲུའི་འཕྲིགས་བློ་སྤྲོངས་ལས༔ བཅུལ་ཞུགས་དར་མའི་གདིང་ཕྱིན་པས༔ འགྲོ་ལུགས་རྣམ་པ་བཞི་དག་ལས༔ ལྟ་བའི་གདིང་འགྲོས་ཕྱུགས་ཀྱིས་འགྲོ༔ དེ་ཡང་སྣང་སྲིད་ལྟ་འདི་དང་༔ གནས་གདོན་ལམ་འདི་འཁྱམ་པོ་

Dharma Samudra　　　　Jigme Lingpa　　　　*Chod Yül*

གུན༔ བགུག་ལ་ར་ཤུག་བདས་པ་བཞིན༔ གཉན་སར་རང་དབང་མེད་པར་གུུར༔ གནས་ དེར་སྐྱེབས་མ་ཐག་ཉིད་དུ༔ དུག་ཤུལ་འབར་བའི་སྲངས་སྲབས་ཀྱིས༔ སླ་འདི་གུན་གྱི་ཀྲང་ པ་ནས༔ བཟུང་སྟེ་བྱུད་ལ་ལན་གསུམ་བསྒོར༔ དབང་ཆེན་གཞི་ལ་བརྫབས་པར་བསམ༔ ཅག་པུ་སྨྲན་བཅས་ཤུགས་ཀྱིས་བརྐྱུར༔ སླ་འདི་ཇི་ལྟར་དྱིངས་ཆེཡང༔ མི་ལྟོངས་མི་སྲིད་ ཇི་ཁོལ་འགྱོ༔ རྣལ་འབྱོར་བཏུལ་ཤུགས་རྐྱང་གྱུར་ན༔ རིམ་པས་བློ་དང་སྤྲར་ཏེ་བྱ༔

I prostrate to the queen of space, the lady of great bliss, Yeshe Tsogyal. The true nature, the Great Perfection, cuts the root of samsara in one stroke, thus it transcends the cutter and the cut. But for those who enjoy elaboration and accomplishing the path of crazy wisdom activity, I will teach the pith instructions for offering one's body as food.

The articles you need to do this are: to overpower the arrogant, a wild animal's skin with the claws intact. To symbolize the descending view, a small tent, and to show the ascending conduct, a khatvanga. To have authority over the demons, a thighbone trumpet. To overpower appearances, a damaru drum. To dominate the hosts of dakinis, have bells, tinkling bells, and tassels with chevrons made of tiger skin, leopard skin, cotton cloth, and small plaits of human hair. In brief, to practice crazy wisdom activity, prepare the necessary, suitable things.

Then, in a sacred power spot, without having an arrogant mind that insults the demons, or thoughts of the eight worldly concerns, arouse heroic confidence through the four immeasurables. Whatever appearances arise must be crushed instantly. At that moment, if you don't use your contemplation to overpower appearances, it is as if spies have intercepted your secret message. Therefore, perform fearless activities with awareness.

With the sound of **PHET**, from your heart center comes a nine-pointed vajra of meteoric iron—solid, firm, heavy and strong. It blazes with light and masses of flames, striking like lightning on that fearful power spot. The hordes of demons dwelling there are *unable to scatter and escape. Think that their bravery and strength are broken and they are stuck there. Then, abandon pretense, shyness and so on, the ordinary doubts and hesitation. With strong confidence in crazy wisdom activity, walk in the four different ways. From among these, the best way to walk is with the power of realization of the perfect view.*

Further, summon all the demons—those of the entire phenomenal existence, the local demons, and the demons who wander around. Herd them like goats and sheep into that frightening place where they are powerless. As soon as you arrive at that spot, assume the manner and gestures of blazing wrathfulness. Holding the demons by their feet, swing them around your head three times and think that they crash onto that powerful ground. Forcibly cast down your tent and mat. Even if the demons seem spacious and easy-going, it is impossible that they won't become provoked and frantic. If your yogic discipline is weak and ineffectual, apply this according to the level of your realization.

DE NE RANG NYI KE CHIG GI
Then, instantly oneself becomes

SANG WA YE SHE KHA DRO MA
Sangwa Yeshe Khandroma, the secret wisdom dakini.

CHE CHUNG SI PE TÖ DANG NYAM
As large as the entire universe,

NAM JUR DZOG PE KUR CHE LA
Her body is generated complete in every aspect.

མི་རྐང་གླིང་བུ་དྲག་ཏུ་འབུད༔

MI KANG LING BU DRAG TU BÜ
Loudly blow the human thighbone trumpet.

ལྟ་བའི་དར་བསྒྲེད་བྲོ་བརྡུང་བྱ༔

TA WE NGAR CHE DRO DUNG JA
Forcefully generate the power of realization and perform the dance.

ཕཊ༔ འཇིགས་མེད་བརྟུལ་ཞུགས་སྤྱོད་པའི་རྣལ་འབྱོར་ང་༔

PHET JIG ME TÜL ZHUG CHÖ PE NAL JOR NGA
PHET I am a fearless yogi who practices crazy wisdom activity.

འཁོར་འདས་མཉམ་པར་བརྡལ་བའི་དགོངས་སྤྱོད་ཀྱིས༔

KHOR DE NYAM PAR DAL WE GONG CHÖ CHI
Through realization activities which encompass samsara and nirvana as equal,

བདག་འཛིན་ལྷ་འདྲེའི་སྟེང་དུ་བྲོ་ཞིག་བརྡུང་༔

DAG DZIN LHA DRE TENG DU DRO ZHIG DUNG
I dance and trample on the demons of ego-clinging

གཉིས་འཛིན་འཁོར་བའི་རྣམ་རྟོག་དུལ་དུ་རློག༔

NYI DZIN KHOR WE NAM TOG DÜL DU LOG
And grind samsaric, dualistic thinking into dust.

རྩ་བརྒྱུད་རིག་འཛིན་བླ་མ་བྲོ་ལ་བྱོན༔

TSA JÜ RIG DZIN LA MA DRO LA JÖN
Vidyadhara lamas of the root lineage, come to the dance!

YI DAM PA WO JA TSO DRO LA JÖN
Ocean of yidams and dakas, come to the dance!

KHA DRO NE NYÜL MA TSOG DRO LA JÖN
Hosts of dakinis and those who roam everywhere, come to the dance!

TÜL ZHUG LAM DU LONG PAR JIN JI LOB
Grant your blessings for my accomplishing the path of crazy wisdom activity.

PHET   **SHAR CHOG LÜ PHAG LING DU DUNG TSA NA**
PHET   While dancing on the eastern continent of Purvavideha,

PA WO KHA DRÖ DRO RA DUM LA CHIL
On the arena of the dakas and dakinis, which is perfectly round,

ZHE DANG JAL PÖ GO LA CHEM SE CHEM
I stomp on the heads of the kings of anger.
CHEM SE CHEM

ME LONG YE SHE LING BU CHU RU RU HUNG HUNG HUNG
The trumpet of mirror-like wisdom blows.
CHU RU RU HUNG HUNG HUNG

Dharma Samudra   Jigme Lingpa   *Chod Yül*

PHET
PHET **LHO YI DZAM BÜ LING LA DUNG TSA NA**
While dancing on the southern continent of Jambudvipa,

PA WO KHA DRÖ DRO RA ZUR SUM WAL
On the arena of the dakas and dakinis, which is a sharp triangle,

NGA JAL SHIN JE GO LA CHEM SE CHEM
I step on the head of the arrogant Lord of Death.
CHEM SE CHEM

NYAM NYI YE SHE THÖ NGA TRO LO LO   HUNG HUNG HUNG
The skullcup drum of equanimity wisdom resounds.
TRO LO LO   HUNG HUNG HUNG

PHET
PHET **NUB CHI BA LANG CHÖ LA DUNG TSA NA**
While dancing on the western continent of Godaniya,

PA WO KHA DRÖ DRO RA DA GAM CHIL
On the arena of the dakas and dakinis, which is perfectly semi-circular,

Dharma Samudra   Jigme Lingpa   *Chod Yül*

འདོད་ཆགས་སྲིན་མོའི་མགོ་ལ་ཆེམས་སེ་ཆེམ༔

DÖ CHAG SIN MÖ GO LA CHEM SE CHEM
I tread on the heads of the female cannibal demons of attachment. **CHEM SE CHEM**

སོར་རྟོག་ཡེ་ཤེས་དྲིལ་གཡེར་ཁྲོ་ལོ་ལོ༔ ཧཱུྃ་ ཧཱུྃ་ ཧཱུྃ༔

SOR TOG YE SHE DRIL YER TRO LO LO HUNG HUNG HUNG
The bells and jingles of discriminating awareness wisdom ring. **TRO LO LO HUNG HUNG HUNG**

཈ཊ༔ བྱང་གི་སྒྲ་མི་སྙན་ལ་བརྡུངས་ཙ་ན༔

PHET **JANG GI DRA MI NYEN LA DUNG TSA NA**
PHET While dancing on the northern continent of Uttarakuru,

དཔའ་བོ་མཁའ་འགྲོའི་བྲོ་ར་གྲུ་བཞི་ལམ༔

PA WO KHA DRÖ DRO RA DRU ZHI LAM
On the arena of the dakas and dakinis, which is a shimmering square,

ཕྲག་དོག་དམ་སྲིའི་མགོ་ལ་ཆེམས་སེ་ཆེམ༔

TRAG DOG DAM SI GO LA CHEM SE CHEM
I trample the heads of the samaya corruptors of jealousy. **CHEM SE CHEM**

བྱ་གྲུབ་ཡེ་ཤེས་ཅོད་པན་པུ་རུ་རུ༔ ཧཱུྃ་ ཧཱུྃ་ ཧཱུྃ༔

JA DRUB YE SHE CHÖ PEN PU RU RU HUNG HUNG HUNG
The tassels of all-accomplishing wisdom flutter.
PU RU RU HUNG HUNG HUNG

ཕཊ༔ དབུས་ཕྱོགས་ལྷུན་པོའི་རྩེ་རུ་བརྡུངས་ཚ་ན༔

PHET   Ü CHOG LHUN PÖ TSE RU DUNG TSA NA
PHET While dancing on the central continent of Mt. Meru,

དཔའ་བོ་མཁའ་འགྲོའི་བྲོ་ར་བྱིན་རེ་ཆགས༔

PA WO KHA DRÖ DRO RA JIN RE CHAG
On the arena of the dakas and dakinis, which is splendid and charming,

གཏི་མུག་ཤི་འདྲེའི་མགོ་ལ་ཆེམས་སེ་ཆེམ༔

TI MUG SHI DRE GO LA CHEM SE CHEM
I crush the heads of the ghosts of ignorance.
CHEM SE CHEM

ཆོས་དབྱིངས་ཡེ་ཤེས་ཧཱུྂ་ལུ་རུ་རུ༔ ཧཱུྂ་ ཧཱུྂ་ ཧཱུྂ༔ ཕཊ༔

CHÖ YING YE SHE HUNG LU CHU RU RU HUNG HUNG HUNG   PHET
The melodious HUNG of dharmadhatu wisdom sounds.
CHU RU RU   HUNG HUNG HUNG   PHET

ཅེས་བརྡུང་ཞིང་གཏད་མེད་བཏང༔ དེ་ནས་ཙོག་པུ་འབུབས་པ་ནི༔ གཞི་དེའི་སྟེང་འདི༔ གདུག་པ་ཅན༔ གན་རྐྱལ་བསྒྱེལ་བའི་ཡན་ལག་ལྔ༔ གནམ་ལྕགས་ཕུར་བུ་བཏབ་པར་བསམ༔

Dance in that way, maintaining your mind without reference points. Then, pitch a small tent on the ground of the cruel demon, who lies on its back with its five limbs extended. Meditate that you pound in stakes of meteoric iron.

ཕཊ༔ ཤར་ཕྱོགས་རྡོ་རྗེ་མཁའ་འགྲོ་མས༔

PHET   SHAR CHOG DOR JE KHA DRO ME
PHET The vajra dakini of the eastern direction

བྱམས་པ་ཆེན་པོའི་ཕུར་པ་ཁྱེར༔

JAM PA CHEN PÖ PHUR PA CHER
Carries the stake of great loving-kindness.

ལྷོ་ཕྱོགས་རིན་ཆེན་མཁའ་འགྲོ་མས༔

LHO CHOG RIN CHEN KHA DRO ME
The ratna dakini of the southern direction

སྙིང་རྗེ་ཆེན་པོའི་ཕུར་པ་ཁྱེར༔

NYING JE CHEN PÖ PHUR PA CHER
Carries the stake of great compassion.

ནུབ་ཕྱོགས་པདྨ་མཁའ་འགྲོ་མས༔

NUB CHOG PE MA KHA DRO ME
The padma dakini of the western direction

དགའ་བ་ཆེན་པོའི་ཕུར་པ་ཁྱེར༔

GA WA CHEN PÖ PHUR PA CHER
Carries the stake of great rejoicing.

བྱང་ཕྱོགས་ལས་ཀྱི་མཁའ་འགྲོ་མས༔

JANG CHOG LE CHI KHA DRO ME
The karma dakini of the northern direction

བཏང་སྙོམས་ཆེན་པོའི་ཕུར་པ་ཁྱེར༔

TANG NYOM CHEN PÖ PHUR PA CHER
Carries the stake of great equanimity.

དབུས་ཕྱོགས་སངས་རྒྱས་མཁའ་འགྲོ་མས༔

Ü CHOG SANG JE KHA DRO ME
The buddha dakini of the central direction

JANG CHUB SEM CHI PHUR PA CHER
Carries the stake of bodhichitta.

DAG DZIN LHA DRE GO WO DANG
By piercing the head

LHU TSIG ZHI LA TAB PA YI
And four limbs of the demon of ego-clinging,

YO GÜL ME PAR NE PAR JUR PHET
It is transfixed, unable to move. **PHET**

Having said that, remain in equanimity, not focusing on yourself, others, or the demons. Then recognize the demons and engage in actually giving your body.

PHET RANG NANG Ö SAL DE WA CHEN PÖ YING
PHET Perception itself is the luminous space of great bliss.

BE TSÖL TRÖ PA DRAL WE NAM KHA LA
In the sky, which is free from contrived effort,

TSA WE LA MA DRUG PA DOR JE CHANG
Is the root lama as Vajradhara, the lord of the six families,

གོང་ད་ཉེན་བརྒྱུད་བླ་མ་ཡི་དམ་ལྷ༔

GONG DA NYEN JÜ LA MA YI DAM LHA
And the gurus and yidams of the mind-to-mind, symbolic,
and oral transmission lineages,

མཁའ་འགྲོ་ཆོས་སྐྱོང་སྲུང་མ་སྤྲིན་ལྟར་གཏིབས༔

KHA DRO CHÖ CHONG SUNG MA TRIN TAR TIB
Along with the dakinis, dharmapalas, and protectors.
They gather like clouds,

མ་འགགས་འཇའ་ཚོན་ཐིག་ལེའི་ཀློང་དུ་གསལ༔

MA GAG JA TSÖN THIG LE LONG DU SAL
Unobstructed and clear, in a vast, circular rainbow.

ཞེས་པས་ཚོགས་ཞིང་གསལ་བཏབ་ལ༔ ལྷ་འདྲེས་གཙོ་བྱས་སེམས་ཅན་ཀུན༔ བྱིད་ཤེས་གུས་ཡིས་སྐྱབས་འགྲོར་དམིགས༔

Thus, vividly invoke that field of refuge and think that all beings, led principally by the demons, take refuge with fervent devotion.

ཕཊ༔   རང་བྱུང་གི་རིག་པ་བཅོས་མེད་འདི༔

PHET   RANG JUNG GI RIG PA CHÖ ME DI
PHET   Because this unfabricated, self-existing awareness

སྐྱབས་ཡུལ་གྱི་ངོ་བོར་མ་རིག་པས༔

CHAB YÜL JI NGO WOR MA RIG PE
Is not recognized as the essence of the objects of refuge,

སྡུག་བསྔལ་གྱི་རྒྱ་མཚོར་བྱིངས་པ་རྣམས༔

DUG NGAL JI JA TSOR JING PA NAM
Beings are drowning in the ocean of suffering.

Dharma Samudra   Jigme Lingpa   *Chod Yül*

KU SUM JI GONG PE CHAB TU SÖL
May the wisdom mind of the three kayas protect us.

Repeat that three times.

Then, develop bodhichitta:

PHET   **NANG WA LA NGÖ POR DZIN PE SEM**
PHET   The mind that clings to appearances as solidly existing

TÜL ZHUG CHI CHÖ PE TSAR CHE NE
Is severed by the activities of crazy wisdom.

YANG DAG GI NE LUG TOG JE CHIR
So that the perfectly pure nature may be realized,

RE DOG DANG DRAL WAR SEM CHE DO
I generate bodhichitta free from hope and fear.

Repeat that three times.

Dharma Samudra   Jigme Lingpa   Chod Yül

དེ་ནས་མཎྜལ་ནི། ལྷག་པ་རི་རབ། ཡན་ལག་གླིང་བཞི། ཉིང་ལག་གླིང་ཕྲན། མགོ་བོ་ལྷ་གནས། མིག་གཉིས་ཉི་ཟླ། དོན་སྙོད་ལྟ་མིའི་དཔལ་འབྱོར་དུ་བསམས་ལ།

Then, for the mandala offering, think that the torso of the body is Mt. Meru, the limbs are the four continents, the fingers are the subcontinents, the head is the god realm, the eyes are the sun and moon, and the inner receptacles and organs of the body are the wealth of gods and men.

ཕཊ྄། གཅེས་འཛིན་གྱི་ཕུང་པོ་སྒྱུ་མའི་ལུས།

PHET CHE DZIN JI PHUNG PO JU ME LÜ
PHET This illusory body, this cherished aggregate,

མཎྜལ་གྱི་ཚོམ་བུར་རབ་བཀོད་ནས།

MAN DAL JI TSÖM BUR RAB KÖ NE
Is arranged as the offering substance of the mandala.

ཚོགས་ཞིང་གི་ལྷ་ལ་བློས་མེད་འབུལ།

TSOG ZHING GI LHA LA TÖ ME BÜL
Without expectations, I offer it to the assembly of the deities.

བདག་འཛིན་གྱི་རྩ་བ་ཆོད་པར་ཤོག། ཕཊ྄།

DAG DZIN JI TSA WA CHÖ PAR SHOG **PHET**
May the root of ego-clinging be cut. **PHET**

དེ་ནས་བླ་མའི་རྣལ་འབྱོར་ནི།

Then, Guru Yoga:

ཕཊ྄། དབྱིངས་ཟག་མེད་ཆོས་སྐུའི་ནམ་མཁའ་ལ།

PHET YING ZAG ME CHÖ KÜ NAM KHA LA
PHET In the stainless space of the dharmakaya,

Dharma Samudra   Jigme Lingpa   Chod Yül

མདངས་འཇའ་ཟེར་ཐིག་ལེར་འཁྲུགས་པའི་དབུས༔

DANG JA ZER THIG LER TRUG PE Ü
Amid a brilliant, circular mass of rainbow light,

ཕ་དུས་གསུམ་ཀུན་མཁྱེན་པདྨ་འབྱུང༔

PHA DÜ SUM KÜN CHEN PE MA JUNG
Is Padmakara, the father who knows all the three times,

ཚུལ་བརྟུལ་ཞུགས་སྤྱོད་པའི་ཧེ་རུ་ཀ༔

TSÜL TÜL ZHUG CHÖ PE HE RU KA
In the style of a heruka performing crazy wisdom activity.

མ་མཁའ་འགྲོ་རྒྱ་མཚོའི་ཚོགས་དང་བཅས༔

MA KHA DRO JA TSÖ TSOG DANG CHE
He is accompanied by the mothers, a vast assembly of dakinis.

སྐུ་མཚན་དཔེའི་གཟི་བྱིན་ཏ་ལ་ལ༔

KU TSEN PE ZI JIN TA LA LA
His body is radiant with the major and minor marks of a buddha. **TA LA LA**

གསུང་གང་འདུལ་ཆོས་སྒྲ་ཨུ་རུ་རུ༔

SUNG GANG DÜL CHÖ DRA U RU RU
His speech is the sound of the Dharma, taming beings according to their needs. **U RU RU**

ཐུགས་འོད་གསལ་རྡོ་རྗེ་སྙིང་པོའི་ངང༔

THUG Ö SAL DOR JE NYING PÖ NGANG
His mind is the state of luminosity, the indestructible essence.

U MÖ GÜ DRAG PÖ SÖL WA DEB
I, your child, supplicate you with strong devotion.

CHI NAM TOG DRAR LANG LHA DRE ZUG
Outwardly, concepts have arisen as enemies; these are the demons' form.

NANG RE DANG DOG PE NYI DZIN SEM
Inwardly, dualistic clinging is their mind of hope and fear.

BAR NANG WA NA TSOG CHEN NGEN KÜN
In between, all sorts of unfortunate conditions appear.

CHÖ ZAB MO DÜ CHI CHÖ YÜL JI
May the profound practice of Chod

DÜ DA TA TEN THOG DI RU CHÖ
Destroy these demons right now, on this very seat.

YING CHÖ KÜ JAL SA ZIN PA RU
So that I may hold the royal seat of the space of dharmakaya,

PHA JE TSÜN LA ME JIN JI LOB   PHET PHET PHET
Father, Jetsun Lama, please grant your blessings.
PHET PHET PHET

ཅེས་བརྗོད་ཚོགས་ཞིང་རང་ལ་བསྟིམ༔ གཉིས་མེད་དང་དུ་མཉམ་པར་གཞག༔

Having prayed in that way, the field of refuge dissolves into oneself. Rest in nondual equanimity.

ཕཊ༔ དེ་ནས་བག་ཆགས་སྙིགས་མའི་ལུས༔

PHET   **DE NE BAG CHAG NYIG ME LÜ**
PHET   Then see your gross body, which is obscured by habitual tendencies,

ཆོ་ཞིང་སྣུམ་ལ་བློས་ཆེ་བའི༔

TSO ZHING NUM LA TÖ CHE WE
As big and fat and greasy.

དབུས་ལས་དངས་མའི་རིག་པ་ནི༔

Ü LE DANG ME RIG PA NI
From within that, the essential awareness

བྲོས་མའི་རྣམ་པར་ཕཊ་ཅེས་དབྱེ༔

TRÖ ME NAM PAR PHET CHE YE
In the form of Troma, separates upward by the sound of **PHET**.

ཞལ་གཅིག་ཕྱག་གཉིས་གྲི་ཐོད་ཅན༔

ZHAL CHIG CHAG NYI DRI THÖ CHEN
She has one face and two arms, and holds a hooked knife and skullcup.

དེ་ཡིས་རང་ལུས་ཐོད་པ་ཕྲལ༔

DE YI RANG LÜ THÖ PA TRAL
She slices the skull from one's body.

སྟོང་ཁམས་ཁྱབ་པའི་མི་མགོ་ཡི༔

TONG KHAM CHAB PE MI GO YI
Encompassing the entire universe, this human head

སྐྱེད་བུ་གསུམ་གྱི་ཁར་བཞག་ནང༔

JE BU SUM JI KHAR ZHAG NANG
Is placed on a hearth of three skulls.

འབྱུང་ལུས་ཚོགས་སུ་བཤམས་པ་དེ༔

JUNG LÜ TSOG SU SHAM PA DE
This body made of the elements is arranged as the feast offering.

འབྲུ་གསུམ་འོད་ཀྱིས་བདུད་རྩིར་སྦར༔

DRU SUM Ö CHI DÜ TSIR BAR
With the light of the three syllables it blazes as the nectar of amrita.

ཨོཾ་ཨཱཿཧཱུྂ་དང་ཧ་ཧོ་ཧྲཱིཿ

OM AH HUNG DANG HA HO HRI
OM AH HUNG and **HA HO HRI**

ཅི་མང་བརྗོད་པས་སྦྱངས་སྤེལ་བསྒྱུར༔ ཁྱོར་འགྱེད་ཡིན་དེ་ཞིད་ལས༔ སྐྱེད་ཚལ་ཟས་གོས༔ སྨན་ལ་སོགས༔ ཡིད་ལ་ཅི་འདོད་དོ་བོར་སྒྱུར༔ དམར་འགྱེད་རང་ཉིད་ཁྲོས་ནག་མས༔ སྐྱགས་མའི་ལུས་ཀྱི་བགས་པ་བཤུས༔ སྟོང་གསུམ་ཁྱབ་པར་བཀྲམ་པའི་སྟེང༔ གཟུགས་ སྒྲ་དྲི་རོ་རེག་བྱ་ལྔར་སྤྲོས༔ ཉན་པའི་འདུན་ས་ལྷུར་བསམ༔ རག་འགྱེད་བདག་གཞན་སེམས་ཅན་ཀྱི༔ ཕོག་མེད་ནས་བསགས་ནད་གདོན་དང༔ སྡིག་སྒྲིབ་ཐམས་ཅད་ནག་བུན༔ གྱི༔ བསྲེས་ཏེ་གཟུགས་ཕུང་ལ་བསྟིམས་པ༔ ལྷ་འདྲེས་ཟོས་བས་ཁོའི་ལུས༔ པོལ་བ་ལྷ༔ བུར་གྱུར་པར་བསམ༔ མཆོད་སྦྱིན་མགྲོན་རྣམས་འདིར་འབོད༔

By reciting these syllables as many times as possible, purify, increase, and transform the offering. If it is the endless generosity of the striped feast, generate gardens, food, clothing, medicine, and so forth. Increase the natures of whatever is desired. For the endless generosity of the red feast, you become Troma Nagmo,

Dharma Samudra   Jigme Lingpa   *Chod Yül*

and stripping off the skin of your own gross body, spread it out to encompass the three thousand worlds. On top of it, pile up heaps of bodies, aggregates, flesh, and blood. Envision it to be like a slaughterhouse. As the endless generosity for the black feast, gather what has been accumulated since beginningless time by all sentient beings, yourself and others—diseases, obstacles, evil deeds, and obscurations. Amassed like a big black cloud, they dissolve into the heaps of bodies, which the demons devour. Think that the demons' bodies then become like charcoal. Invite in this way all the guests of your offering and generosity.

PHET CHÖ YÜL TSA SUM DAM CHEN NE
PHET You who are objects of offering, beginning with the Three Roots and the samaya protectors,

DE JE JUNG PÖ TSO JE PE
And you who are the objects of generosity, principally the eight classes of spirits,

JIN YÜL LEN CHAG DRE DÖN YEN
As well as the karmically-connected demons and obstructers,

TÜL ZHUG CHÖ PE NE DIR JÖN
Come to this place of crazy wisdom activity.

DE RING JIG ME NAL JOR NGE
Today I, the fearless yogi,

འཁོར་འདས་གཉན་འབྱེད་སྒྱུ་མའི་ལུས༔

KHOR DE SHEN JE JU ME LÜ
Offer this illusory body that differentiates between samsara and nirvana.

སྟོང་གསུམ་ཆོན་ཡངས་ཀ་པ་ལར༔

TONG SUM CHÖN YANG KA PA LAR
In the skullcup as vast as the three thousand worlds,

བམ་ཆེན་ཚོགས་ཀྱི་འཁོར་ལོར་བཤམས༔

BAM CHEN TSOG CHI KHOR LOR SHAM
The corpse is arranged as the ganachakra offering

ཟག་མེད་ཡེ་ཤེས་བདུད་རྩིར་བསྒྱུར༔

ZAG ME YE SHE DÜ TSIR JUR
And transformed into the nectar of stainless wisdom.

འདོད་དགུར་འཆར་བའི་ཅོ་འཕྲུལ་ཅན༔

DÖ GUR CHAR WE CHO TRÜL CHEN
With a magical display in which all desirable things have arisen

གཅེས་འཛིན་མེད་པར་འབུལ་ལགས་ཀྱིས༔

CHE DZIN ME PAR BÜL LAG CHI
I make this offering without holding it dear.

སྟོན་ཆེན་མགྲོན་ལ་གཤེགས་སུ་གསོལ༔

TÖN CHEN DRÖN LA SHEG SU SÖL
Please come as guests to this great party.

མཆོག་ཆེན་ཐོད་རྔ་སྐད་རེ་གསངས༔

CHOG CHEN THÖ NGA KE RE SANG
The drum of a supreme skullcup beats brightly.

ཞིང་ཆེན་གཡང་གཞི་བརྗིད་རེ་ཆེཿ

ZHING CHEN YANG ZHI JE RE CHE
The supreme skin is magnificent.

མི་རྐང་གླིང་བུ་གདངས་རེ་སྙནཿ

MI KANG LING BU DANG RE NYEN
The thighbone trumpet blows melodiously.

དྲིལ་གཡེར་ཆོད་པན་དངས་རེ་སྒྲོཿ

DRIL YER CHÖ PEN DANG RE TRO
The bells, tinkling bells, and tassels swing joyfully.

བྱ་རྒོད་ཤ་ལ་འཐིབས་པ་བཞིནཿ

JA GÖ SHA LA THIB PA ZHIN
Just like vultures landing on flesh,

སྐད་ཅིག་ཉིད་ལ་གཤེགས་སུ་གསོལཿ ཕཊཿ

KE CHIG NYI LA SHEG SU SÖL   PHET
Please come here this very instant. **PHET**

དེ་ནས་འབུལ་ཞིང་བསྔོ་བ་ནིཿ

Then, the offering and dedication:

ཕཊཿ གདོད་མའི་མགོན་པོ་མན་ཆད་ནསཿ

PHET   DÖ ME GÖN PO MEN CHE NE
PHET   To all of you—down from the primordial protector

རྩ་བའི་བླ་མ་ཡན་ཆད་ཀྱིཿ

TSA WE LA MA YEN CHE CHI
And up to the root lama

Dharma Samudra Jigme Lingpa *Chod Yül*

JÜ SUM RIG DZIN LA MA DANG
And the vidyadhara lamas of the three lineages,

YI DAM KHA DRO CHÖ CHONG LA
As well as the yidams, dakinis, and dharmapalas—

BAM CHEN DÜ TSI CHÖ PA BÜL
I offer the amrita of the great corpse.

LHA DRE TSO JE DAG ZHEN JI
May I and others, and particularly the demons,

TSOG NYI DZOG SHING DRIB NYI JANG
Perfect the two accumulations and purify the two obscurations.

TÜL ZHUG DRO DÖN THAR CHIN NE
Having perfected crazy wisdom activity and the benefit of beings,

NANG WA Ö SAL JU MAR JONG
May appearance be accomplished as illusory clear light,

YA NGA BAG TSA CHÖ KUR DRÖL
And fear and anxiety be liberated in the dharmakaya.

Dharma Samudra　　　Jigme Lingpa　　　*Chod Yül*

HE RU KA TAR JIN JI LOB
Please bless me to become a heruka.

PHET JIG TEN DE DANG MA DE CHI
PHET To those in the world and beyond the world,

DE JE JUNG PO MI MA YIN
The eight classes of spirits and the non-humans,

LOG DREN SHA ZE DÖN TSOG LA
And to the hosts of flesh-eating demons who lead beings astray,

TONG SUM CHAB PE ZHING PAG TENG
On a human skin the size of the three thousand worlds

SHA TRAG RÜ PE PHUNG POR BÜL
I offer heaps of flesh, blood, and bones.

DAG TU DZIN NA NGA RE ZHEN
If I cling to this self, I am being weak.

CHÖ DU MA NÜ CHÖ RE LÖ
If you cannot use this, you are being lazy.

རིང་ན་རྗེན་པར་འུར་མིད་ཐོང་ས༔

RING NA JEN PAR CHUR MI THONG
If you are in a hurry, swallow the raw flesh whole.

ལྷོད་ན་དུམ་བུར་ཚོས་ལ་ཟོ༔

LHÖ NA DUM BUR TSÖ LA ZO
If you have time, cut it into pieces and cook it.

རྡུལ་ཕྲན་ཙམ་ཡང་མ་བཞག་ཅིག༔

DÜL TREN TSAM YANG MA ZHAG CHIG
Don't leave even one morsel uneaten.

ཕཊ༔   འཁོར་ཚེ་ཐོག་མ་མེད་པ་ནས༔

PHET **KHOR TSE THOG MA ME PA NE**
PHET For those who, from beginningless time in samsara,

ཤ་འཁོན་ཆགས་པའི་ལན་ཆགས་དང་༔

SHA KHÖN CHAG PE LEN CHAG DANG
Have had resentment and other habitual tendencies,

གློ་བུར་ལྷགས་པའི་སྙིང་རྗེའི་མགྲོན༔

LO BUR LHAG PE NYING JE DRÖN
And those who have suddenly arrived, all the guests of my compassion,

ཁས་ཞན་དབང་ཆུང་མ་ལུས་ལ༔

KHE ZHEN WANG CHUNG MA LÜ LA
Including those with little strength, who always listen to others,

Dharma Samudra   Jigme Lingpa   *Chod Yül*

སོ་སོ་གང་ལ་ཅི་འདོད་ཀྱིས༔

SO SO GANG LA CHI DÖ CHI
As whatever each individual wants

འདོད་ཡོན་མི་ཟད་གཏེར་དུ་བསྔོ༔

DÖ YÖN MI ZE TER DU NGO
I dedicate this inexhaustible treasure of desirable things.

འབྲེལ་པ་ཐོགས་ཚད་སངས་རྒྱས་ཤིང༔

DREL PA THOG TSE SANG JE SHING
May whoever is connected with this feast attain unobstructed enlightenment

བུ་ལོན་ལན་ཆགས་བྱང་བར་ཤོག༔ ཕཊ༔

BU LÖN LEN CHAG JANG WAR SHOG PHET
And be cleansed of all karmic debts and habitual tendencies. **PHET**

ཅེས་བརྗོད་བློས་པ་མེད་པར་བྱིན༔ སྟོང་ཉིད་དང་ལ་མཉམ་པར་གཞག༔ དེ་ཚེ་ལུས་ལ་ གཅེས་འཛིན་དང་༔ འདིགས་སྲུང་འདུ་འཕྲོག་ལྟོ་སྐྱེས་ནུ༔ ལུས་ནི་ལྷ་འདྲེ་བྱིན་ནས་ མེད༔ སེམས་ནི་གཞི་མེད་རྩ་བ་བྲལ༔ འདི་བས་སངས་རྒྱས་ཉིད་ཀྱིས་ཀྱང་༔ གཞིགས་པ་ མེད་སྙམ་གདེང་བསྐྱེད་ལ༔ གང་ཤར་རང་དོ་ཙ་གདར་བཅད༔ ཕོགས་བཅས་བདུད་དང་༔ ཕྱི་རྒྱན་འབྱུང་བདག་གཅན་གཟན་མི་ཁྱོད་སོགས༔ ཕོགས་མེད་བདུད༔ ཟང་ཀྱེན་དགའ་སྲུག སེམས་ཆགས་པ་དང་ཆགས་སྲུང་གི་རྣམ་རྟོག་སོགས༔ དགའ་བྱོར་བདུད་དང་༔ རང་འགྱུར་ བདེ་སྐྱིད་མངོན་རྫོགས་སོགས༔ སྙེམས་བྱེད་བདུད༔ ཞེ་ཆོམ་དང་ཁུ་འཕྲག་ལ་སོགས༔ ཕཊ༔ཅེས་དབྱེར་སུ་གཅོད་པ་ཡིན༔ དེ་ཡང་དུས་ཆོད་ལ་མཆོད་ན་ཕོ་རངས་ཆོགས་ གཉིས་རྟོགས་པའི་ཕྱིར༔ དགར་འགྱེད་བདུད་རྩིའི་དཔོར་སྤྱར༔ ཉིན་གུང་ལན་ཆགས་སྦྱང་ བའི་ཕྱིར༔ ཁྲ་འགྱེད་གང་ལ་འཆམས་པར་བསྔོ༔ ནུབ་མོ་བཀྲ་ཤིས་ལམ་སྟོང་ཕྱིར༔

Dharma Samudra   Jigme Lingpa   *Chod Yül*

བདག་འཛིན་ཆར་ག་ཆོད་དམར་འགྱེད་གཏོང་༔ སྟོང་ལ་སྟེག་སྟོང་དག་འབྱེད་བྱ༔ གུན་གུང་
འདུན་པ་བསྒྱུར་བ་སྟེ༔ གཙོ་བོ་དམིགས་པས་ཉམས་སུ་བླང་༔ དེ་ཚེ་ཚོགས་འཕུལ་ཅི་བྱུང་ཡང་༔
ཉམས་དང་བྲལ་བའི་ལྟ་བས་གཅུན༔ གལ་ཏེ་རྣལ་འབྱོར་དབྱིངས་ཆུང་ནས༔ སྟོང་
འཆོབས་འཆུན་པར་དགའ་བའམ༔ ལྟ་འདི་དབྱིངས་ཆེས་མ་ལྟོངས་ན༔ གེང་དུས་དགར་
པོའི་དམིགས་པ་བྱ༔ ཕཊ་ཅེས་རང་ཉིད་སྐད་ཅིག་གིས༔ གེང་དུས་དགར་པོ་མི་འབར་བ་
ཤིན་ཏུ་ཚོ་པོ་ལས་བྱུང་བའི༔ མེ་ཡིས་སྟོང་གི་འདིག་རྟེན་དང་༔ ཁྱེད་པར་ལྷ་འདྲེའི་གནས་
རྟེན་བསྲེགས༔ མཐར་ནི་གེང་དུས་མེ་དང་བཅས༔ འོད་ཡལ་སྟོང་པའི་དང་ལ་གཞག༔ འགོ་
དང་སྲུང་བ་ལ་ཡང་ཟབ༔ ཚར་ཆོད་དུས་སུ་མ་བྱུང་དང་༔ གནོད་འདྲེ་གདུག་པ་ཡང་གཏོང་
ན༔ རིག་པ་ཁྲོས་མའི་སྐུར་གསལ་བས༔ སྒྲིག་མའི་ལུས་ཀྱི་ལགས་པ་བཞུས༔ སྟོང་
གསུམ་ཁེངས་པའི་གཡང་གཞིའི་སྟེང་༔ ནུ་རྣམས་གཅལ་དུ་བཀྲམ་པ་ལ༔ འདི་གདོན་ཟས་
ལ་གདུང་བའི་མོད༔ ཁྲོས་མས་གཡང་བའི་འུབ་ཀྱིས་དྲིལ༔ སྐྱལ་དང་རྒྱའི་ཞགས་པས་
བསྡམས༔ རྒྱུད་ལ་བསྐོར་ཞིང་བརྡབས་པ་ཡིས༔ ནུ་ཕྱུག་རྣམས་མྱོག་དག་ཏུ་སོང་༔ སྐྱལ་
པའི་གཅན་གཟན་དུ་མ་ཡིས༔ ཕག་མ་མེད་པར་ཟོས་པར་བསམ༔ དབྱིངས་རིག་བསྲེས་ཏེ་
མཉམ་པར་གཞག༔ དེས་ནི་ཆར་ཆོད་དེས་འབྱུང་ཞིང་༔ འདི་གདོན་གདུག་པ་ཆར་ཆོད་
འགྱུར༔ གུན་ལ་གཅིས་འཛིན་བློ་སྤོངས་ཏེ༔ ལྷ་བའི་གདོད་གིས་ཞིན་པ་གཅིས༔ དེ་ཚེ་ཆར་
ཆོད་འདུ་བའི་སྟོངས༔ སྟོངས་ཆོད་འདུ་བའི་ཆར་ཆོད་དང་༔ གཞིས་ཀ་འདུ་བའི་འདྲེས་མ་
དང་༔ འདྲེས་མ་འདུ་བའི་བག་ཆགས་དང་༔ ཆར་སྟོངས་གཞིས་ཀ་མཐར་ཕྱིན་གྱི༔ རྟགས་
རྣམས་ཉམས་དང་སྣང་ཏེ་སྐྱེང་༔ དོན་ལ་བདག་མེད་གུན་བཟང་མོ༔ ཡུམ་ཆེན་ཤེས་རབ་པར་
ཕྱིན་མའི༔ དགོངས་པ་སྐྱོང་དུ་གྱུར་ཙ་ན༔ གཅོད་ཡུལ་ལམ་དུ་ལོངས་བའོ༔ སམཡ༔

Praying thus, give without holding anything back and meditate within the state of emptiness. At that time, if you hold your body dear, or fear and hesitation arise in your mind, think that your body does not exist; it has already been given to the demons. Your mind is groundless and rootless; it can't be found by the demons, since even the buddhas can't see it. Arouse a courageous mind, recognizing deep down that whatever arises is one's own display. There are substantial, obstructing demons [external conditions such as the elements, wild animals, outlaws, and so on], insubstantial demons [internal conditions such as happy and sad moods, and thoughts of attachment, anger and so on], demons of excitement [being conceited about one's own happiness and so on], and demons of uncertainty [doubt, hesitation, and so forth]. Shout **PHET** and sever those into the space of emptiness.

Further, to indicate the times of the day for the feasts: in the morning, in order to complete the two accumulations, increase the white feast as the nature of amrita. In mid-day, in order to purify habitual tendencies, dedicate the striped feast in whatever way is appropriate. In early evening, in order to accomplish crazy wisdom activity, give the red feast to sever ego-clinging. At night, purify evil deeds by the black feast. All of these change with one's intention, so mainly practice the visualization.

At this time, no matter what illusory reactions arise, reduce them with the view that is beyond temporary experiences. If the practitioner's realization is small, it is difficult to handle the provocation that arises or the demons may be diffident and can't be aroused. If so, you should do the meditation on the white skeleton. Shouting **PHET**, instantly you become a white skeleton blazing with fire. From that enormous fire another fire arises, which burns the threefold world, particularly the dwelling place of the demons. To conclude, the skeleton, the fire, and their light subside and dissolve into emptiness. Also, this practice provides special protection against contagious disease. If signs of accomplishment have not arisen, then one has to put pressure on the malevolent demons. Visualize your awareness in the form of Troma and spread out the skin of your gross body to the extent of the three thousand worlds. On top of that scatter a display of flesh and bones, which the demons and obstructors devour longingly. At that moment, Troma quickly folds up the field of skin and ties it with a noose made of snakes and intestines. She whirls it overhead and then smashes it on the ground. Think that the flesh and bones of the demons become pulp, which many emanated wild animals consume. Then, rest evenly with space and awareness intermingled. Through that practice, signs of *accomplishment will definitely arise. The cruel and obstructing demons will be subdued. The mind that holds everything dear will be given up. It is very important to retain the confidence of the view. At that time, signs of being provoked may seem like signs of accomplishment, or signs of accomplishment may seem like signs of being provoked. Or both signs appear mixed, or they seem mixed because of habitual tendencies. To perfect both the signs of being provoked and accomplishing, you should conduct yourself according to your experiences and signs. Ultimately, egolessness is Samantabhadri, the Great Mother Prajnaparamita. If you can encompass that realization, you can accomplish the path of Chod practice.* **SAMAYA**

To conclude, do the dedication and aspiration prayers:

AH GE DANG MI GE TOG TSOG RANG DRÖL LA
AH All thoughts, whether virtuous or unvirtuous, are self-liberated.

RE DANG DOG PE TSEN MA MI MIG CHANG
The characteristics of hope and fear cannot be found.

NANG CHE TEN DREL LU ME GE TSOG JÜN
However, since interdependent appearances inevitably continue as the accumulation of virtue,

ZAG ME CHÖ CHI YING SU NGO WAR JA
Dedicate this within the undefiled dharmadhatu.

PHET   KÜN DZOB LÜ CHI JIN PA LA TEN NE
PHET   By giving this body of relative truth

KAL PAR SAG PE BU LÖN LEN CHAG JANG
May karmic debts and habitual tendencies, accumulated for aeons, be purified.

DÖN DAM CHÖ CHI DEN PE JÜ DRÖL TSE
When my being has been liberated by the Dharma of absolute truth

DAG GI DÜ PA DANG POR CHE WAR SHOG
May these demons be born as my first disciples.

DE TSE MA CHÖ RANG ZHAG NYUG ME DÖN
Whenever the unfabricated, self-existing, innate truth

MI SÜN LHA DRE JÜ LA CHE NE CHANG
Arises in the mindstreams of the wild demons,

NGAR DZIN TRÜL PE JE SU MI DRANG WAR
Without following after confused ego-clinging

JAM DANG NYING JE SHE JÜ LEN PAR SHOG
May their mindstreams be saturated with love and compassion.

Dharma Samudra   Jigme Lingpa   *Chod Yül*

བདག་ཀྱང་བཏུལ་ཞུགས་སྤྱོད་པ་མཐར་ཕྱིན་ནས༔

DAG CHANG TÜL ZHUG CHÖ PA THAR CHIN NE
For myself, having perfected the yogic activity of crazy wisdom,

སྐྱིད་སྡུག་རོ་སྙོམས་འཁོར་འདས་ཆོས་སྐུར་འབྱོངས༔

CHI DUG RO NYOM KHOR DE CHÖ KUR JONG
May happiness and sadness be one equal taste, and may samsara and nirvana be accomplished as the dharmakaya.

ཕྱོགས་ལས་རྣམ་རྒྱལ་འབྲེལ་ཚེ་དོན་ལྡན་གྱིས༔

CHOG LE NAM JAL DREL TSE DÖN DEN JI
Victorious in all directions, may I have a meaningful connection with everyone,

ཕྲིན་ལས་མཐར་ཕྱིན་འཇའ་ལུས་འགྲུབ་པར་ཤོག༔ པྷཊ༔

TRIN LE THAR CHIN JA LÜ DRUB PAR SHOG PHET
Accomplish buddha activity, and attain the rainbow body. **PHET**

སྨྲ་བསམ་བརྗོད་མེད་ཤེས་རབ་ཕ་རོལ་ཕྱིན། །

MA SAM JÖ ME SHE RAB PHA RÖL CHIN
Inconceivable, inexpressible Prajnaparamita

མ་སྐྱེས་མི་འགག་ནམ་མཁའི་ངོ་བོ་ཉིད། །

MA CHE MI GAG NAM KHE NGO WO NYI
Unborn, unceasing, by nature like the sky,

སོ་སོ་རང་རིག་ཡེ་ཤེས་སྤྱོད་ཡུལ་བ། །

SO SO RANG RIG YE SHE CHÖ YÜL WA
Experienced by self-reflexive awareness' discerning pristine cognition.

Dharma Samudra Jigme Lingpa *Chod Yül*

དུས་གསུམ་རྒྱལ་བའི་ཡུམ་གྱི་བཀྲ་ཤིས་ཤོག །

DÜ SUM JAL WE YUM JI TRA SHI SHOG
Mother of the Victorious Ones of the three times, please bring forth auspiciousness.

ཐབས་མཁས་ཐུགས་རྗེ་ཤཱཀྱའི་རིགས་སུ་འཁྲུངས། །

THAB KHE THUG JE SHAK YE RIG SU TRUNG
Born through skillful means and compassion in the Shakya family,

གཞན་གྱིས་མི་ཐུབ་བདུད་ཀྱི་དཔུང་འཇོམས་པ། །

ZHEN JI MI THUB DÜ CHI PUNG JOM PA
You vanquished the forces of evil that others could not subdue.

གསེར་གྱི་ལྷུན་པོ་ལྟ་བུར་བརྗིད་པའི་སྐུ། །

SER JI LHÜN PO TA BUR JI PE KU
Your body is resplendent like a golden mountain.

ཤཱཀྱའི་རྒྱལ་པོ་ཁྱོད་ཀྱིས་བཀྲ་ཤིས་ཤོག །

SHAK YE JAL PO CHÖ CHI TRA SHI SHOG
King of the Shakyas, please bring forth auspiciousness.

ཀུན་ཏུ་བཟང་མོ་ཤེས་རབ་ཕ་རོལ་ཕྱིན། །

KÜN TU ZANG MO SHE RAB PHA RÖL CHIN
Most Excellent Lady Samantabhadri—Prajnaparamita,

དབྱིངས་ཕྱུག་རྒྱལ་ཡུམ་རྡོ་རྗེ་རྣལ་འབྱོར་མ། །

YING CHUG JAL YUM DOR JE NAL JOR MA
Queen of Space, Mother of the Buddhas—Vajrayogini,

དབྱངས་ཅན་ལྷ་མོ་ཡེ་ཤེས་མཚོ་རྒྱལ་ཞབས། །

YANG CHEN LHA MO YE SHE TSO JAL ZHAB
Goddess of Eloquence Sarasvati—Yeshe Tsogyal,

བླ་མ་སྐུ་གསུམ་མཁའ་འགྲོས་བཀྲ་ཤིས་ཤོག །

LA MA KU SUM KHAN DRÖ TRA SHI SHOG
Three Kaya Guru Dakini, please bring forth auspiciousness.

རྒྱ་གར་པཎ་ཆེན་བོད་ལ་བཀའ་དྲིན་ཆེ། །

JA GAR PEN CHEN BÖ LA KA DRIN CHE
Great Indian pandita so kind to Tibet,

པདྨ་འབྱུང་གནས་སྐུ་ལ་འདས་འབྱུངས་མེད། །

PE MA JUNG NE KU LA DE TRUNG ME
Pema Jungne, unborn and undying,

ད་ལྟ་ལྷོ་ནུབ་སྲིན་པོའི་ཁ་གནོན་མཛད། །

DA TA LHO NUB SIN PÖ KHA NÖN DZE
You now tame the rakshasas in the southwest,

ཨོ་རྒྱན་རིན་པོ་ཆེ་ཡིས་བཀྲ་ཤིས་ཤོག །

OR JEN RIN PO CHE YI TRA SHI SHOG
Orgyen Rinpoche, please bring forth auspiciousness.

ཅེས་བརྗོད་ལྷ་བའི་དངམདངས་བསྒྱངས། སྤྱིང་རྗེ་ཆེན་པོའི་རྩེས་ཞེན་པས། བདེ་སྡུག་གཏོང་ལེན་དམིགས་པ་དང༌། ཆོས་ཀྱི་སྟྱིན་པ་རྣམས་དག་བྱ༔ འབྲེལ་ཐོགས་བཟང་ངན་ཐར་ལམ་འགོད༔ ས་མ་ཡ༔ མ་མ་ཀོ་ལིང་ས་མནྟ༔ བདེ་སྡུག་གཏོང་ལེན་ནི། བདག་གི་བདེ་བ་ལྷ་འདྲེར་གཏོང་བ་དང༌། ལྷ་འདྲེའི་སྡུག་བསྔལ་རང་གིས་ལེན་པའོ། ཆོས་ཀྱི་སྟྱིན་པ་ནི། མཐར།

Dharma Samudra   Jigme Lingpa   *Chod Yül*

Having said that, maintain the clarity of the view. Using the transformative power of great compassion, envision giving your happiness in exchange for others' suffering. Give the completely pure gift of the Dharma. Whatever you encounter, whether good or bad, will lead to liberation. **SAMAYA MA MA KO LING SA MANTA**
As for giving and taking happiness and suffering, one's own happiness is given to the demons and their suffering is taken onto oneself. As for the gift of the Dharma, conclude with:

CHÖ NAM THAM CHE JU LE JUNG
Of all things which proceed from a cause

DE JU DE ZHIN SHEG PE SUNG
The Tathagata has explained their cause

JU LE GOG PA GANG YIN PA
And likewise their cessation.

GE JONG CHEN PÖ DI KE SUNG
This is the doctrine of the Great Ascetic.

Say that and:

DIG PA CHI YANG MI JA ZHING
Do not engage in any negative activity.

དགེ་བ་ཕུན་སུམ་ཚོགས་པར་སྤྱད།

GE WA PHÜN SUM TSOG PAR CHE
Practice virtue perfectly.

རང་གི་སེམས་ནི་ཡོངས་སུ་གདུལ།

RANG GI SEM NI YONG SU DÜL
Completely tame your own mind.

འདི་ནི་སངས་རྒྱས་བསྟན་པ་ཡིན།

DI NI SANG JE TEN PA YIN
This is the teaching of the Buddha.

ཞེས་དང་།

Say that and:

འབྱུང་པོ་གང་དག་འདིར་ནི་ལྷགས་གྱུར་ཏམ།

JUNG PO GANG DAG DIR NI LHAG JUR TAM
May the elemental spirits who are living here or visiting,

ས་འམ་འོན་ཏེ་བར་སྣང་འཁོད་ཀྱང་རུང་།

SA AM ÖN TE BAR NANG KHÖ CHANG RUNG
Living on the earth, under it, in the sky, or wherever,

སྐྱེ་དགུ་རྣམས་ལ་རྟག་ཏུ་བྱམས་བྱེད་ཅིང་།

CHE GU NAM LA TAG TU JAM JE CHING
Always be loving towards beings

ཉིན་དང་མཚན་མོ་ཆོས་ལ་སྤྱོད་པར་ཤོག །

NYIN DANG TSEN MO CHÖ LA CHÖ PAR SHOG
And practice the Dharma day and night.

ཅེས་སོགས་ཤིས་བརྗོད་བཟང་པོ་བྱའོ།།

Recite those and other auspicious verses.

Dharma Samudra   Jigme Lingpa   *Chod Yül*

གདངས་རྟ་ནི།
The trumpet melodies are:

ༀ སྦྲང་ལ་རིང་བ་བུང་བའི་སྐད་ལྟ་བུ།
OM Long and pleasing like the humming of a bee.

ཧཱུྃ རྨས་ལ་འཚེར་བ་རྟའི་སྐད་ལྟ་བུ།
HUNG Powerful and dignified like the neighing of a horse.

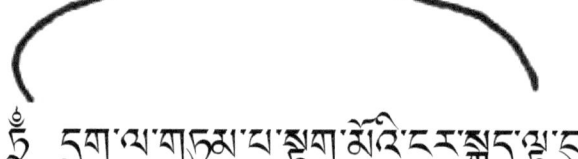

ཧཱུྃ དྲག་ལ་གཅུམ་པ་སྟག་མོའི་ངར་སྐད་ལྟ་བུ།
TRANG Wrathful and cruel like the roar of a tigress.

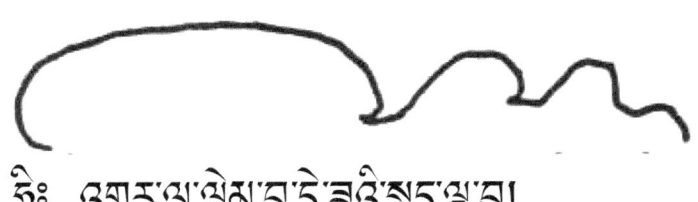

ཧྲཱིཿ འགྱུར་ལ་ཕྱེམ་བ་དྲི་ཟའི་སྐད་ལྟ་བུ།

HRI Moving and vibrating like the voices of gandharvas.

ཨཱཿ འགྱུར་ཕྱེམ་གོང་འདྲ་ནས་གཤམ་འདེགས་ཚམ་བྱེད་པ་ལ་ མཁའ་འགྲོའི་སྒྲུག་གུ་ཟེར། །

AH Moving and vibrating like the last one above, but rising up at the end with what is called the "whistle of the dakinis."

བོད་རྒྱལ་ལོ་ ༢༡༡༨ ལྕགས་མོ་ལུག་ཟླ་ ༥ ཚེས་ ༢༠ ཕྱི་ལོ་ ༡༩༩༡ ཟླ་ ༧ ཚེས་ ༢ ལ་ དེ་འུ་མིག་གི་བོད་ཀྱི་སྔ་འགྱུར་བའི་བདུད་མཚམ་སྦྱོར་བའི་འདུས་སྡེ་དང་གཞན་ཡང་ཕྱོགས་ཀྱི་སློབ་ལྕུན་ ལ་མཁན་ཆེན་དཔལ་ལྡན་ཤེས་རབ་ཀྱིས་ཟབ་ཆོས་འདིའི་ལྗིད་ཀྱི་ཁྲིད་ལུང་གནང་བའི་སྐབས་ དེར་མདོ་ཁམས་རྡོ་ཤུལ་དུ་སྔ་འགྱུར་བའི་བསྟན་ཞབས་སུ་སྨྲེས་པའི་སྐལ་པ་ཅན་དཔའ་གི་ བཙེ་ཚོ་དབང་དོན་རྒྱལ་དང་ཚོས་མཛད་མ་སྟོད་དྲེ་དབང་མོས་བསྒྱུར། སྤྱར་ཡང་དེ་གཉིས་ ཀྱིས་ཞུས་གཏན་ནན་ཁྱལ་བགྱིས་པའི་དགེ་བས་སེམས་ཅན་བདེ་བ་དང་སངས་རྒྱས་བསྟན་ པ་དར་རྒྱས་ཡུན་གནས་དང་ཁྱད་པར་འགྲོ་ཀུན་གྱིས་བདུད་བཞི་ཐད་ཀར་གཅོད་ནས་བརྟུལ་ ཞུགས་ལམ་དུ་ལོངས་པར་ཤོག་ཅིག ཅེས་འགལ་མཆིས་ཀུན་རྩ་གསུམ་དམ་ཅན་དང་ཕྱོགས་ ཀྱི་མོས་ལྡན་སྤྱན་སྔར་འཆགས།

On the twentieth day of the fifth month of the Tibetan Iron Sheep Year, 2118, the second day of the seventh month of the Western year 1991, Khenchen Palden Sherab gave the transmission and practice instructions of this profound teaching to several disciples from the Padmsambhava Buddhist Center of New Mexico and from other places. At that time, Khenpo Tsewang Dongyal, a monk of the Pang family, who had the good fortune to be born among the teachings of the Early Translation school in the area of Doshul in Do Kham, translated this text with the Dharma practitioner Ann Helm. Later, they carefully checked and finalized the translation. By the virtue of doing this, may the happiness of beings and the teachings of the Buddha flourish and continue for a long time. In particular, may all beings directly sever the four demonic forces and accomplish the path of crazy wisdom activity. All faults and mistakes in this translation are confessed in the presence of the Three Roots, samaya-bound protectors, and devoted practitioners.

| Dharma Samudra | Jigme Lingpa | *Chod Yül* |

༄༅། །དཔལ་ལྡན་པདྨ་བསམ་ཡས་གླིང་། །

PALDEN PADMA SAMYE LING
618 BUDDHA HIGHWAY
SIDNEY CENTER, NEW YORK 13839

PADMASAMBHAVA.ORG

༄༅། །མ་གཅིག་ལབ་སྒྲོན་གྱི་བསྐྱེད་རྫོགས་གསོལ་འདེབས་མགུར་མ་བཞུགས་སོ། །

Song of Supplication of the Creation and Completion
Stages of Machig Labdron

By Raga Asye

༄༅། །མ་གཅིག་ལབ་སྒྲོན་གྱི་བསྐྱེད་རྫོགས་གསོལ་འདེབས་མགུར་མ་བཞུགས་སོ། །

Song of Supplication of the Creation and Completion Stages of Machig Labdron

By Raga Asye

Dharma Samudra

**By practicing on this may all sentient beings
achieve the perfect true-nature state of the lama.
May their highest aspirations be fulfilled
for the benefit of all sentient beings.**

© 2019 by Dharma Samudra

All rights reserved

All rights reserved. No part of this material may be reproduced in any form or by any means, electronic or mechanical, including photocopying, recording, or by any information storage and retrieval systems, without prior permission from the authors.

Published by Dharma Samudra

Padmasambhava Buddhist Center
Palden Padma Samye Ling
618 Buddha Highway
Sidney Center, NY 13839
(607) 865-8068

padmasambhava.org

The Song of Supplication of the Creation and Completion Stages of Machig Labdron

NAMO GURU DAKINI YE
Homage to the Guru Dakini!

NE CHI WÖ TSUG GI DRU GANG SA
One cubit over the top of my head,

DEN PE MA NYI DA SUM TSEG TENG
On a three-tiered seat of lotus, sun, and moon

JA Ö PHUNG TRIG PE GUR KHANG NA
Inside a tent radiating masses of light,

RANG DE PA GANG YÖ LA MA DANG
Inseparable from my own Lama, in whom I have faith,

DÖN YER ME PHAG ZHI CHE PE YUM
Is the mother of the four kinds of noble beings,

Dharma Samudra   Raga Asye   *Song of Supplication of Machig Labdron*

MA LAB CHI DRÖN MA KU DOG KAR
The white Machig Labdron.

U RAL PA SIL BÜ KU JAB NÖN
Her hair, loose, falls on her back, and

ZHAL ZHI DZUM CHEN SUM NAM KHA ZIG
With a smiling face, she gazes into space with her three eyes.

KU DAR KAR PHÖ KA LUNG GI CHÖ
She wears a deep-sleeved gown of white silk which flaps in the wind,

KU KE PAR DAR MAR KE RAG CHING
And a red belt is tied around her waist.

ZHAB DOR JE CHIL MO TRUNG GI ZHUG
Her legs are folded in the vajra posture, and

THUG DA TENG AH YIG NGAG CHI KOR
At her heart, on a moon, is the syllable AH surrounded by the mantra.

CHAG YE PE SER JI DA MA RU
Her right hand beats a golden damaru,

Dharma Samudra   Raga Asye   *Song of Supplication of Machig Labdron*
2

དེ་འགྲོལ་བས་སྟོང་གསུམ་སྒྲ་ཡིས་གང་། །
DE TRÖL WE TONG SUM DRA YI GANG
Filling the three thousand universes with its sound.

གནས་འོག་མིན་ཆོས་དབྱིངས་ཞིང་ཁམས་ནས། །
NE OG MIN CHÖ YING ZHING KHAM NE
From the realm of dharmadhatu, Akanishtha,

སྲས་སངས་རྒྱས་བྱང་སེམས་རྒྱ་མཚོའི་ཚོགས། །
SE SANG JE JANG SEM JA TSÖ TSOG
Hosts of her sons and daughters, oceans of buddhas and bodhisattvas

དཔེ་ཤོག་ཆ་རླུང་གིས་བསྐྱོད་བཞིན་བྱོན། །
PE SHOG CHA LUNG GI CHÖ ZHIN JÖN
Arrive as leaves swirling in the wind,

དེ་ཐམས་ཅད་མ་གཅིག་སྐུ་ལ་ཐིམ། །
DE THAM CHE MA CHIG KU LA THIM
And all dissolve into her body.

ཕྱག་གཡོན་པས་དངུལ་དཀར་དྲིལ་བུ་ལ། །
CHAG YÖN PE NGUL KAR DRIL BU LA
Her left hand holds a bell of white silver

དེ་སིལ་སིལ་སྒྲ་ཡིས་ཕྱོགས་བཅུར་གང་། །
DE SIL SIL GRA YI CHOG CHUR GANG
Whose tinkling sound fills the ten directions.

གནས་ཉི་ཤུ་རྩ་བཞིའི་མཁའ་འགྲོའི་ཚོགས། །
NE NYI SHU TSA ZHI KHAN DRÖ TSOG
Hosts of dakinis of the twenty-four places

Dharma Samudra   Raga Asye   *Song of Supplication of Machig Labdron*

PE KHA WA BU YUG TSUB ZHIN JÖN
Arrive as snowflakes in a blizzard,

DE THAM CHE YUM JI KU LA THIM
And all dissolve into the mother's body.

CHAB KÜN DÜ MA CHIG LAB DRÖN MA
Machig Labdron, you who unite all the objects of refuge,

NYING RÜ PE TENG NE SÖL WA DEB
I pray to you from the depths of my heart!

LÜ THOB KA DAL JOR RIN CHEN DI
Grant me your blessings so that I may use well

DAG NYING PO LÖN PAR JIN JI LOB
This precious body of freedoms and endowments so difficult to obtain.

DRA CHI DAG NAM ONG CHA ME PE
Since my enemy, the Lord of Death, will come without warning,

LO JÖ ME DRUB PAR JIN JI LOB
Bless me to achieve a regretless mind.

| Dharma Samudra | Raga Asye | Song of Supplication of Machig Labdron |

ཁོང་ཆོས་ཀྱི་རྒྱལ་པོའི་ཁྲིམས་ར་ནས། །

KHONG CHÖ CHI JAL PÖ TRIM RA NE
In the court of the King of Karma

རང་ངོ་གནོང་མེད་པར་བྱིན་གྱིས་རློབས། །

RANG NGO NONG ME PAR JIN JI LOB
Bless me so that I may not feel that I failed.

གནས་རིགས་དྲུག་གང་དུ་སྐྱེས་ཀྱང་རུ། །

NE RIG DRUG GANG DU CHE CHANG RU
Of any of the six realms where I may be born,

དེ་སྐྱེ་སྒོ་ཆོད་པར་བྱིན་གྱིས་རློབས། །

DE CHE GO CHÖ PAR JIN JI LOB
Bless me so that I may cut the entranceway.

སྐྱབས་མི་བསླུ་བདེན་པ་དཀོན་མཆོག་གསུམ། །

CHAB MI LU NGE PA KÖN CHOG SUM
The Three Jewels are without doubt an infallible refuge:

སེམས་ཡིད་ཆེས་སྐྱེ་བར་བྱིན་གྱིས་རློབས། །

SEM YI CHE CHE WAR JIN JI LOB
Bless me that I may develop confidence in them.

མ་འགྲོ་དྲུག་ཕ་མ་དྲིན་ཅན་ལ། །

MA DRO DRUB PHA MA DRIN CHEN LA
Bless me so that I may give rise to love and compassion

བྱམས་སྙིང་རྗེ་སྐྱེ་བར་བྱིན་གྱིས་རློབས། །

JAM NYING JE CHE WAR JIN JI LOB
Towards my mothers of the six realms, as kind as parents.

Dharma Samudra   Raga Asye   *Song of Supplication of Machig Labdron*

DÖN RANG SEM CHÖ KU JEN PA LA
My own mind is really the naked dharmakaya:

DE TEN PA THOB PAR JIN JI LOB
Bless me so that I may reach stability in it.

MA LAB CHI DRÖN ME KU SUNG THUG
The body, speech, and mind of Machig Labdron,

PE CHU LA CHU ZHAG CHI ZHIN DU
Just as water settles into water,

DE DAG DANG YER ME CHIG JUR NE
Become inseparably one with mine.

GANG DREL TSE DE CHEN DREN PAR SHOG
Hence, may I lead whoever I meet to great bliss!

DAG DE TAR SÖL WA TAB PE THÜ
By the power of such a prayer,

MA YUM CHEN Ö ZHU DAG LA THIM
The great mother melts into light and dissolves into oneself.

Dharma Samudra　　Raga Asye　　*Song of Supplication of Machig Labdron*

DÖN RANG SEM TRÖ DREL JEN PAR BÜ
Only one's own naked mind, free from elaborations, is left.

DA TSUR TÖ RANG GI SEM LA TÖ
Now look inwards, look to your own mind.

SEM TE PE MI THONG NGÖ PO NI
Looking at your mind, there is nothing to see.

CHÖ TONG PA NYI DE RANG GI SEM
Things are phenomena-emptiness, and that is your own mind.

SEM ME PA MA YIN CHI YANG CHAR
It is not an absence of mind: whatever arises,

CHÖ RIG PE YE SHE RANG GI SEM
Phenomena as primordial awareness, is your own mind.

SEM DE NA DE WE NGO WOR TÖ
If your mind feels blissful, look at the essence of bliss.

CHÖ DE TONG CHAG JA CHEN PO YIN
Phenomena as bliss-emptiness are Mahamudra.

Dharma Samudra   Raga Asye   *Song of Supplication of Machig Labdron*

སེམས་གསལ་ན་གསལ་བའི་ངོ་བོར་ལྟོས། །
SEM SAL NA SAL WE NGO WOR TÖ
If your mind is clear, look at the essence of clarity.

ཆོས་གསལ་སྟོང་ཕྱག་རྒྱ་ཆེན་པོ་ཡིན། །
CHÖ SAL TONG CHAG JA CHEN PO YIN
Phenomena as clarity-emptiness are Mahamudra.

སེམས་སྟོང་ན་སྟོང་པའི་ངོ་བོར་ལྟོས། །
SEM TONG NA TONG PE NGO WOR TÖ
If your mind is empty, look at the essence of emptiness:

ཆོས་མི་རྟོག་ཕྱག་རྒྱ་ཆེན་པོ་ཡིན། །
CHÖ MI TOG CHAG JA CHEN PO YIN
Phenomena without concepts are Mahamudra.

ཚུར་བལྟས་པས་མཐོང་རྒྱུ་ཅི་ཡང་མེད། །
TSUR TE PE THONG JU CHI YANG ME
Looking inwardly, there is nothing to see whatsoever.

ཆོས་ཐ་མལ་ཤེས་པ་རྗེན་པར་བུད། །
CHÖ THA MAL SHE PA JEN PAR BÜ
There is nothing else than the naked, ordinary awareness of phenomena.

ཕར་བལྟས་པས་ཐམས་ཅད་འཇའ་ཚོན་བཞིན། །
PHAR TE PE THAM CHE JA TSÖN ZHIN
Looking outwardly, everything is like a rainbow.

གཟུགས་སོ་སོར་གསལ་ཡང་ངོ་བོར་སྟོང་། །
ZUG SO SOR SAL YANG NGO WOR TONG
Every form appears yet is empty by nature:

Dharma Samudra   Raga Asye   *Song of Supplication of Machig Labdron*

ཆོས་སྣང་སྲིད་སྒྱུ་མའི་རང་བཞིན་ཡིན། །
CHÖ NANG SI JU ME RANG ZHIN YIN
Phenomena are the universe of illusory nature.

སེམས་དུག་ལྔའི་རྟོག་པ་ཅི་ཤར་ཡང་། །
SEM DUG NGE TOG PA CHI SHAR YANG
Whatever thought of the five poisons arises in the mind

དེ་རང་ངོ་བལྟས་པས་རང་སར་ཞི། །
DE RANG NGO TE PE RANG SAR ZHI
Is pacified in itself by looking directly at its essence.

ཆོས་དུག་ལྔ་རང་གྲོལ་གདམས་ངག་ཡིན། །
CHÖ DUG NGA RANG DRÖL DAM NGAG YIN
This is the special instruction for the self-liberation of the five poisons.

སེམས་ཀྱི་དུག་སྣང་བ་ཅི་ཤར་ཡང་། །
SEM CHI DUG NANG WA CHI SHAR YANG
Whatever pleasant or unpleasant appearance arises in the mind

དེ་རང་ངོ་བལྟས་པས་རང་སར་ཞི། །
DE RANG NGO TE PE RANG SAR ZHI
Is pacified in itself by looking directly at its essence.

ཆོས་རོ་སྙོམས་ཕྱག་རྒྱ་ཆེན་པོ་ཡིན། །
CHÖ RO NYOM CHAG JA CHEN PO YIN
Phenomena of equal taste are Mahamudra.

སེམས་སྐྲག་སྣང་སྣ་ཚོགས་ཅི་ཤར་ཡང་། །
SEM TRAG NANG NA TSOG CHI SHAR YANG
Whatever fearful appearances arise in the mind

Dharma Samudra   Raga Asye   *Song of Supplication of Machig Labdron*

དེ་ངོ་བོར་བལྟས་པས་རང་སར་ཞི། །
DE NGO BOR TE PE RANG SAR ZHI
Are pacified in themselves by looking directly at their essence.

ཆོས་གཅོད་ཡུལ་ཕྱག་རྒྱ་ཆེན་པོ་ཡིན། །
CHÖ CHÖ YUL CHAG JA CHEN PO YIN
Phenomena to be cut by Chod are Mahamudra.

སེམས་སྡུག་བསྔལ་སྣང་བ་ཅི་ཤར་ཡང་། །
SEM DUG NGAL NANG WA CHI SHAR YANG
Whatever painful appearances arise in the mind

དེ་ངོ་བོར་བལྟས་པས་རང་སར་ཞི། །
DE NGO BOR TE PE RANG SAR ZHI
Are pacified in themselves by looking directly at their essence.

དེ་དམ་ཆོས་སྡུག་བསྔལ་ཞི་བྱེད་ཡིན། །
DE DAM CHÖ DUG NGAL ZHI JE YIN
This is the holy Dharma that pacifies suffering.

སེམས་ཡོད་མེད་རྟག་ཆད་ཀུན་དང་བྲལ། །
SEM YÖ ME TAG CHE KÜN DANG DRAL
Mind is free from all extremes of existence, nonexistence, permanence, and annihilation.

དེ་དམ་ཆོས་དབུ་མ་ཆེན་པོ་ཡིན། །
DE DAM CHÖ U MA CHEN PO YIN
This is the holy Dharma of the Great Madhyamaka.

Dharma Samudra   Raga Asye   *Song of Supplication of Machig Labdron*
10

དེ་སེམས་ལ་མ་རྫོགས་ཆོས་གཅིག་མེད། །

DE SEM LA MA DZOG CHÖ CHIG ME
There is not a single phenomenon that is not perfect in mind.

དེ་དམ་ཆོས་རྫོགས་པ་ཆེན་པོ་ཡིན། །

DE DAM CHÖ DZOG PA CHEN PO YIN
This is the holy teaching of the Great Perfection.

ཡར་རྒྱལ་བའི་ཐུགས་དང་རང་གི་སེམས། །

YAR JAL WE THUG DANG RANG GI SEM
The mind of the high Victorious Ones, one's own mind,

མར་འགྲོ་དྲུག་སེམས་རྣམས་ངོ་བོ་གཅིག །

MAR DRO DRUG SEM NAM NGO WO CHIG
And that of the low beings of the six realms are of a single essence.

དེ་ལྟ་བ་འཁོར་འདས་དབྱེར་མེད་ཡིན། །

DE TA BA KHOR DE YER ME YIN
Thus samsara and nirvana are inseparable.

སེམས་འདི་བསྒོམ་གཏད་སོ་མེད་པར་ཞོག །

SEM DI GOM TE SO ME PAR ZHOG
Without focused meditation, rest in this mind:

དེ་ཐ་མལ་ཤེས་པ་རྗེན་པ་ཡིན། །

DE THA MAL SHE PA JEN PA YIN
It is naked ordinary awareness.

སེམས་བལྟ་བྱ་ལྟ་བྱེད་མེད་པར་ཞོག །

SEM TA JA TA JE ME PAR ZHOG
Rest in this mind, without looker or thing to look at:

Dharma Samudra   Raga Asye   *Song of Supplication of Machig Labdron*

དེ་ཕྱག་རྒྱ་ཆེན་པོའི་ཉམས་ལེན་ཡིན། །
DE CHAG JA CHEN PÖ NYAM LEN YIN
That's the practice of Mahamudra.

ཆོས་ལྟ་བ་སྤྱོད་པ་མ་བསླད་པ། །
CHÖ TA WA CHÖ PA MA LE PA
Dharma is undefiled view and conduct:

རང་སྡོམ་གསུམ་མིག་འབྲས་ལྟ་བུར་སྲུངས། །
RANG DOM SUM MIG RE TA BUR SUNG
Protect the three vows as your eyeballs.

དེ་བཀའ་ཕྱག་ཆུ་བོ་གཉིས་འདྲེས་ཡིན། །
DE KA CHAG CHU WO NYI RE YIN
This is the convergence of the two rivers of the Kadampa and Mahamudra traditions.

དོན་རང་སེམས་བརྟན་པ་ཐོབ་པ་ཡིན། །
DÖN RANG SEM TEN PA THOOB PA YIN
The attainment of stability in one's own true mind

དེ་འབྲས་བུའི་མིང་དུ་བཏགས་པ་ཡིན། །
DE DRE BÜ MING DU TAG PA YIN
Is given the name "result,"

ཆོས་གསང་སྔགས་ལུགས་ཀྱི་འབྲས་བུ་ཡིན། །
CHÖ SANG NGAG LUG CHI DRE BU YIN
The result of the Dharma of Secret Mantra.

| Dharma Samudra | Raga Asye | *Song of Supplication of Machig Labdron* |

12

ཆོས་བཅུ་གསུམ་མར་མེའི་དོགས་ལ་བྲིས། །ཁྱེད་ཚོ་གཅིག་སྒྲུབ་པའི་སྙིང་དུས་ཅན། མ་
ལབ་སྒྲོན་བརྒྱུད་འཛིན་རྟོ་མོ་དེས། མི་ད་ལ་དད་སྟེན་བསྐུར་ཞེར་བས། ཚིག་དེ་ལ་དད་ལྡན་
ཐུགས་དམ་མཛོད། ཅེས་ཡོལ་སྟོད་ཆོས་རིའི་སྐྱ་རགས། ར་ག་ཨ་སྱས་ཤོ་གུ་རི་ཕུག་ནས་རྟོ་
མོ་ལ་སྦྱེལ་བ་དགེའོ། མངྒ་ལཾ།

On the thirteenth day this was written by the light of a butter lamp. "The nun who holds the lineage of Machig Labdron and who has the heartfelt wish to attain realization in one life, requested me to send a support of devotion. Make these words your dedicated heart practice!" In the cave of Shogu this was sent to the nun by Raga Asye of Yoltö Chöri. May it bring virtue! Mangalam!

།བླ་མ་འཆི་མེད་ཐུགས་དམ་དང་། །ཕྱག་བྲིས་དཔེ་ལས་ཕི་ལིབ་ཀྱིས། །བཤུས་བསྒྱུར་
མཛད་དགེས་བསོད་ནམས་ཀྱིས། །ཡུམ་ཆེན་ཤེར་ཕྱིན་འགྲུབ་གྱུར་ཅིག །

This heart practice of Lama Chimed was copied and translated from his manuscript by Philippe Turrenne. By the merit of this virtuous activity may all realize the state of the Great Mother Prajnaparamita! (This colophon was written by Ven. Khenchen Palden Sherab Rinpoche and Ven. Khenpo Tsewang Dongyal Rinpoche.)

Endnotes

[1] Mahayana is a Sanskrit term that can be translated as "Great Path." Its goal is the benefit of both self and others; more specifically, it is to attain enlightenment in order to help liberate all other sentient beings from the sufferings of samsara.

[2] The Sutra Mahayana is the portion of the teachings that were spoken by the Buddha directly to assemblies of students, and in the most general terms, relating to the practice of meditation.

[3] The Tantra Mahayana is based on texts called tantras. It shares the same goal as the Sutra Mahayana, but utilizes a very wide range of physical and mental techniques, called "skillful means," to bring rapid realization of the ultimate nature.

[4] A series of more than thirty sutras, of widely varying length, all of which establish the view of the inherent emptiness of self and phenomena, which is then realized through philosophical study, logic analysis, and meditation.

[5] Dzogchen [Tib.] or Atiyoga [Skt.], which can be translated as "Great Perfection," is the highest of the Inner Tantras.

[6] Guru Padmasambhava is the great realized being who is recognized in Tibetan Buddhism as the immediate rebirth of Buddha Shakyamuni, and the source of all of the Buddha's

teachings in Tibet. He is the root guru of practitioners in Nyingma lineages.

[7] The term 'vajra' is Sanskrit; it corresponds to the Tibetan *dorje*. It can mean many things depending on the context. Here, it means "indestructible" or "unshakeable."

[8] Kaya [Skt.] or *ku* [Tib. sku] literally means "body." Yet when it's used to describe enlightened beings, it becomes very difficult to translate. It signifies something like "dimension," "field [of energy, activity]," or "basis."

[9] The name Prajnaparamita can be used to designate the enlightened quality of transcendental wisdom, as well as a group of sutras that expound this wisdom. Here, the term is being used as a name for a dharmakaya buddha.

[10] Each "poison" is the obscured energy of one of the "wisdoms." For example, the poison of pride or arrogance is an obscured energy. Its pure energy is the wisdom of equanimity, which sees all phenomena as equal in perfection.

[11] Akanishtha [Skt.] or *Ogmin* [Tib. 'og min] can be translated as "none higher," indicating the highest state of realization.

[12] Terma [gter ma] literally means "hidden treasure." In the Nyingma tradition, these are teachings that originated from the mind of Guru Padmasambhava, were transcribed by Yeshe Tsogyal, and then hidden by them in many areas. The stated purpose of this system of transmitting the teachings is to preserve the integrity of the teaching, and make it available in a fresh form to students of later generations as needed. Terma are not rediscovered

randomly: each terma has an intended revealer, known as a terton.

[13] This number is based on the ancient system of counting years, in which each solar year is equal to two lunar years.

[14] The attainment of the highest state of enlightenment in this life is called the "transcendental wisdom rainbow body" [Tib. 'ja 'lus], which is achieved by fully accomplished Dzogchen practitioners at the time of death. They dissolve the elements of the body into rainbow light.

[15] *Wang*, *lung*, and *tri* are the three components that are required in order to begin practicing any Vajrayana practice. They must be conferred by a qualified vajra master.

[16] Siddhas are individuals, male and female, who have completely mastered the tantric practices of the Vajrayana.

[17] Nagarjuna (c. 150–250 CE) was one of the six great commentators, or the "Six Ornaments" of the Buddha's teachings. His teachings, which mainly employ subtle and sophisticated reasoning, provide the foundation for the Madhyamaka school, which propounds the Middle Way philosophy. Nagarjuna was also connected to the nagas— powerful, god-like serpent beings—and he received the hidden Prajnaparamita sutras from them. The nagas were charged with protecting these sutras for future times.

[18] Asanga was a famous Indian master who lived in the 4th century CE. He received sutra teachings directly from the Future Buddha Maitreya, and transcribed them as the *Five Treatises of Maitreya*. These became the foundation of

the Mind Only philosophical school, which is known as *Chittamatra* in Sanskrit, and *Yogachara* in Tibetan.

[19] The Madhyamaka or "Middle Way" philosophical school teaches freedom from all extremes, which was succinctly laid out in Nagarjuna's verse at the end of the *Heart Sutra* practice: "Unceasing and unborn; neither nonexistent nor everlasting; neither coming nor going; neither several in meaning nor with a single meaning."

[20] A Mahayana school founded by Asanga. Its view is that all phenomena are merely mind—habitual tendencies stored in the alaya consciousness of an individual mindstream, manifesting as one's physical body, external objects, and environment.

[21] The eight great vidyadharas were Vimalamitra, Humkara, Manjushrimitra, Nagarjuna, Prabhahasti, Dhanasamskrita, Shantigarbha, and Rombuguhya, with Guru Padmasambhava often being considered the ninth vidyadhara.

[22] The eighty-four mahasiddhas were ancient Indian tantric masters, including Nagarjuna. Their life stories were recounted by Abhayadatta. For a complete list, along with the very interesting translations of the meanings of their Sanskrit names, refer to rigpawiki.org.

[23] A conceptual framework based on the idea that there is an "I" that is separate from an "other," a "higher" from a "lower," or any dualistic separation of existing entities.

[24] There were two famous masters with this name in the history of Chod. Aryadeva (3rd century) was Nagarjuna's

foremost student and considered the co-founder of the Madhyamaka school. Another master, referred to as "Aryadeva the Brahmin" was active in India in the 9th century. He is the author of the text referred to below.

[25] The new wave of translations that were being made of Indian sutra and tantra teachings, beginning in the later ninth century, became the focus for the development of a number of "New," or *Sarma* schools of practice in Tibet. The Sakya and Kadampa schools emerged, along with several Kagyu schools and the Shije and Chod schools. It was at this point that the Ancient Tradition acquired the name *Nyingma*, which means "Old."

[26] A *dorje lobpon* is a qualified Vajrayana master, the spiritual authority who gives empowerment, transmits the teachings, and leads Vajrayana practices.

[27] Samye [bsam yas] Monastery, which means "inconceivable," was the first monastery built in Tibet in the 8th century. King Trisong Deutsen sponsored the building process, Guru Padmasambhava subdued the demons that were obstructing the construction, and Khenpo Shantarakshita became the first abbot.

[28] In Tibetan this individual is called the *dorje chopon* [rdo rje mchod dpon]—the one who performs the ritual actions such as arranging the shrine and making the offerings.

[29] Vajrapani is one of the eight great bodhisattvas. He embodies the power of the buddhas, and is known as the "Lord of the Secrets." He is especially responsible for the transmission of Tantras to the human realm.

[30] The first volume contains instructions on Calm Abiding meditation, the second, instructions on meditation and conduct, and the third, instructions on meditation with the result.

[31] Nyangral Nyima Ozer (1124–1192) was a mind emanation of King Trisong Deutsen and the first of the "five sovereign tertons." He revealed many termas, including a dakini terma cycle of Troma Nagmo.

[32] The twenty-fifth day of each lunar month is celebrated as the Day of the Dakinis, with an appropriate practice and offerings.

[33] AH is the seed syllable of Prajnaparamita.

[34] The four syllables of HA RA NI SA represent the wisdom dakinis of the four directions. Machig Labdron herself is the wisdom dakini of the central direction.

[35] Gugul, or guggulua, is a common incense ingredient also called myrrh, or dhoop in India. It is made from the sap of the *Commiphora* tree.

[36] This was an indication of the emergence of the dakini's third eye.

[37] The third eye is a defining mark of a dakini, as well as of other semi-wrathful and wrathful enlightened beings.

[38] Pechas are traditional woodblock printed books, with wide, short pages, wrapped in special cloths, and stored in specially constructed pigeonhole bookcases, often as part of a shrine itself.

[39] It is traditional for Tibetans, especially masters of the Dharma, to be given a succession of names as they progress through different levels of ordination and realization.

[40] Drapa Ngonshe [grwa pa mngon shes] received his ordination at Samye Monastery. During his years as a monastic, he gave Machig Labdron and her sister their vows, and then taught the Prajnaparamita to Machig Labdron. Later in life, he returned his monastic vows and became a great terton. He is particularly renowned for revealing the *Four Medical Tantras* [gyud zhi], which are the foundational scriptures of Tibetan medicine. In his later years, he also received the Shije teachings from Padampa Sangye and the Chod teachings from Machig Labdron.

[41] Highly enlightened beings appear in the human realm by choice, having formed aspirations to help all sentient beings. Machig Labdron is proclaiming her intention to fulfill her promises.

[42] Choton Sonam Lama's [skyo ston bsod nams bla ma, dates unknown] elder brother was Zurpoche Shakya Jungne, one of great masters named "Zur" in our lineage prayers.

[43] "Little nun" is an affectionate and respectful diminutive.

[44] *Tho* [thod pa] means "forehead"—or in this context, "skullcup"—and *bhadra* means "excellent," "great," "beautiful," and "skillful."

[45] This describes the semi-wrathful countenance of a powerful realized yogi.

[46] *Tendrel* [rten 'brel] refers to interdependent origination,

"coincidence," and the interlinked causes and conditions that come together to produce an event. By carefully considering these, the result of an action may be discovered.

[47] According to many histories, Topa Bhadra took the children with him and supervised their early training. He returned to Tibet, bringing Drupse and Drupchungma to their mother when she was forty-two. Both children were already well trained, and ready to receive Machig Labdron's instructions. Drupse, whose tantric name was Tonyon Samdrup, became the holder of her Dharma lineage.

[48] The "Red Copper Castle" [Zangs ri mkhar dmar] is a red rock at the southern point of the Copper Mountain overlooking the Tsangpo River. Machig Labdron lived in a meditation cave nearby for most of the rest of her life.

[49] Pandita is a Sanskrit term for a learned master. In Tibet, *khepa* [mkhas pa] signifies a master learned in the traditional "five sciences" curriculum.

[50] Until this time, all "official" Dharma transmission had been one-way: from India to Tibet, and thus from Sanskrit to Tibetan.

[51] Shugseb Jetsun Rinpoche founded the Shugsep [shug gseb] Nunnery located thirty miles from Lhasa on the slopes of Mount Gangri Thokar. This nunnery, now re-established in India, upholds the practice of the Nyingma traditions of Chod.

[52] *The Hundred-fold Dialogue of the Dakini* [mkha' 'gro'i zhu lan brgya rtsa].

[53] *From the Cycle of the Great Compassionate One Overcoming*

Samsara and Nirvana: The Condensed Offering of the Illusory Body [thugs rje chen po 'khor 'das zil gnon las sgyu lus mchod sbyin bsdus pa bzhugs so].

[54] *From the Heart Essence of Longchenpa: The Bellowing Laugh of the Dakini* [klong chen snying gi thig le las gcod yul mkha' 'gro'i gad rgyangs bzhugs].

[55] T*roma Nagmo: A Practice Cycle for Realization of the Wrathful Black Dakini*, is Dudjom Lingpa's Troma cycle, and is an exceptional terma in that it is a complete path of Vajrayana, containing all the practices from Ngondro through to the Dzogchen practices of Trekcho and Togal.

[56] Raga Asye (1613–1678), who is also known by his Tibetan name Karma Chagme, was one of the most highly realized and accomplished scholars and yogis. He was a member of a branch of the Karma Kagyu school in eastern Tibet called Neydo Kagyu [gnas mdo bka' brgyud], which was closely linked with the Nyingma. He studied with the most famous Nyingma and Kagyu masters of his time.

[57] *The Precious Garland: A Collection on Chod* [gcod tshogs las rin chen 'phreng ba].

[58] Sangphu Neuthog [gsang phu ne'u thog] was the most famous monastic college of its time, with masters of many lineages. Thus Longchenpa had the opportunity to receive great scholarly knowledge from Kadam, Sakya, and Kagyu masters. He found monastic life difficult, however, and left for the hermitage life fairly soon.

[59] Rigdzin Kumaradza was an austere, nomadic yogi who

practiced and taught the Dzogchen teachings in the lineage of Vimalamitra. He was also one of the masters of the great Third Karmapa, Rangjung Dorje.

[60] Samye Chimphu [bsam yas chims phu] was the sacred place of Guru Padmasambhava's speech. It is a mountain retreat situated four hours walk above Samye Monastery. During the last twelve centuries, numerous great masters have meditated in the caves at this hermitage.

[61] The *Seven Treasuries*, or *Dzod Dun* [mdzod bdun], are Longchenpa's most famous works. They present the whole of Buddhist thought from a *Nyingthig* viewpoint. The *Ngalso Korsum* (*Trilogy of Comfort and Ease*) and the *Rangdrol Korsum* (*Trilogy of Self-Liberation*) provide in-depth introductions to Dzogchen.

[62] He was also responsible for the publication of the Derge version of the "Collection of Nyingma Tantras," or *Nyingma Gyudbum*, having collected and preserved many rare texts and compiled them with the earlier collection of Ratna Lingpa. Without this activity, most of the Early Translation school texts would have been lost.

[63] The five aggregates [phung po lnga] taught by Buddha Shakyamuni and chanted in the *Heart Sutra*, are form, feeling, perception, mental formation, and consciousness. They exhaustively encompass every thing that we associate with the body, and every thing that we associate with the mind.

[64] *Bardo* literally means "between." Here it specifically refers to the "bardo of becoming," [srid pa'i bar do]—the period during which our mindstream, having separated from our

body, makes the challenging transition to the next lifetime. This is one of six bardo experiences in one's lifetime.

[65] The Tibetan names for these four are (1) the tangible demon [thogs bcas bdud], (2) intangible demon [thogs med bdud], (3) exhilaration demon [dga' brod bdud], and (4) arrogance demon [snyems byed kyi bdud].

[66] Chandrakirti was a famous Indian scholar and master associated with Nalanda Monastic University, who taught according to the Prasangika Madhyamaka philosophical school.

[67] This marks the beginning of the generation stage, or *kyerim* [bskyed rim]. We are instructed to visualize ourself as the wisdom dakini. We remain in this visualization stage until page 16.

[68] It has twenty-four principal spots of the dakinis, and "Eight Great Cemeterics." In the Venerable Khenpo Rinpoches' book *Key to Opening the Wisdom Door of Anuyoga*, the twenty-four principal spots are listed as: (1) Zalendara; (2) Pullima-malaya; (3) Arbuta; (4) Rameshvara; (5) Oddiyana; (6) Godavari; (7) Devikota; (8) Molava; (9) Lampaka; (10) Kamarupa; (11) Odra; (12) Trishanku; (13) Koshala; (14) Kalinga; (15) Kanchika; (16) Himalaya; (17) Pretapuri; (18) Grihadevata; (19) Maru; (20) Saurashtra; (21) Suvarnadvipa; (22) Nagara; (23) Kulanta; and (24) Sindhu.

The eight charnel grounds for the wrathful mandala are listed as:

(1) Most Fierce [shar du gtum drag], in the east

(2) Endowed with Skeletons [lhor keng rus can], in the south
(3) Blazing Vajra [nub tu rdo rje 'bar ba], in the west
(4) Dense Thicket [byang du tshang tshing 'khrigs pa], in the north
(5) Auspicious Grove [mer bkra shis tshal], in the southeast
(6) Black Darkness [mun pa nag po], in the southwest
(7) Resonant with "Kilikili" [rlung du ki li ki li'i sgra sgrog pa], in the northwest
(8) Wild Cries of "Ha Ha" [ha ha rgod pa], in the northeast

[69] The vajra is found in two major designs. The more common five-pointed vajra, usually paired with the bell in Vajrayana practices, is generally used. The nine-pointed vajra visualized here is used only during practice on wrathful deities.

[70] Bodhgaya, once a small village on the bank of the Nairanjana River, was where Buddha Shakyamuni attained enlightenment. Nowadays it is the center of the pilgrimage route for Buddhists from all traditions.

[71] The Tibetan text is composed in several specific poetic meters: here the meter is the "Flying Garuda." This metrical structure makes it possible to incorporate dance with the chanted text in a dignified style. Translations into other languages, to date, lack a regular meter to which a dance may be fitted.

[72] Generally, when reading or reciting in English, it is appropriate to use either Sanskrit term 'yogi' or 'yogini'— whichever applies to oneself. The Tibetan word *naljor* [rnal 'byor] is not gender specific. However, it was frequently taken to indicate a male practitioner, as in the translation here. The Tibetan word *naljorma*, denotes a female practitioner, and

has one additional syllable that cannot be freely substituted without changing the poetic meter.

⁷³ Traditionally, Tibetan dance would be performed outdoors, in a courtyard, or out in a field. Khenpo Tsewang Rinpoche is using the "nightclub" analogy because Western students tend to think of dancing in an indoor space.

⁷⁴ ཨ༔ The thigle on the top represents the element of space. The half-moon below it represents the air element. The HA syllable represents fire. The 'a syllable represents water. And the vowel mark at the bottom represents earth.

⁷⁵ Samaya vows are oaths or pledges to keep and maintain specific practices, usually but not always received at the time of receiving a tantric empowerment. Yogis and yoginis must keep the vows they have chosen to take.

⁷⁶ In Tibetan Buddhist teachings, ghosts are held to "exist" no more and no less than any other aspects of the phenomenal world. The term used here is *dre* ['dre], which can mean both a ghost and a demon. It can also be the spirit of a dead person, an imp, an evil spirit, or a devil. For an extensive categorization of *dre*, see the *Riwo Sang Chod* fire puja sadhana published by Dharma Samudra on pages 9 and 10. Other related and overlapping terms are *shin* [gshin], which means the "dead;" *dud* [bdud] means "mara" or "demon;" and *sin* [srin], which means "cannibal demon" or "raksha."

⁷⁷ Garab Dorje's [Tib.; dga' rab rdo rje] name in Sanskrit is Surati Vajra, which literally means "Indestructible Joy." He is also referred to as Prahevajra and Pramodavajra. Garab Dorje was the first human vidyadhara in the Dzogchen lineage.

He was immaculately conceived and born to the daughter of King Uparaja (Indrabhuti) of Oddiyana. Garab Dorje received all the scriptures, tantras, and oral instructions of Dzogchen from Vajrasattva and Vajrapani in person. Having achieved complete enlightenment through the effortless path of the Great Perfection, Garab Dorje transmitted his teachings to Manjushrimitra. Guru Padmasambhava also received teachings from the wisdom form of Garab Dorje.

[78] The khatvanga is a tantric implement of Indian origin with very complex symbolism. It is usually shown as a tall staff topped with a trident and five-colored ribbons. It is one of the major attributes of Guru Padmasambhava, as well as his dakini consorts Yeshe Tsogyal and Mandarava.

[79] The Tibetan *jetsun* or *jetsunma* are honorific Tibetan terms applied to revered teachers and great saints and lamas.

[80] Vajravarahi, Dorje Phagmo [rdo rje phag mo], or "Diamond Sow" is the root of all emanations of dakinis. She is also a female deity who is the consort of Hayagriva and Chakrasamvara. She may be depicted as black or red in color, and has a small sow's head protruding from her head.

[81] For rhythmical repetition of the chant, the Tibetan syllable DANG is sometimes inserted, as OM AH HUNG dang HA HO HRI. DANG means "and."

[82] Atsaras in this story are irritating, harmful spirits. The term may be a variation of the Indian language "*apsara*," which typically refers to a seductive female spirit sent to distract ascetics.

[83] This is a simple version of the Dependent Origination mantra.

[84] This familiar verse concludes many chanting practices.

[85] *Riwo Sang Chod*, page 20.

[86] *Dudjom Tersar Ngondro* [ngag don du pa zhug], page 37.

[87] The text offers the translation, "Behold the emptiness-awareness, the true face of the lama!"

[88] *Dudjom Tersar Ngondro*, page 42.

BIBLIOGRAPHY

Nyoshul Khenpo Jamyang Dorje 2005. *A Marvelous Garland of Rare Gems: Biographies of Masters of Awareness in the Dzogchen Lineage*. Richard Barron, translator, Padma Publishing, Junction City, CA.

Sangye, Padampa, *Lion of the Siddhas: The Life and Teachings of Padampa Sangye*, 2008. Translated and edited by David Molk with Lama Tsering Wangdu Rinpoche. Snow Lion Publications, Ithaca, NY.

Gyatso, Janet, 1998. *Apparitions of the Self: The Secret Autobiographies of a Tibetan Visionary*. Princeton University Press, Princeton, NJ.

Edou, Jérôme, 1996, *Machig Labdron and the Foundations of Chod*. Snow Lion, Boston and London.

Allione, Tsultrim, 1984. *Women of Wisdom*. Arkana Publications, London and New York.

Simmer-Brown, Judith, 2001. *Dakini's Warm Breath: The Feminine Principle in Tibetan Buddhism*, Shambhala Publications Inc, Boston, MA.

Harding, Sarah, ed., 2003. *Machik's Complete Explanation: Clarifying the Meaning of Chod*. Snow Lion Publications, Ithaca, NY.

Zong Rinpoche, Kyabje, 2006. *The Oral Instructions of Kyabje Zong Rinpoche: Chod in the Ganden Tradition.* David Molk, ed. Snow Lion Publications, Ithaca, NY.

Go Lotsawa, *Deb thar Ngon po*, ~ 1476, translated as *The Blue Annals*, Roerich, George N., 1996 (reprint). Motilal Banarsidass Publishers Private Limited, Delhi, India.
[biographies of Padampa Sangye and his *Shije* lineage holders, and Machig Labdron and her *gcod* lineage holders.] Books XII and XIII, pp. 867–981, 982–1005.

Dilgo Khyentse and Padampa Sangye, *The Hundred Verses of Advice: Tibetan Buddhist Teachings on What Matters Most.* trans. Padmakara Translation Group, Shambhala, London, 2005.

List of Figures

1. Statue of Machig Labdron,
   Lama Jomo Lorraine .... front cover
2. Padmasambhava Buddhist Center Insignia i
3. His Holiness Dudjom Rinpoche,
   photographer unknown vi
4. Khenchen Palden Sherab Rinpoche,
   West Palm Beach, Florida 2000,
   photograph by Debin Harbin vi
5. Lama Chimed Namgyal, West Palm Beach,
   Florida 1994, photograph by Mimi Bailey vi
6. Offerings, Padma Samye Ling gonpa murals vii
7. Buddha Shakyamuni, Padma Samye Ling
   gonpa murals xxii
8. Ven. Khenchen Palden Sherab Rinpoche,
   Padma Samye Ling, 2005,
   photographed by Ron Wagner 2
9. Guru Padmasambhava, Padma Samye Ling
   gonpa murals 14
10. Padampa Sangye, Padma Samye Ling
    gonpa murals 17
11. Guru Padmasambhava's Lama Dance Above Samye
    Monastery, Padma Samye Ling gonpa murals 18
12. Machig Labdron, Padma Samye Ling
    gonpa murals 23
13. Yeshe Tsogyal, Padma Samye Ling gonpa murals 38

List of Figures

14. Longchenpa, Padma Samye Ling gonpa murals 41
15. Jigme Lingpa, Padma Samye Ling gonpa murals 43
16. Ven. Khenpo Tsewang Dongyal Rinpoche, Chod Ritual Retreat, Padma Samye Ling, 2014, photograph by Lama Pema Dragpa 46
17. PHET Syllable, calligraphy by Ven. Khenpo Tsewang Dongyal Rinpoche 57
18. Buddha Samantabhadri, Sangwa Yeshe, and Troma Nagmo, personal thangka of Her Eminence Dudjom Sangyum Kuzhok Rigdzin Wangmo 72
19. Sangwa Yeshe, Padma Samye Ling Vajrakilaya Medicine Buddha Temple 74
20. OM Melody, calligraphy by Ven. Khenchen Palden Sherab Rinpoche 81
21. HUNG Melody, calligraphy by Ven. Khenchen Palden Sherab Rinpoche 81
22. TRANG Melody, calligraphy by Ven. Khenchen Palden Sherab Rinpoche 82
23. HRI Melody, calligraphy by Ven. Khenchen Palden Sherab Rinpoche 82
24. AH Melody, calligraphy by Ven. Khenchen Palden Sherab Rinpoche 82
25. Five Continents from Above, Padma Samye Ling gonpa murals 87
26. Side View of the Five Continents, Padma Samye Ling gonpa murals 88
27. HUNG syllable, calligraphy by Ven. Khenchen Palden Sherab Rinpoche 89
28. Orgyen Vajradhara, Padma Samye Ling gonpa murals 104

29. Troma Nagmo, Padma Samye Ling
    gonpa murals 112
30. Buddha Shakyamuni Teaching His Five First Students,
    Padma Samye Ling gonpa murals 150
31. Prajnaparamita, Sangwa Yeshe, Padampa Sangye,
    and Machig Labdron, Padma Samye Ling
    Vajrakilaya Medicine Buddha Temple 160
32. Insignia of the Nyingma School of Tibetan Buddhism,
    Padma Samye Ling gonpa murals 188
33. Sadhana of the *Bellowing Laugh of the Dakini*
    revealed by Jigme Lingpa 191
34. *Song of Supplication of the Creation and Completion
    Stages of Machig Labdron* by Raga Asye 239
35. Venerable Khenpo Rinpoches, 2000,
    photograph by Debi Harbin 278
36. Khenchen Palden Sherab Rinpoche, 2000,
    photograph by Debi Harbin 279
37. Khenpo Tsewang Dongyal Rinpoche, 2000,
    photograph by Debi Harbin 283
38. Padma Samye Ling Monastery and
    Retreat Center, 2007, photograph by Kelly Noskov,
    retouched by Sandy Mueller 290
39. Padma Samye Chökhor Ling Monastery, Sarnath,
    India 1996, photograph by Debi Harbin 291
40. Orgyen Samye Chökhor Ling Nunnery, Sarnath,
    India 1997, photograph by Edna de Jesús 291
41. Padma Samye Jetavan Miracle Stupa, Shravasti,
    India 2006, photograph by
    Lama Jomo Lorraine 292
42. Gochen Monastery, Tibet, 2006,
    photographer unknown 292
43. Palm Beach Dharma Center, West Palm Beach,
    Florida 2014, photograph by Greg Kranz 293

List of Figures

44. Palden Sherab Pema Ling, Jupiter, Florida 2014,
    photograph by Kirby Shelstad 293
45. Yeshe Tsogyal Temple, Nashville, Tennessee 2018,
    photograph by Michele Webber 294
46. Padma Gochen Ling, Monterey, Tennessee 2009,
    photograph by Michael Nott 294
47. Pema Tsokye Dorje Ling, San Juan,
    Puerto Rico 2009, photograph by
    Beba Pema Drolma 295
48. Padma Samye Ling Monastery and
    Retreat Center, 2013,
    photograph by Jen Curry 295
49. Four-Armed Mahakala, Padma Samye Ling
    gonpa murals 296
50. Ekajati, Padma Samye Ling
    gonpa murals 296
51. Dorje Legpa, Padma Samye Ling
    gonpa murals 296
52. Rahula, Padma Samye Ling
    gonpa murals 296
53. Mantra that Purifies Mishandling
    a Dharma Text 298
54. Venerable Khenpo Rinpoches,
    Padma Samye Ling, 2005,
    photographed by Ron Wagner .... back cover

All gonpa wall and mural photographs are used with permission.
© Padmasambhava Buddhist Center

Venerable Khenpo Rinpoches

About the Authors

Ven. Khenchen Palden Sherab Rinpoche (1938–2010)

Venerable Khenchen Palden Sherab Rinpoche was a renowned scholar and meditation master of the Nyingma school of Tibetan Buddhism. He was born on May 10, 1938 in the Doshul region of Kham in eastern Tibet, near the sacred mountain Jowo Zegyal. On the morning of his birth, a small snow fell with flakes in the shape of lotus petals. Among his ancestors were many great scholars, practitioners, and tertons.

His family was semi-nomadic, living in the village during the winter and moving with the herds to high mountain pastures in the summer, where they lived in yak hair tents. The monastery for the Doshul region is known as Gochen Monastery, founded by the great terton Tsasum Lingpa, and his father's family had the hereditary responsibility for administration of the business affairs of the monastery. His grandfather had been both administrator and chantmaster in charge of the ritual ceremonies.

Khenchen Rinpoche began his education at Gochen Monastery at age four. He entered Riwoche Monastery at age fourteen, completing his studies there just before the Chinese invasion of Tibet reached the area. Among his root teachers was the illustrious Khenchen Tenzin Dragpa (Katok Khenpo Ashe).

In 1959, Khenchen Rinpoche and his family were forced into exile, escaping to India. After the tumultuous period following their escape, in 1967 he was appointed head of the Nyingma department of the Central Institute of Higher Tibetan Studies in Sarnath by His Holiness Dudjom Rinpoche, the Supreme Head of the Nyingma school of Tibetan Buddhism. He held this position of abbot for seventeen years, dedicating all his time and energy to ensure the survival and spread of the Buddha's teachings.

Venerable Khenchen Palden Sherab Rinpoche moved to the United States in 1984 to work closely with His Holiness Dudjom Rinpoche. In 1985, he and his brother, Venerable Khenpo Tsewang Dongyal Rinpoche, founded the Dharma Samudra Publishing Company. In 1988, they founded the Padmasambhava Buddhist Center (PBC), which has centers throughout the United States, as well as Puerto Rico, Russia, and India, among others. The principal center is Palden Padma Samye Ling, located in Delaware County, upstate New York. PBC also includes a traditional Tibetan Buddhist monastery and nunnery at the holy site of Deer Park in Sarnath, and the Miracle Stupa for World Peace at Padma Samye Jetavan, which is in Jetavan Grove in Shravasti, India.

Khenchen Palden Sherab Rinpoche traveled extensively within the United States and throughout the world, giving teachings and empowerments, conducting retreats and seminars, and establishing meditation centers. He authored three volumes of Tibetan works, and co-authored over thirty-five books in English with Venerable Khenpo Tsewang Dongyal Rinpoche. His collected Tibetan works include:

About the Authors

Advice from the Ancestral Vidyadhara, a commentary on Padmasambhava's *Stages of the Path, Heap of Jewels*

Blazing Clouds of Wisdom and Compassion, a commentary on the hundred-syllable mantra of Vajrasattva

Clouds of Blessings, an explanation of prayers to Terchen Tsasum Lingpa, and other learned works, poems, prayers and sadhanas

The Essence of Diamond Clear Light, an outline and structural analysis of The *Aspiration Prayer of Samantabhadra*

The Mirror of Mindfulness, an explanation of the six bardos

Opening the Eyes of Wisdom, a commentary on Sangye Yeshe's *Lamp of the Eye of Contemplation*

Opening the Door of Blessings, a biography of Machig Labdron

The Ornament of Stars at Dawn, an outline and structural analysis of Vasubandhu's *Twenty Verses*

The Ornament of Vairochana's Intention, a commentary on the *Heart Sutra*

Lotus Necklace of Devotion, a biography of Khenchen Tenzin Dragpa

Pleasure Lake of Nagarjuna's Intention, a general summary of Madhyamaka

The Radiant Light of the Sun and Moon, a commentary on

Mipham Rinpoche's *The Sword of Wisdom That Ascertains Reality*

The Smile of Sun and Moon: A Commentary on the Praise to the Twenty-One Taras

Smiling Red Lotus, a short commentary on the prayer to Yeshe Tsogyal

Supreme Clear Mirror, an introduction to Buddhist logic

Waves of the Ocean of Devotion, a biography-praise to Nubchen Sangye Yeshe, and *Vajra Rosary*, biographies of his main incarnations

White Lotus, an explanation of prayers to Guru Rinpoche

About the Authors

VEN. KHENPO TSEWANG DONGYAL RINPOCHE

Venerable Khenpo Tsewang Dongyal Rinpoche was born in the Doshul region of Kham in eastern Tibet, on June 10, 1950. On that summer day in the family tent, Khenpo Rinpoche's birth caused his mother Pema Lhadze no pain. The next day, upon moving the bed where she had delivered the baby, his mother found growing a beautiful and fragrant flower, which she plucked and offered to Chenrezig on the family altar.

Soon after Khenpo Tsewang was born, three head lamas from Jadchag Monastery came to his home and recognized him as the reincarnation of Khenpo Sherab Khyentse, who had been the former head abbot at Gochen Monastery. Sherab Khyentse was a renowned scholar and practitioner who spent much of his life in retreat.

Khenpo Rinpoche began his formal schooling at age five when he entered Gochen Monastery. However, his first Dharma teacher was his father, Lama Chimed Namgyal Rinpoche. The Chinese invasion of Tibet interrupted his studies, and he escaped to India with his family in 1959. There his father and brother continued his education until he entered the Nyingmapa Monastic School of northern India, where he studied until 1967. Khenpo Rinpoche then entered the Central Institute of Higher Tibetan Studies, which at the time was part of Sanskrit University in Varanasi, where he received his BA degree in 1975. He also attended Nyingmapa University in West Bengal, where he received another BA and an MA in 1977.

In 1978, His Holiness Dudjom Rinpoche enthroned Venerable Khenpo Tsewang Dongyal Rinpoche as the abbot of the Wish-fulfilling Nyingmapa Institute in Boudanath, Nepal, where he taught poetry, grammar, and philosophy. Then, in 1981, His Holiness appointed Khenpo Rinpoche as the abbot of the Dorje Nyingpo center in Paris, France. Finally, in 1982, he asked Khenpo Tsewang to work with him at the Yeshe Nyingpo center in New York. From that time until His Holiness Dudjom Rinpoche's mahaparinirvana in 1987, Khenpo Rinpoche continued to work closely with him, often traveling with His Holiness as his translator and attendant.

In 1988, Khenpo Tsewang Dongyal Rinpoche and his brother, Venerable Khenchen Palden Sherab Rinpoche, founded the Padmasambhava Buddhist Center. Since that time, he has served as a spiritual director at the various Padmasambhava Buddhist centers throughout the world. He maintains an active traveling and teaching schedule. Khenpo Rinpoche is the author of *Light of Fearless Indestructible Wisdom: The Life and Legacy of His Holiness Dudjom Rinpoche*, published in both Tibetan and English. He has also authored a book of poetry on the life of Guru Rinpoche entitled *Praise to the Lotus Born: A Verse Garland of Waves of Devotion*, and a unique two-volume cultural and religious history of Tibet entitled *Six Sublime Pillars of the Nyingma School*, which details the historical bases of the Dharma in Tibet from the 6th to 9th centuries. At present, *Six Sublime Pillars* is one of the only books to convey the Dharma activities of this period in such depth, and His Holiness Dudjom Rinpoche encouraged Khenpo Tsewang to complete it, describing the work as an important contribution to the history of the Kama lineage.

Along with these, Khenpo Tsewang Dongyal Rinpoche has co-authored over thirty-five Dharma books in English with Venerable Khenchen Palden Sherab Rinpoche.

Padma Samye Ling Shedra Series

The Venerable Khenpo Rinpoches have taught the Dharma in the United States for more than thirty years. In that time, they have given over a decade of shedra teachings. These clear and profound teachings include detailed summaries and commentaries by great Nyingma masters such as Kunkhyen Longchenpa and Mipham Rinpoche. Each of the PSL Shedra Series books distills the essential meaning of the Nyingmapa shedra program that the Venerable Rinpoches received in Tibet as the last generation of lamas to be taught in the traditional monastic setting, which had carefully preserved the lineage teachings for centuries.

The PSL Shedra Series is developing into a complete and comprehensive Nyingma shedra curriculum that will serve as the basis for the present and future study of the Buddhadharma in PBC Centers. It is our hope that these books will provide a solid framework for traditional Tibetan Buddhist study by people in the English-speaking world, whose busy lives do not easily allow for more extended periods of retreat and study.

With the PSL Shedra Series, the Venerable Khenpo Rinpoches are directly sustaining and glorifying the study curriculum that has enabled the Buddhadharma to be successfully carried from generation to generation. By developing intelligent, thorough analysis, practitioners establish a reliable foundation for realizing the path of enlightenment. The PSL Shedra Series currently includes:

(Nine Yanas)   *Turning the Wisdom Wheel of the Nine Golden Chariots*

(Vol. 1)   *Opening the Clear Vision of the Vaibhashika and Sautrantika Schools*

(Vol. 2)   *Opening the Clear Vision of the Mind Only School*

(Vol. 3)   *Opening the Wisdom Door of the Madhyamaka School*

(Vol. 4)   *Opening the Wisdom Door of the Rangtong & Shentong Views: A Brief Explanation of the One Taste of the Second and Third Turning of the Wheel of Dharma*

(Vol. 5)   *Opening the Wisdom Door of the Outer Tantras: Refining Awareness Through Ascetic Ritual and Purification Practice*

(Vol. 6)   *Splendid Presence of the Great Guhyagarbha: Opening the Wisdom Door of the King of All Tantras*

(Vol. 7)   *Key to Opening the Wisdom Door of Anuyoga: Exploring the One Taste of the Three Mandalas*

Other Publications by the Authors

Advice from a Spiritual Friend: A Commentary on Nagarjuna's Letter to a Friend

The Beauty of Awakened Mind: Dzogchen Lineage of the Great Master Shigpo Dudtsi

The Buddhist Path: A Practical Guide from the Nyingma Tradition of Tibetan Buddhism (formerly entitled *Opening to Our Primordial Nature*)

Ceaseless Echoes of the Great Silence: A Commentary on the Heart Sutra (English and Spanish)

The Dark Red Amulet: Oral Instructions on the Practice of Vajrakilaya

Discovering Infinite Freedom: The Prayer of Kuntuzangpo

Door to Inconceivable Wisdom and Compassion

The Essential Journey of Life and Death
    Volume I: Indestructible Nature of Body, Speech, and Mind
    Volume II: Using Dream Yoga and Phowa as the Path

Heart Essence of Chetsun: Voice of the Lion (restricted)

Illuminating the Path: Ngondro Instructions According to the Nyingma School of Vajrayana Buddhism (English and Spanish)

Inborn Realization: A Commentary on His Holiness Dudjom Rinpoche's Mountain Retreat Instructions

Cutting Through Ego

Liberating Duality with Wisdom Display: The Eight Manifestations of Guru Padmasambhava

Light of Fearless Indestructible Wisdom: The Life and Legacy of His Holiness Dudjom Rinpoche

Light of Peace: How Buddhism Shines in the World

Lion's Gaze: A Commentary on the Tsig Sum Nedek

Mipham's Sword of Wisdom: The Nyingma Approach to Valid Cognition

The Nature of Mind (formerly entitled *Pointing Out the Nature of Mind: Dzogchen Pith Instructions of Aro Yeshe Jungne*)

Prajnaparamita: The Six Perfections

Praise to the Lotus Born: A Verse Garland of Waves of Devotion

The Seven Nails: The Final Testament of the Great Dzogchen Master Shri Singha

The Smile of Sun and Moon: A Commentary on the Praise to the Twenty-One Taras

Supreme Wisdom: Commentary on Yeshe Lama (restricted)

Tara's Enlightened Activity

Uprooting Clinging: A Commentary on Mipham Rinpoche's Wheel of Analytic Meditation

Walking in the Footsteps of the Buddha: The Path to Freedom

Opening the Door of the Dharma Treasury Practice Guides

A series of condensed instructions on some of the main practices of the Padmasambhava Buddhist Center and Nyingma Lineage

- Volume 1: *Practice Guide for a Eulogy Praising the Twelve Deeds in the Life of the Buddha*

- Volume 2: *Commentary on the Blessing Treasure: A Sadhana of the Buddha Shakyamuni*

- Volume 3: *Practice Guide of the Seven Line Prayer of Padmasambhava*

- Volume 4: *Practice Guide for the Contemplation of the Four Thoughts That Turn the Mind From Samsara*

- Volume 5: *Practice Guide for the Contemplation of Vows and Conduct in the Nyingma Tradition*

More information about these and other works by the Venerable Khenpo Rinpoches can be found online at:
padmasambhava.org/chiso

Padmasambhava Buddhist Center

Venerable Khenchen Palden Sherab Rinpoche and Venerable Khenpo Tsewang Dongyal Rinpoche established the Padmasambhava Buddhist Center (PBC) to preserve the authentic message of Buddha Shakyamuni and Guru Padmasambhava in its entirety, and in particular to teach the tradition of Nyingmapa and Vajrayana Buddhism. It is dedicated to world peace and the supreme good fortune and well-being of all. PBC now includes over twenty centers in the United States, Russia, Canada, and Puerto Rico, in addition to monastic institutions in India, Russia, and the United States.

The Samye Translation Group was founded by the Venerable Khenpo Rinpoches to commemorate and preserve the great ancient tradition of translation that was firmly established during the glorious Tibetan Buddhist era of the seventh through tenth centuries. As a reflection of gratitude for the unique activities of these enlightened translators, the Samye Translation Group has published Dharma books that cover all nine yana teachings of the Nyingma school of Tibetan Buddhism, including shedra philosophy books.

For more information about the Venerable Khenpo Rinpoches' activities, the Samye Translation Group, or Padmasambhava Buddhist Center, please contact:

Padma Samye Ling
618 Buddha Highway
Sidney Center, NY 13839
(607) 865-8068
padmasmabhava.org

Padma Samye Chökhor Ling Monastery • Sarnath, India

Orgyen Samye Chökhor Ling Nunnery • Sarnath, India

Padma Samye Jetavan Miracle Stupa • Shravasti, India

Gochen Monastery • Tibet

Palm Beach Dharma Center • West Palm Beach, Florida

Palden Sherab Pema Ling • Jupiter, Florida

Yeshe Tsogyal Temple • Nashville, Tennessee

Padma Gochen Ling • Monterey, Tennessee

Pema Tsokye Dorje Ling • San Juan, Puerto Rico

Palden Padma Samye Ling • Sidney Center, New York

Dharma Protectors: Four-Armed Mahakala,
Ekajati, Dorje Lekpa, and Rahula

༄༅། །རྣམ་དག་བདུད་རྩི། །ཨོཾ་ཉྩེ་སྔོན་དྲོ་རུང་བྱོན། །རྗེས་སུ་བཟུང་།

ཨེ་མ་ཧོ། ཉི་ཟླ་གྲགས་པ་འདི་དཔེའི་ཆོས་ཉིད་ནང་དུ་བཀག་ནས་དཔེའི་ཆ་དེར་ཅེ་འདར་
བགོམས་ཀྱང་ཉེས་པ་མེད་འབྱུང་བར་འདམ་དཔལ་ཏུ་རྒྱུད་ལས་གསུངས་སོ། །